The Story of the American Merchant Marine

John Randolph Spears

Alpha Editions

This edition published in 2024

ISBN : 9789362990242

Design and Setting By
Alpha Editions
www.alphaedis.com
Email - info@alphaedis.com

As per information held with us this book is in Public Domain.
This book is a reproduction of an important historical work. Alpha Editions uses the best technology to reproduce historical work in the same manner it was first published to preserve its original nature. Any marks or number seen are left intentionally to preserve its true form.

Contents

CHAPTER I IN THE BEGINNING .... - 1 -

CHAPTER II EARLY GROWTH .... - 13 -

CHAPTER III EVOLUTION OF THE SMUGGLER AND THE PIRATE .... - 23 -

CHAPTER IV BEFORE THE WAR OF THE REVOLUTION .... - 34 -

CHAPTER V MERCHANTMEN IN BATTLE ARRAY .... - 49 -

CHAPTER VI EARLY ENTERPRISE OF THE UNITED STATES MERCHANT MARINE .... - 57 -

CHAPTER VII FRENCH AND OTHER SPOLIATIONS .... - 68 -

CHAPTER VIII THE BRITISH AGGRESSIONS .... - 76 -

CHAPTER IX THE BEGINNINGS OF STEAM NAVIGATION .... - 86 -

CHAPTER X PRIVATEERS, PIRATES, AND SLAVERS OF THE NINETEENTH CENTURY .... - 101 -

CHAPTER XI THE HARVEST OF THE
SEA BEFORE THE CIVIL WAR ....- 112 -

CHAPTER XII THE PACKET LINES
AND THE CLIPPERS ....- 122 -

CHAPTER XIII DEEP-WATER
STEAMSHIPS—PART I ....- 138 -

CHAPTER XIV DEEP-WATER
STEAMSHIPS—PART II ....- 148 -

CHAPTER XV THE CRITICAL
PERIOD ....- 158 -

CHAPTER XVI DURING A HALF
CENTURY OF DEPRESSION ....- 169 -

Footnotes..- 194 -

CHAPTER I
IN THE BEGINNING

THE first vessel built within the limits of the United States for commercial uses was a sea-going pinnace of thirty tons named the *Virginia*. Her keel was laid at the mouth of the Kennebec River, in Maine, on an unnamed day in the fall of 1607. The story of this vessel, though brief, is of great interest because, in part, of certain peculiarities of rig and hull which, in connection with a sea-going vessel, now seem astounding, but chiefly because it portrays something of the character of the men who, a little later, laid the foundations of the American Republic.

The adventure which led to the building of the *Virginia* grew out of that wonderful harvest of the sea, the cod fishery on the banks of Newfoundland. For more than a hundred years before she was built many fishermen of Europe had been sailing to the Banks in early spring and returning home each fall. Throughout the sixteenth century there were from 100 to 300 fishing vessels there every year, excepting only those years when wars raged the hardest. In 1577, for instance, as the records show, 350 vessels sailed for the Banks, gathered their harvest, went ashore in the bay where St. John, Newfoundland, now stands, cured the catch on flakes built on the beach, and then sailed for home well satisfied.

Though dimly seen now, those fishermen, as they flocked across the sea in the spring, form one of the most striking pictures in history. For no one had ever charted the western limits of that waste of waters. The Banks lay beyond a belt of the sea famous, or infamous, as the "roaring forties." And yet in ships so rude that the hulls were sometimes bound with hawsers to hold them together these men anchored where black fogs shut them in, where sleet-laden gales were a part of their common life, where bergs and fields of ice assaulted them, and where irresistible hurricanes from the unknown wilds beyond came to overwhelm them. To these real dangers they added others that, though born of the imagination, were still more terrifying. They saw evil spirits in the storm clouds, and demons came shrieking in the gales to carry their souls to eternal torment.

Even in pleasant weather life was hard. Masters ruled their crews by torture. To punish an obstinate sailor they wrapped a stout cord around his forehead and then set it taut until his eyes were popped from the sockets. The food brought from home spoiled. In the best vessels the crew slept in leaking, unwarmed forecastles, while in some of the vessels—those that were but partly decked over—they slept unsheltered. The brine of the sea covered them with sores called sea boils, and their hands dripped blood as they hauled in their cod lines.

Consider further that these fishermen came from four nations that were always at war with each other, either openly or in an underhanded way. And yet the English, the French, the Spanish, and the Portuguese anchored side by side on the Banks, built their flakes side by side on the Newfoundland beach, and when a ship opened her seams as she wallowed in the gale, the crews of the others within reach eagerly lowered their boats to rescue the drowning.

In courage, fortitude, sea skill, and resourcefulness those Banks fishermen had never been surpassed.

This is by no means to say that the fishermen never fought each other. Good fair fighting was a part of the comfort of life as they saw it. But the conditions that eliminated the weaklings naturally created in their minds a standard of justice under which all who survived could work.

Let it be noted now that with all their hardships they were not without compensating rewards. Good digestion waited on appetite. The life ashore while curing the catch—a life where venison and wild fowl replaced their salted meats, and the red people of the region came to visit them—was a time for jollification. But more important than all else they had leisure as well as hard work. For having a share in the catch instead of wages, they obtained enough money, on reaching home, to enable them to pass the winter beside the hearthstone, where they told tales of adventures that stirred the blood. So the love of the sea was cultivated and the race was perpetuated.

Into the midst of these fishermen, as they worked among their flakes upon the Newfoundland beach, came Sir Humphrey Gilbert, on August 5, 1583, who was the forerunner of the New England colonists. He told them he had come to take possession of the country and establish an English colony there. The fishermen saw that such a settlement would interfere with their business, but no resistance was made while he erected a monument and did such other things as the customs of the day required of those taking possession of a new land. One may fancy they saw in Sir Humphrey a man of their own sort. For he had crossed the sea in the ten-ton *Squirrel*, and although she was, as they said, "too small a bark to pass through the ocean sea at that season of the year," he sailed in her when bound for home; he would not ask his men to take a risk which he would not share. And when the storm that overwhelmed him came, he sat down at the stern of the little bark with a book in his hand, and shouted in a cheerful voice to the crew of the *Hind*, which was close alongside:—

"We are as near to heaven by sea as by land."

The sailors of Gilbert's expedition have been called "no better than pirates" (Bancroft), but at worst they were able to cherish the abiding faith of their master as expressed in those words. The seamen who sailed (1530) with William Hawkins in that "tall and goodlie ship of his own," the *Paul*, to the coasts of Africa and Brazil, and with Drake in the *Pelican* in that famous voyage around the world, and with Raleigh's expedition to the coast of North Carolina, were recruited from among these fishermen, to whom adventure was as the breath of life. And the men who did the actual work of building the *Virginia* were of the same class.

As the reader remembers, the first charter of Virginia as a colony provided for two colony-planting companies. One, the London Company, settled its colonists in what is now the State of Virginia, while the other, the West-of-England or Plymouth Company, was to people the northern coast. In May, 1607, the Plymouth Company sent two vessels to establish a fishing colony on what is now the coast of Maine. One of the vessels was a "fly-boat" called the *Gift of God*. A fly-boat was a flat-bottomed, shoal-draft vessel handy for exploring inland waters. The other was "a good ship" named the *Mary and John*. These ships shaped their course to an island off the coast then well known to the fishermen, and now called Monhegan, "a round high Ile," where they arrived on August 9. On the 18th they located their settlement on a peninsula, on the west side of the mouth of the Kennebec, which was "almost an island." There they erected dwellings, a storehouse, and a church, with a fort enclosing all. Then "the carpenters framed a pretty pinnace of about 30 tons, which they called the *Virginia*, the chief shipwright being one Digby of London." A plan of the fort as "taken by John Hunt, the VIII day of October in the yeere of our Lorde 1607," is reproduced in Brown's *Genesis of the United States*. This chart is important because it shows under the guns of the fort a small vessel which was, no doubt, the "pretty pinnace" *Virginia*.

While the dimensions of the *Virginia* were not recorded, we can get a fair idea of her size from Charnock's *History of Marine Architecture* (II, 431), where a smack named the *Escape Royal*, in 1660, was of 34 tons burden and 30 feet 6 inches long by 14 feet 3 inches wide, and 7 feet 9 inches deep. The 30-ton *Virginia* was not far from these dimensions. She carried a spritsail and a jib. As the sail spread was insufficient for driving the vessel in light airs and confined waters, oars were provided. The hull was partly decked, enough to protect the cargo.

The crew had to be content with an awning when the wind was light. When the wind was heavy, they had to face the gale, as was the custom on the Banks. And yet the *Virginia* was built by men who intended to use her not only in the fishery and the coasting trade with the Indians, but for oversea trade as well. It is a matter of record, too, that she made at least one voyage from England to the Chesapeake, and it is believed that some of the Kennebec colonists sailed in her upon that voyage.

Curiously enough, however, the Kennebec colony failed somewhat ingloriously. The winter was long and severe. A fire destroyed the storehouse and the provisions that had been brought from England. The unexplored wilderness oppressed them. In fact, while they would face a hurricane at sea in an open boat, the terrors of the wilderness, though chiefly of their own imagining, drove them away, and they were hard pressed at home to find excuses for what they had done.

In the meantime a settlement was made at Jamestown, Virginia. Of the 105 colonists at Jamestown, 48 were described as gentlemen, 12 as laborers, 4 as carpenters, and the others as servants and soldiers. The servants were white slaves, who were not, however, held for life. The ships with this oddly assorted colony arrived in the Chesapeake on April 20, 1607. Of the things done at Jamestown two only need be considered here. They began creating a merchant marine in 1611 by building a shallop of twelve or thirteen tons' burden. A Spaniard who visited the colony at that time noted that the iron used in the boat had been taken from a wreck at Bermuda—a fact that shows the colonists had not had enough interest in ship-building to bring iron for that purpose from home.

The truth is the Virginia colonists never had much interest in shipping, save only as they built many vessels of small size for use in local transportation on their inland waters. The reason for this condition of affairs is pointed out in Bruce's *Economic History of Virginia*. The money crop was, as it is now, in many parts of the State, tobacco. Tobacco had been introduced into England in 1586. The settlers found the Indians cultivating it on the James River, but they gave little heed to it until 1612, when John Rolfe, the first American "squaw man," began producing it partly for his own use and partly because he was trying to find some product that could be exported to England with profit. Thus Rolfe's garden was the first American agricultural experiment station. Under cultivation the leaf produced was of better quality than that obtained from the Indians, and when a trial shipment was sent to England the success of the venture was great. Thereupon the colonists became so eager to produce it that the authorities felt obliged to prohibit the crop unless at least two acres of grain were grown at the same time by each planter.

The demand for Virginia tobacco increased until the merchants sent their agents to the colony to buy and pay for the crop long before it was harvested; they even sent ships to lie there for months before the harvest in order to have first chance to secure it. Why should the Virginians build or buy ships under such circumstances?

Now consider some of the conditions surrounding the first New England settlers. Many fishermen had visited the New England coast before a settlement was made there. These adventurers found full fares and they looked upon the coast at a season when it was not "stern."

It was to this coast that the Pilgrims came.

Of the well-known story of the Pilgrims it seems necessary to recall here, first of all, the fact that they were Englishmen who had lived for several years among the Dutch, a people who described themselves upon their coinage as a nation whose "way is on the sea." More than a thousand ships were built every year in Holland where the Pilgrims were sojourning, and everybody lived in a seafaring atmosphere. Though a distinct people, the Pilgrims necessarily absorbed, as one may say, something of the Dutch aptitude for trade and sea life. Thus, when ready to migrate to America, they were able to secure the capital they needed for the venture from merchants who were acquainted with the success that had attended the fishing voyages to the coast.

It is worth noting, too, that Captain Thomas Jones, of the *Mayflower*, had fished in Greenland waters, and that Mate Robert Coppin was carried as the pilot of the ship because he had been on the parts of the coast to which the expedition was bound. The Pilgrims intended to settle somewhere near the Hudson River, but on November 11, 1620, the *Mayflower* was found at anchor under Cape Cod. While lying there a number of the company came to think that a settlement there would serve their purpose well, and the reasons given in support of this proposition are of interest because they show what business ideas animated these Pilgrims. The location, they said, "afforded a good harbor for boats." It was "a place of profitable fishing." "The master and his mate and others experienced in fishing" preferred it to the Greenland fishery where whaling made large profits. Moreover, the situation was "healthy, secure and defensible." While the desire for "freedom to worship God" was perhaps uppermost in their talk, as it was in their writings, the Pilgrims were "intensely practical in applying their theories of Providence and Divine control to the immediate business in hand," as Weeden says, in his *Economic History of New England*.

After settling at Plymouth, as the reader remembers, life was hard during the first years. But the poetic rhapsodies about the "stern and rock-bound coast" do not convey an accurate idea of the agricultural possibilities of the region. Some of the farm lands of eastern Massachusetts are among the most prolific and profitable in the nation. The average yield of Indian corn per acre in Massachusetts in 1907 (see Year Book, Department of

Agriculture) was exceeded only by that of Maine (another part of the "stern and rock-bound coast") and that of the irrigated lands of Arizona. Arizona averaged 37.5 bushels per acre, Maine 37, and Massachusetts 36. Consider, too, that it was in April, "while the birds sang in the woods most pleasantly," that Squanto and Hobomoc, red neighbors, taught these Englishmen how to fertilize the fields with fish, and to plant corn in fields that the Indians had cleared. And corn, produced on these fields, formed the first cargo of the first American sea-trader of which we have a definite record.

Through various causes not necessary to enumerate the Pilgrims got on so poorly that it was not until 1624 that they began ship-building. The prosperity that came to them in that year was due to success in fishing. They took enough cod to freight a ship for England. The profit on the cod was so much beyond the immediate need of the people that they launched "two very good and strong shallops (which after did them greate service)."

As it happened, in the year following the building of these shallops the Pilgrims produced such an abundant crop of corn that they had some to sell. Accordingly they loaded a shallop with it, and sent it, under Winslow, to the Kennebec, where he traded it for 700 pounds of beaver skins.

A year later a more important, or at any rate a more profitable, voyage was made. Some English merchants who had maintained a trading-post on Monhegan Island sent word down the beach that they were going to abandon it and would sell the remainder of their goods at a bargain. Although in the years that had passed the Pilgrims had, at times, come so near to starvation that men had been seen to stagger in the street because they were faint with hunger, they had persisted. They had caught and sold fish. They had produced forest products and corn for sale. They had traded with the Indians for furs. They had traded with the fishermen who came over from England, and they had made a profit on every deal—they had not lived in Holland for nothing. When a bargain in trade goods on Monhegan Island was offered, they had capital to make a purchase, and going there with a shallop they secured stuff worth £400. Then, on finding at the mouth of the Kennebec some other goods that had been taken from a French ship wrecked on that coast, they bought an additional £100 worth, which was all their boat would hold, as one may suppose. For as soon as they reached Plymouth Bay they cut their shallop in two and lengthened her, so that when another opportunity was offered to buy goods at a bargain she would have a larger capacity.

Recall, now, a number of events occurring in America before, and at about the time of, the first voyages of the Pilgrim shallops. Henry Hudson had sailed in the *Half Moon* up the river that bears his name (September, 1609), and the Dutch, after building a few fur-buying posts in that country, had begun a permanent settlement on the lower end of Manhattan Island (1623). Adrien Block, a Dutch explorer, had built a "yacht" on Manhattan Island (during the winter of 1614-1615), that was used later in the coasting trade. At New Amsterdam the Dutch built many small boats for gathering furs on the Hudson, and they repaired ships coming to the port when there was need. But as late as October 10, 1658, J. Aldrichs wrote a letter from that town saying, in connection with a "galliot" that was needed for local use (N. Y. C. docs. II, 51):—

"We are not yet in condition to build such a craft here."

At a still earlier date the French had made a permanent settlement in Canada. In the long story of the French in America it is of interest to note first that the Bretons and Basques had been among the pioneers on the Newfoundland fishing banks. It is not difficult to believe that the Basques were there before Cabot's time.

Of the French explorers we need to recall but one, Samuel de Champlain, "young, ardent, yet ripe in experience, a skilled seaman and a practiced soldier," who had been leading a strenuous life in the West Indies. In 1603 he made a voyage to the St. Lawrence River. In 1604 he helped to make a settlement on the St. Croix River, where he remained until the next year. When a badly needed relief ship came in 1605, he explored the New England coast down around Cape Cod.

In 1608 Champlain built a trading-post where Quebec now stands, and in 1616 there were two real home-builders there, a farmer named Louis Hebert and Champlain himself. In 1626 the population numbered 105, all told. It is not unlikely that the French ship, from which the Pilgrims obtained enough cheap goods to fill their shallop, in their second voyage to the Maine coast, had been wrecked while on a voyage to Quebec. The seafaring merchants of New England inevitably took much interest in the development of this colony from a rival nation.

Still more interesting, though in a different way, were the settlements of the West Indies. The Spaniards had introduced the sugar-cane and negro slavery, an economic combination of the greatest importance to the commerce of the world; for while the Spaniards maintained, as far as possible, a monopoly of their own trade, both slavery and sugar-planting spread all over the islands. Moreover, Spanish exclusiveness was to lead to adventures on the part of some New Englanders.

In 1605 the crew of an English ship took possession of Barbados. On February 17, 1625, an English ship "landed forty English and seven or eight negroes" on the island, and thus began building a colony that was of the utmost importance to New England traders in later years. In 1676 the export of sugar "was capable of employing 400 sail of vessels, averaging 150 tons."

In the meantime (1619), a Dutch privateer had come to Jamestown, Virginia, where "twenty Africans were disembarked," and sold to planters who were to use negro slaves, for many years thereafter, with profit, in the production of tobacco. And slaves, sugar, and tobacco were among the first articles of merchandise to bring profit to the New England ship-owners.

Most interesting of all, however, were the centres of population established upon the New England coast. The English fishermen who came to the coast after the arrival of the Pilgrims, occasionally landed men to remain through the winter in order to trade for furs and procure a supply of provisions—venison, wild fowl, etc.—for the use of the crews of the ships that were to return in the spring.

Of this character was a settlement made at Cape Ann in 1623. The Rev. John White, of Dorchester, England, having become interested in the fishermen, persuaded some merchants to send out people to form a colony. The whole business was badly managed; in 1626 the merchants abandoned the colony, and most of the people returned to England. But one Roger Conant and "a few of the most honest *and industrious* resolved to stay." They removed, however, to a point on the coast known as Naumkeag, where they made a settlement which they named Salem.

In the meantime White had been working faithfully in England to promote the interests of these men, and in 1628 sixty or seventy emigrants were sent over to join them. In 1629 White and other English Puritans procured a charter for "a colony under the title of The Governor and Company of Massachusetts Bay." The settlers who came to America and lived under this charter were the "Puritans" of American history, a fact that seems worth especial mention because a modern mark of intelligence in New England is found in the ability to distinguish between the "Pilgrims" who formed the colony on Plymouth Bay, or the "Old Colony," and the "Puritans" who made the settlements at the head of Massachusetts Bay.

The colonists who came over in 1628 explored the head of the bay, and some of them located where Charlestown now stands. With its dancing waters, its green islands, and its views of the distant blue hills from which the Indians had already called it Massachusetts, the region was enchanting, and the Puritan explorers described it in such glowing colors that 200 more settlers were brought over the next year. The Puritans were the original "boomers" of America.

Among the 200 who arrived in 1629 there were wheelwrights, carpenters, and ship-builders. The ship-builders went up the Mystic River to the place where Medford now stands, and established a shipyard. A considerable number of the emigrants of 1630 joined them. This was the first American shipyard, properly so called.

It is also to be noted that some of these emigrants, under the lead of John Winthrop, located on the peninsula opposite Charlestown, which was distinguished by a three-pointed hill and a "Backbay," where they built a town named Boston.

The French, having a water-road to the far-away regions of the Great Lakes, became wholly absorbed in the fur trade. The Dutch on the Hudson, though less favorably situated, had a western outlet through the Iroquois Indian country, and did a large business in furs. The English on Barbados, having a favorable climate, a fertile soil, and slaves, were preparing to supply all Englishmen with sugar, while the English on the Chesapeake, having facilities similar to those at Barbados, were already astonishing the commercial world with their product of tobacco.

The New Englanders had no considerable back country from which they could draw furs; they had no water route to the interior, and at that time they were unable to produce any crop from the soil for which a good market could be found in Europe. But what they lacked in these respects they made up by hard work in the development of such resources as their country afforded. The histories of New England are full of tales of privation and suffering endured during the first years of their existence, and the stories are all true. But as soon as those settlers had learned how to supplement their prayers for daily bread by well-directed efforts to secure it, hunger fled. They then saw that the waters laving their feet were inviting them to go afloat to seek fortune in the uttermost parts of the earth, and they accepted the invitation.

On July 4, 1631 (the fact that it was on July 4 has attracted the attention of more than one New Englander as a "beautiful coincidence"), the ship-builders on the Mystic launched their first sea-going vessel. "The bark, being of thirty tons," was named the *Blessing of the Bay*. Her owner, Governor John Winthrop, recorded his reason for building her:—

"The general fear of want of foreign commodities, now that our money was gone, set us on work to provide shipping of our own."

That statement was characteristic of the people as well as of Winthrop. A "want"—any want—"set them on work" to provide for themselves.

The *Blessing of the Bay* was not a "bark" according to modern nomenclature. She was a vessel of one mast, and much like the vessel built by the less persistent people in the earlier settlement at the mouth of the Kennebec. On August 31 she "went on a voyage to eastward," to trade with the Indians, beyond a doubt, and to pick up such business as might be offered by the few settlers and the fishermen to be found along shore. The fishing and trading station which "fishmongers in London" had built on the Piscataqua, at which no planting was done, was probably the most important point visited.

Another incident of this year, 1631, is of almost as much interest as the launch of the *Blessing of the Bay*. One John Winter established a shipyard on Richmond Island, off Cape Elizabeth (near the site of the modern Portland), Maine. Some time in December Winter began to build there a ship for merchants in Plymouth, England. As already noted, other ships had been built in America by Europeans for European use, but Winter's work may be called the beginning of the American business of building ships for export.

Three facts about Winter's shipyard may be correlated. In 1638 sixty men were at work in it. During the year a 300-ton ship brought a cargo of wines and liquors to the island. "It was a sporadic" settlement, and it "dwindled away."

Winthrop's *Blessing of the Bay* appears to have been the first New England vessel to open trade with the Dutch on Manhattan Island. She went there in 1633, perhaps sooner. In 1627 the Dutch had invited "friendly commercial relations" with the Pilgrims by sending the governor of the colony "a rundlet of sugar and two Holland Cheeses," with a letter in which they offered to "accommodate"—to give credit. But the Pilgrims were shy because the Dutch had been trading with the Connecticut Indians, a region claimed by the English; the Dutch had come even to the head of Buzzard's Bay, where the Pilgrims were maintaining a post for the fur trade. However, in September, 1627, the Dutch sent Isaac de Rasieres with a small trial cargo in the "barque Nassau" to see what he could do, and he proved a worthy forerunner of the great race of American commercial travellers. For he carried soldiers and trumpeters along, not to fight, but to do honor to the occasion by means of salutes and blaring music; and he chose these men from among the residents of New Amsterdam who had known some of the Pilgrims in Holland. Indeed, some of them were related to the Pilgrims. Naturally, after "the joyful meeting of kindred as well as friends," and after much fine talk and the display of goods,—especially of "wampum,"—De Rasieres made what he called "the beginning of a profitable trade."

Wampum (bits of sea-shell) was the coin of the red men. The chief mint of the continent was on Long Island. All red men, at that time, were much more anxious to get wampum than the silver coin of the white man. The Pilgrims were glad to buy the wampum because the Indians of New England had but little, and were eager to get it.

It was no doubt to secure a supply of wampum and such West India products as sugar and salt, in which the Dutch traded, that Winthrop sent his *Blessing of the Bay* to Manhattan Island.

Certain details of the earlier voyages should now prove interesting. For instance, Winthrop's vessel was at first engaged in trading on her owner's account. She was not a freighter, looking for cargo to carry at a price per ton, but a floating store, so to say, carrying merchandise for sale or exchange. The distinction between the freighter and the ship trading on owners' account is to be kept in mind.

After the New Englanders had spread to Connecticut there is a record of the employment of the *Blessing of the Bay* as a freighter. She carried goods from Massachusetts Bay to Connecticut at 30*s.* per ton.

In 1629 the freight rate between England and Massachusetts Bay was £3 per ton. Passengers were carried at £5 each, and horses at £10 each. The goods rate increased after a time.

That the oversea rates were remunerative is manifest from the increase in the number of ships finding employment in the trade. In 1635 the Secretary to the Admiralty learned that forty ships were regularly employed in the trade, of which "six sail of ships, at least" belonged to the Americans.

The profits in the trade on owners' account were also recorded. In 1636 Thomas Mayhew and John Winthrop, Jr., as partners, sent a vessel to the Bermudas, then called the Summer Islands, where she sold corn and pork and bought oranges, lemons, and potatoes. Perhaps that was the first importation of Bermuda potatoes. The profit on the venture was "twenty od pounds."

The *Richmond*, a 30-ton vessel, built by Winter at Richmond Island, Maine, carried 6000 pipe-staves from the island to England, where they were sold at a profit of a little over £25 per thousand.

An idea of the profits on some of the voyages "eastward" to trade with the Indians can be had from the records of the Pilgrims, who, with their shallops, became experts in that line. Between 1631 and 1636, inclusive, the Pilgrims bought and shipped 12,150 pounds of beaver skins and 1156 of otter. "Ye parcells of beaver came to little less than 10,000 li. [pounds]. And ye otter skins would pay all ye charges," as Governor Bradford wrote. As otter skins sold for from 14 to 15*s.* a pound, "ye charges" in a business that gave a profit of "little less than £10,000" did not exceed £867. And this profit was made, although the Pilgrims had to buy some of their trade goods on credit and pay 40 per cent interest per annum on the sum thus borrowed.

It was at this period of the history of the American merchant marine that Captain Thomas Wiggin, an observing shipmaster from Bristol, England, wrote a letter about the New Englanders, in which he said:—

"The English, numbering about two thousand, *and generally most industrious*, have done more in three years than others in seven times that space, and at a tenth of the expense."

CHAPTER II
EARLY GROWTH

ALTHOUGH geographical conditions were in most respects against them, it is manifest from any study of the New Englanders that their chief mercantile interests, during the earliest years, were concentrated in the fur trade. The Pilgrims devoted their first surplus crop to that trade, and the first voyage of Winthrop's *Blessing of the Bay* was to "eastward." According to the contracts, they had come to make fishing stations; yet the large profits made on such furs as they were able to secure kept their minds fixed on the Indian trade. But, happily, at an opportune moment a man came to Salem who was able to see that enduring prosperity could be found by the colonists only in the fisheries; and by example as well as precept he speedily led them to accept his view. Curiously enough, as it must seem in our modern view of the profession, this man was a clergyman, the Rev. Hugh Peter (written also Peters).

Few more stirring stories are to be found in the history of New England than the biography of Hugh Peter. He was born in England, of wealthy parents, in 1599, graduated at Cambridge in 1622, and immediately took holy orders. Very soon, however, he had (or made) such trouble with the church authorities that he had to flee from the country. Then he served an English congregation in Rotterdam until 1634, when he came to New England and was made pastor of the Puritans at Salem.

In 1641 Peter was sent as ambassador to treat with the Dutch of New Amsterdam for a settlement of the disputes over the territory of Connecticut, and the records of his work, especially the proposals which he submitted (N. Y. C. docs. I, 567), show that he was a master of diplomacy. His work with the Dutch led the colonists to send him as their ambassador to England, when the civil war began there. Being a Puritan, he naturally joined the hosts of Cromwell and with such energy and zeal as were characteristic of the man.

In June, 1645, he was made "Chaplain of the Train," and a little later private secretary to Cromwell. He was with his chief at the storming of the castle at Winchester and when the dour hosts swept over the works at Basing. As a special honor, and because of his eloquence, Cromwell sent him on each occasion to tell Parliament how the battles were won; and the reader who would like to learn what a preacher had to say about such fighting as was done in those battles can find one of the addresses in Carlyle's *Cromwell*. Having been sent on a mission to Holland, he delivered a sermon which stirred the audience until "crowds of women" stripped the wedding rings from their fingers to aid in providing funds for the work of the great Commoner.

For his zeal he was arrested soon after the Restoration. "His trial was a scene of flagrant injustice," and he was condemned, hanged, and quartered. But he faced his accusers and death as he had faced all else in life. He was placed on the gallows while one of his friends was yet hanging there, and was compelled to look on while the corpse was lowered and cut to pieces. When this had been done, one of the executioners turned, and rubbing his bloody hands together, said to Peter:—

"How like you this?"

But Peter, in a voice of unconcern, replied—

"I thank God I am not terrified at it; you may do your worst."

When Hugh Peter came to Salem, he found the people of the colony, with few exceptions, living in log houses that had thatched roofs and dirt floors. They were frontiersmen, a thin line of population stretched along the beach. Although there were masters and servants, there was less division of labor than that fact would now seem to imply. Owners and servants worked together. They cut timber in the forest for lumber and fuel; they built houses of all needed kinds; they cultivated the soil and they cared for their cattle. The New World was almost without form and void, but the divine power of labor was moving upon the wastes. A natural-born leader was needed, however, and Hugh Peter was the man for the hour. He saw that the fur trade was slipping away and that some other resource must be provided. Better yet, he saw that the fisheries would provide a permanent prosperity, and he began to preach the gospel of good fish markets in far countries. No record of his arguments remains, but we may easily learn what he said by reading the contemporary writings of John Smith, who used the facts vigorously, as Peter did beyond a doubt.

In 1619 "there went" to America, said Smith, a ship "of 200 tuns ... which with eight and thirty men and boys had her freight, which she sold for £2100 ... so that every poor sailor that had but a single share had his charges and sixteen pounds ten shillings for his seven months work." In 1620 three different ships "made so good a voyage that every sailor that had a single share had twenty pounds for his seven months work, which is more than in twenty months he should have gotten had he gone for wages anywhere."

If a statement of the gains of a foremast hand would serve as an effective argument in England, it would be much more effective in New England, where many men low in the social scale were finding opportunities to rise—where, indeed, men who had come over as indentured servants had already become capitalists able to join in a venture afloat. The profits of the merchants were also known and printed, however, even though not considered a matter of first importance by Smith. Thus there was a statement that "the charge of setting forth a ship of 100 tuns with 40 persons to make a fishing voyage" was £420 11s. The average take of fish on the American coast would sell for £2100, of which £700 would be the share of the merchant supplying the outfit costing £420 11s. His profit on the voyage would therefore be near 100 per cent, even though the prevailing rate of interest on borrowed money were 40 per cent. The shipowner took a third of the income from the voyage, and made a still larger profit, for a hundred-ton ship could be built in New England, as Randolph noted, for £4 per ton.

With these facts in hand Hugh Peter went among his people preaching the gospel of enterprise with as much enthusiasm no doubt as he felt and displayed later in preaching religious doctrines before Cromwell's men. As a result of his work he "procured a good sum of money to be raised to set on foot the fishing business, and wrote into England to raise as much more." Further than that, the General Court, as the governing body of the colony was called, appointed six men to fish "for general account."

The Salem people made money from the first. The business spread to nearby Marblehead, and the people there became so much interested that when a minister in the pulpit told them that they ought to seek the "kingdom of heaven to the *exclusion* of all earthly blessings," one of the congregation interrupted him by saying, "You think you are preaching to the people at the Bay. Our *main* end is to catch fish."

By 1640 the Salem people had made such progress and profits in their fishery that they were able to launch a ship of 300 tons, a monster of a vessel for the day and place. Moreover, Boston people were so wrought up by Peter's enterprise in this matter that they also built a ship at the same time, the *Trial*, of 160 (or 200) tons.

Unhappily for Salem, her people had no leader after Peter sailed for England, and Boston soon gained the ascendancy in commerce as in politics. But for many years Salem was a port of vast importance in the story of our merchant marine.

In the meantime (1636), the *Desire*, a ship of 120 tons, was built at Marblehead for the fishing business. It is likely that Peter inspired the people there to build her. She was engaged in fishing for two years and then made a voyage in the slave trade, and thus acquired enduring notoriety.

Of much more importance than these large vessels in promoting the shipping interests of the colonists were the small vessels, smacks, and shallops, which men of limited means built and used. A seven-ton shallop could be built for £25, and in the hands of her owners she was well able to go fishing. Friends and neighbors united their labor as well as their accumulations of capital in sending the small boats to sea. Even the dugout canoe which a man could make for himself was used in the bay fisheries, and the whole world was within the reach and grasp of a man who had the courage and enterprise to launch forth in a dugout canoe of his own making. It was in and through such men that the American colonists *were gaining the sea habit.*

The cod was the fish of chief importance, though other varieties were sent abroad, and used at home in enormous quantities. Mackerel, though some were eaten and some exported, were used chiefly for bait. Sturgeon eggs were made into caviare then, as now, while the flesh of the sturgeon was smoked and sold—perhaps as the flesh of some more delicate fish. Hake, halibut, and haddock were of some importance, but the one fish that ranked next after the cod was the alewife.

It is said that alewives were so called because their well-rounded abdomens reminded the fishermen of such of their wives as were too fond of malt drinks! Millions of alewives came to the coast and swarmed up the streams until the channels seemed to be filled solid with the struggling bodies. Seines, scoop-nets, and even the naked hands were used in taking them, but the weir was in common use from the first. Indeed, the Indians used weirs before the white men came.

The people naturally looked upon these swarming fish as common property, and when weirs were built by private enterprise and the owners were thus able to "control the market" to a certain extent, laws were promptly enacted to regulate these primitive "trusts." One John Clark was allowed to build a weir at Cambridge on condition that he sell to no one not an inhabitant of the town "except for bait." The interests of the commonwealth were placed ahead of those of the small community when there was a need of "bait." The price of alewives was fixed at "IIIs 6d per thousand." Another monopolist was to "fetch home the alewives from the weir; and he is to have XVId a thousand and load them himself for carriage; and *to have the power to take any man to help him,* he paying of him for his work."

The importance of alewives to the people is thus shown clearly. The notable uses of alewives were as food, as fertilizers, and as bait, but a few were smoked for export.

The early laws governing the fisheries may well have still further consideration here. After Hugh Peter began arousing an interest in the fisheries, the General Court exempted fishing vessels from all charges for a period of seven years, beginning in 1639. Fishermen and ship carpenters were excused from serving the public on training days. When alewives were taken at the weirs, the fishermen were to be served at statute-made prices before any were to be offered to the public. This was provided for, of course, after the farmers had learned their art well enough to prevent the fear of starvation. Land was set aside for fish-curing stages, and pasture was provided for the cattle which fishermen owned but could not attend to while at sea.

Until 1648 the fishermen, on coming ashore to "make" their catch, were allowed to land, cut timber, and erect their stages for the work regardless of the ownership of the ground where they landed. After that date they were still allowed to do the same things, but they were then required to pay the owner of the land for the use of land and timber. In 1652, to preserve the reputation of the colony product of fish, the law provided for "fish viewers" at "every fishing place," whose duty it was to separate cured fish into grades according to quality.

Some details of the early methods of taking fish on the Banks were recorded. Neither the dory nor the trawl had then been developed. Hand-lines thrown from the deck of the fishing ship were used exclusively. The hooks and lines were imported from England, and Smith records the price: "12 dozen of fishing lines, £6; 24 dozen of fishing hooks, £2." The Indians made fairly good hooks of bones and shells. They spun lines from the fibres of Indian hemp, which they saturated with grease and the wax of the bayberry bush, but the white men would not use any such gear.

Cod lines for use on the Grand Banks were from 50 to 75 fathoms long; the lines now used on the Georges Bank are often as much as 150 fathoms long. Sinkers (conical plummets of lead), were from 3 to 8 pounds in weight according to the strength of the tidal current where the fishing vessel anchored. The enthusiastic John Smith said: "Is it not pretty sport to pull up two pence, six pence and twelve pence as fast as you can haul and veer a line?" But the fishermen who stood at the rail, in freezing weather, hauling a wet line that was 75 fathoms or more in length, and weighted with 8 pounds of lead and a 100-pound codfish, did not find it exactly "pretty sport." Moreover, hauling and veering did not end their work, for when the school of fish was lost, the catch had to be cleaned and salted, even though the men had been at the rail day and night for 48 hours. But the work afforded better opportunities for "getting on," and so they found in it the "pleasing content" of which Smith also speaks.

As the reader knows, stoves were not invented until many years later, but the fishermen made shift by carrying a half hogshead nearly filled with sand. In the centre of the sand they scooped a hole in which the fire was built. By means of such a fire, built on deck, they cooked their food, warmed themselves, and dried their wet clothing. The scene where a fleet of fishermen anchored together on the banks by night, and all together cooked their suppers by the flaring fires, was memorable. One sees how easy it was for the imaginative sailor to name such a tub of fire a "galley," the name applied to the modern ship's kitchen.

In food supplies the New Englanders naturally fared better than their old-country competitors. Being nearer home, they had fresh vegetables for a greater proportion of the time afloat. Food was cheaper, too, and the circumstances or conditions under which the food was produced made them more lavish in using it. They raised their own peas and had barrels of them at home; why should they stint themselves on the Banks? To this day American ships are noted for superior food and hard work. Of course they ate plenty of fish, as all fishermen did, and they caught many sea-birds, of which they made savory dishes.

John Smith emphasizes the fact that in the English ships the catch was divided into three parts, of which the crew received only a third, the two-thirds going to the owner and the merchant who fitted out the expedition. Where one man owned and outfitted the ship, he took the two-thirds, of course. But as Weeden, in his *Economic History of New England* (quoting Bourne's *Wells and Kennebunk*), shows, in 1682-1685, if not earlier, "the capitalist fitting out the expedition with boat, provisions, seines, &c., took one-half the value of the catch, and the other part went to the crew." In the eighteenth century the share of the capitalist was reduced to one-fifth.

The whale fishery of the first half of the seventeenth century was of small importance in comparison with that of later years, but it is still worth mention. The chief source of oil and bone seems to have been found in the whales that died from natural causes and drifted to the beach. But men did go afloat in chase when the spouting spray and vapor were seen from the shore, and laws were provided at an early day to regulate the catch. The General Court, under these laws, took a share of all drift whales—from two barrels to a third of the whole product. In the chase the first harpoon that held its place claimed the whale. It was provided "5ly, that no whael shall be needlessly or fouellishly lansed behind ye vitall." The most important fact here is that at first the men who killed a whale shared equally. Later, when the men of superior skill claimed shares in proportion to the work they did, the "lay" system was evolved. The captain of a ship received from 1 barrel in 17 to 1 in 25; in recent years still more. Mates had from 1 in 30 to 1 in 50. The men who threw the harpoon had 1 in 75, say, while foremast men had still less, even down to 1 in 200 for a green hand. No better system for encouraging men to do as well as they could has ever been devised.

Of similar importance was the custom then prevailing of allowing the crews of merchant ships to carry a "private venture." When Skipper Cornell's Ewoutsen, in a Dutch cruiser, captured four New England ketches "in the neighborhood of Blocx Island," Captain Richard Hollingworth, commanding of one of the four, declared that he was "freighted on account of Wharton and Company, merchants of Boston, with 47 tubs of tobacco; *Item*, 6 tubs of tobacco for Mathew Cartwright and 13 tubs for himself and crew ... in all 66 tubs, with eight hides." The crew owned nearly a fifth of the cargo. (N. Y. C. docs. II, 662.) Seamen before the mast as well as officers took from port, in stated quantities, any commodities which they supposed they could sell to advantage in any of the ports to which the ship was bound. Here or there these goods were exchanged for others, which were again traded at other ports, or carried home to be sold. Wages were not so very low for common sailors, even by modern standards. They received on an average £2 10*s.* per month. Mates had, say, £3 10*s.*, and captains £4 10*s.*, and, rarely, £6 a month. On top of this the private venture was carried free, and the shrewd sailormen often made much more on the private venture than from wages. It is a matter of much importance.

The sailor, having a direct interest in the voyage, made haste to shorten sail when a squall threatened to carry away the masts; he worked with all his might whenever any danger threatened, because she carried his merchandise. More important still is the fact that the custom made merchants of the men, and that is to say, it made them self-respecting and ambitious. There were instances where the crew received no wages whatever; the owner, master, and men were all adventurers together.

There is no more instructive comparison in the history of the nation than that between these early-day merchants of the forecastle and the driven brutes before the mast in the clippers of a later day.

Consider now the influence of the poverty of the builder upon the character of the ship. Capital was so scarce that a man worth £4000 was called wealthy. Ships were built where scarcely a shilling in currency changed hands. The workmen were paid with goods. Where neighbors united to build a vessel, they traded produce of fishery field, or forest to the merchant for such iron, sails, and cordage as they needed, or they gave him a share in the vessel. The merchant traded the produce of the fisheries or forest in Europe for the outfit he gave to the builders. By hard labor and severe economy only were these vessels sent afloat. It was the European fashion of the day to build ships with enormous cabins piled high at the stern end, and to ornament the superstructures with carvings and paints. The New Englanders, having no capital to spare, had to forego the pleasure of ornamenting their ships with decorated superstructures; they were obliged to consider efficiency only. They did not know it at the time, but the fact was that this enforced economy led to an advance in the art of ship-building. On navigating the ships without superstructures, it was seen that the tall cabins had made the ships top-heavy, and had served to strain instead of strengthen the hulls. Moreover, the huge pile of timber had held the ship back in any winds but the fairest. Ships without superstructures were stronger, of greater capacity, swifter and handier.

Then there were the geographical influences which affected the model and rigs of ships. Whether in fishing or coasting voyages, the American ship must be prepared to meet winds from any point of the compass on every day she was out of port. The prevailing winds were westerly, but there was neither trade wind nor monsoon. The ship must therefore be rigged to force her way ahead against adverse winds. For such winds the spritsails, lugs, and others, where the cloth was stretched fore and aft, rather than to yards hung square across the masts, were more convenient. The schooner was a natural evolution of the coasting conditions.

The waters of the harbors were shallow. In England deep-water ports had favored deep hulls, but the American designer who wished to increase the capacity of a hull had to make it wider instead of deeper. Wide beam gave greater stability; a wide ship could carry wide sails and yet "stand up like a church" in a heavy wind. Of course stout masts were needed for wide sails, but the forests were full of enormous pines that could be had, at first, for the cutting. Wide hulls of shoal draft, with wide sails spread upon stout spars, made speedy ships, a fact that even now is not as well understood as it should be. The speedy ships invited their masters to "carry on"—to keep their sails spread full breadth while the gale increased to a weight that would "take the sticks out of" vessels of inferior design. The swift ship, well driven, soon brought fame as well as additional profit to crew and owners, and the pride in the ship which was thus developed led all who were in any way connected with her to look for still further improvements.

The short distances between harbors also had some influence upon the forms of ships. For one thing, short passages favored small vessels with small crews. The greater the number of vessels, the greater the number of captains accustomed to responsibility, a matter of no small importance in its effect upon the formation of the sea habit among a people. Then the short passage naturally led the crew into taking chances; they would risk a growing gale in a short run. Once out of port in "dirty weather," the manifest dangers set all hands thinking of improved ways of shortening sail in an emergency, and of improved shapes of hull and cut of canvas to help a vessel to "claw off" a lee shore. The men who worked in the shipyard building for themselves, and then went afloat, were particularly observant at such times. One of the most common statements to be found in the stories of perils at sea, as related by American shipmasters of other days, is this:

"Every dollar I owned in the world was in that ship, and" for that reason every hardship was endured and every effort made to bring her to port.

In 1624 the Pilgrims exported their first cargo of fish. Boston sent its first cargo away in 1633. The owners of these fish had to pay three or four pounds a ton freight; and an agent in England, who charged a good commission for doing so, found a customer to buy them. The New Englanders saw that the vessel carrying the cargo made a profit for her owner. They saw, too, that an agent in a foreign country across the water would never have quite the interest in selling to advantage that they themselves would have if they were there to sell. In short, if the fish business were to be handled in the most profitable way possible, they must carry the cargo in their own ship direct to the consumer. Hugh Peter preached this doctrine with emphasis, beyond doubt, for it was he who led in building the 300-ton ship at Salem. From catching fish to carrying them to the oversea market was a short passage quickly made. With this in mind, consider the brief story of the voyage of the good ship *Trial*, Captain Thomas Coytemore, made after the fishing business was well in hand.

The *Trial*, as noted, was the ship built in Boston when the people there were stirred to emulation by the work of Hugh Peter in Salem. Loaded with fish and pipe-staves, she sailed away to Fayal (1642). Fayal was chosen because the people there had religious views leading them to eat fish instead of flesh on many days of the year, and they were wine-makers who used many casks every year. The *Trial* found the market at Fayal "extraordinary good," and Captain Coytemore exchanged the fish and staves for wine, sugar, etc., which he carried to St. Christopher's, in the West Indies. There he traded wine for cotton, tobacco, and some iron which the people had taken from a ship that had been wrecked on the coast, and was then visible, though so far under water that the wreckers had abandoned all work upon it. As the New Englanders were exceedingly anxious to get all kinds of iron things used about a ship, Captain Coytemore must needs have a look at the wreck, and after due examination, he determined to try to recover more of the wreckage. Slinging a "diving tub" (doubtless a good stout cask, well weighted, and with the open end down), above the hulk, he got into it, and having been lowered to the sunken deck, made shift to hook good stout grapnels to the valuable things lying within reach.

AN EARLY VIEW OF CHARLESTON HARBOR
From a print in the possession of the Lenox Library

Comparisons, though sometimes odious, may be excused when instructive. The conditions of life in Canada led the French to devote themselves to furs only. The Dutch at Manhattan Island were absorbed in furs and the trade of the West India Company. The Virginians and the English West Indians devoted themselves almost exclusively to producing tobacco and sugar by means of slave labor.

Under the conditions of life in New England, the people became perforce farmers, growing their own food; loggers, cutting timber in the near-by forest for use in building houses, fishing smacks, and ships; fishermen, going afloat in the smacks and then curing the catch on the beach; seamen, who, blow high or blow low, carried the catch in their own ships direct to the consumer; traders, meeting the competition of the keenest merchants in the world; inventors, who, when unable to do their work by methods already in use, promptly improvised something new that would serve the purpose.

CHAPTER III
EVOLUTION OF THE SMUGGLER AND THE PIRATE

AMONG the first acts of the English Parliament for the regulation of the commerce of the American colonies, notable here, was that passed in 1646, by which it was provided that no colonial produce should be carried away to foreign ports except in vessels under the British flag.

Since the days of Raleigh, who had done his utmost to create the sea habit among his countrymen, the English people had been growing jealous of the enterprising Dutch, who then were carrying the commerce of the world. This act was a measure to restrain the freedom of the Dutch carrying trade and to give it to English (including colonial) ships. In 1650, although England was yet torn by civil war, Parliament prohibited all foreign ships from trading with the colonies without first obtaining a license. A year later came the culminating act of the Protector's Parliament, "the famous Act of Navigation," as McCulloch calls it (London edition, 1839, p. 817). It provided that no goods produced or manufactured in *Asia*, *Africa*, or *America* should be imported into any part of the English domain except in ships belonging to English subjects whereof the master and more than half the crew were Englishmen. The importation of *European* goods was prohibited except in English ships, or ships belonging to the country where the goods were produced, or those of the country from which they could only be or were most usually exported. As is well known, this act was intended as a final blow at the Dutch carrying trade.

Consider, now, that "shipping" means one thing, "commerce" or "trade" another. While modern American "commerce" is increasing in a way that seems marvellous, American shipping has been almost entirely driven from the foreign "carrying trade." The English enactments relating to the colonies, from the settlement of Virginia down to and including the "famous Act of Navigation," were all designed to favor all colonial commerce as well as shipping.

After the Restoration, Parliament passed what is known as the Navigation Act of 1660, which was followed by another in 1663, which was still more stringent. The object of these laws, as expressly stated in the later act itself, was in part "the maintaining the greater correspondence and kindness between subjects at home and those in the plantations; keeping the colonies in a firmer dependence upon the mother country; making them yet more beneficial to it; ... it being the usage of other nations to keep their plantation trade exclusively to themselves."

To this end it was first "enacted" (to quote McCulloch), "that certain *specified* articles, the produce of the colonies, and since well known in commerce by the name of *enumerated* articles, should not be exported *directly* from the colonies to any foreign countries, but that they should first be sent to Britain, and there unladen (the words of the act are, *laid upon the shore*), before they could be forwarded to their final destination. Sugar, molasses, ginger, fustic, tobacco, cotton and indigo were originally enumerated; and the list was subsequently enlarged by the addition of coffee, hides and skins, iron, corn [*i.e.* grain], lumber, &c."

That is to say, the colonists were compelled to take the *enumerated* products to England and there lay them "upon the shore." The restriction was laid upon the "commerce" of the colonists; there was no restriction upon the use of colonial ships.

The writer begs the indulgence of intelligent readers while he treats this matter as if for a kindergarten. From the days of McCulloch to the present time no one has sufficiently emphasized the difference between commerce and shipping, a distinction that must be made entirely plain before one can see clearly just how these navigation acts affected the American merchant marine.

Having compelled the colonies to send all their enumerated products to England (it was not necessary to *sell* them there; they could be reëxported under certain regulations), Parliament went still further in its effort to maintain a "greater correspondence and kindness" between the colonists and the home subjects, by enacting, in 1663, that "no commodity of the growth, production or manufacture of Europe, shall be imported into the British plantations but such as are laden and put on board in England, Wales, or Berwick-upon-Tweed," and in English-built shipping with an English crew.

The export *trade* of the colonies was to be restricted for the benefit of the merchants of England; so also was this import trade. Whether so intended or not, the restrictions resulted in a lowering of the prices of the colonial enumerated products when sent to England, because the market was glutted. At the same time the prices of the European products, which the colonist wished to buy, were, with few exceptions, greatly enhanced. The colonial producer was robbed by the artificial reduction of the selling price of his products, and the artificial increase of the price he paid for his European goods—robbed twice by arbitrary laws.

In 1672 Parliament passed another act still further to increase the "correspondence and kindness" existing between the colonials and the subjects living in the mother-country. A heavy tax was laid upon the commerce between the colonies.

"By these successive regulations," says Robertson, "the plan of securing to England a monopoly of its colonies ... was perfected."

It should now be interesting to note the actual influence of all this legislation upon the colonial *merchant marine*. On July 4, 1631, Massachusetts had launched her first ship, a vessel of 30 tons. In 1676 Randolph reported that her people owned 30 ships of from 100 to 250 tons' burden, 200 of from 50 to 100 tons, 200 of from 30 to 50 tons, and 300 of from 6 to 10 tons, the latter being chiefly fishing smacks, though some were engaged in the coasting trade. The colony owned 430 vessels as large or larger than the *Blessing of the Bay*. Many ships were also owned in the other New England colonies. In 1678 New York owned "5 smale ships and a Ketch" that were in the coasting trade.

Sir Josiah Child, a notable Englishman engaged in the trade with America, said, in a book which he wrote on commercial matters:—

"Of all the American plantations his Majesty has none so apt for building of shipping as New England, nor any comparably so qualified for the breeding of seamen, not only by reason of the *natural industry* of that people, but principally by reason of their cod and mackerel fisheries." And to this he adds a statement which for the first time gave expression to what has since been known as the "American Peril." He said, "And, in my poor opinion, there is nothing more prejudicial and in prospect more dangerous to any mother kingdom than the increase of shipping in her colonies."

All this is to say that while Parliament had passed three acts that were confessedly intended to prohibit a part, and hamper all of the colonial *trade*, except that with the mother-country; and while these acts had proved injurious and vexatious to the colonial producers and merchants, the colonial *shipping*, the merchant marine, had had such a vigorous growth that it was alarming the ship-owners who lived in England.

This condition of affairs becomes all the more interesting when it is remembered that a restriction of colonial trade was likely to affect colonial shipping indirectly, at any rate; that is, through a reduction in the amount of cargo to be carried. This injury was sure to appear in any reduction of trade between the colonies, and it was certain to affect the ships trading on owner's account first of all.

One easily finds a variety of reasons why colonial shipping had grown so rapidly in spite of legislation adverse to trade. For one thing, good ships were built in New England for £4 per ton burden—carrying capacity; the cost in England was higher. Charnock says it was a little less than £6 there, while Sir Josiah Child says it was from £7 to £8. Whatever the difference, it is a memorable fact that the mechanics in New England received higher wages than those in the old country.

Naturally many merchants of England bought colony-built ships, and this proved beneficial indirectly to all colonial shipping. The New England shipyards were full of orders the year round. The percentage of the inhabitants engaged in building ships and in supplying the ships' builders with forest and farm products was therefore very large. These forest and farm owners, as well as the shipyard hands and the crews of colonial vessels, helped to cultivate the sea habit among all the people. Then the farms were all within driving distance of navigable water; all farm surplus exported, either abroad or to other colonies, went in ships, and the farmer from the most remote plantation was not unlikely to see his produce loaded upon a ship of some kind. In fact, many a man behind the plough could "hand, reef and steer."

Reference has already been made to the resourcefulness of the American seaman of the period, but it may be said again that the manner of life of the people—the fact that "even at the end of the colonial period the average American led a life of struggling and privation"—made American crews the most efficient in the world. Captain John Gallop, in a sloop of twenty tons, manned by two men and two boys, was, in 1636, not only able to take care of his vessel in a gale of wind but to retake another sloop that had been captured by the Indians. Many vessels traded to the West Indies with but five men and a boy on board. Raleigh had mourned because Dutch ships, in his day, needed no more than half as many sailors as English ships, but in 1676 the New England ships needed less than the Dutch or any other ships. It was when contemplating a New England ship manned by a New England crew that Sir Josiah Child discovered the "American Peril." He saw that a colonial ship manned by a colonial crew *was more efficient* than the same ship manned by any other crew, and that is a most important fact in this story.

A most interesting cause of the growth of the colonial merchant marine is found in the bounties which the navigation laws offered to, and the facilities they provided for, those who would engage in clandestine trade. It was unlawful to carry tobacco from the colonies direct to a foreign port, but the export of fish and staves was permitted. Importations of salt were permitted, but Spanish iron must be purchased in England at a time when Spanish iron was the best in the world for ship-builder's use. The restriction on tobacco lowered the price in the colonies; that on the iron raised the price there. If tobacco were clandestinely exported direct to Spain and iron brought directly home, the ship made far greater profits than in the days before the hated laws. Moreover, the smuggled cargo paid no tariff-for-revenue dues or port charges. And it was easy to smuggle in any kind of a cargo.

In connection with this provision of a bounty on smuggling, consider the influence of the fact that the laws were intentionally unfair to the colonists. The colonists resented the injustice, and all the more because their trade previous to the enactment of the laws had been free. Then the conditions under which the laws were enforced were inquisitorial and otherwise vexatious. A time came when forts were built and revenue cutters were provided for the enforcing of the laws, and the officials of forts and cutters were insolent and overanxious to confiscate accused ships.

Recall, now, the mental attitude of the colonists toward all authority. Some had emigrated from England to escape religious tyranny. Many had come over as indentured servants, looking forward to a time when they should be free, and become men of influence. Then all the conditions of colonial life, and especially its dangers, cultivated a feeling of manly independence of all authority. Finally, the colonists had from the first made at least their local laws according to their own standards of right.

"It is not unknown to you that they look upon themselves as a free State ... there being many against owning the King, or having any dependence on Engld." (Letter dated March 11, 1660.)

In short, the colonists had been rapidly developing the American habit of doing what they happened to believe to be right, regardless of the law in the case, and they called, or were to call, this habit an appeal to the "higher law."

Inspired by honest indignation and an opportunity to increase their profits, the colonial ship-owners and crews, with much unanimity, appealed to the "higher law."

Smuggling began as soon as attempts were made to enforce the law. It was estimated that the losses to the British revenue through the direct sale of tobacco to the Dutch at Manhattan Island previous to the year 1664 amounted to £10,000 a year. When, in 1665, the king took notice of colonial dereliction, by issuing instructions for a strict enforcement of the laws, the General Court of Massachusetts replied that they were not conscious of having "greatly violated" them. In 1776 Edward Randolph was sent over especially "Impowered" to prevent "Irregular Trade," and the letters he wrote to the "Lords Commissioners of the Council of Trade and Plantations"[1] are full of references to the ways of the smugglers. Other letters of the period, especially those of Governor Bellomont, are similarly interesting.

At first the evasions were quite open. It is related that Skipper Clæs Bret loaded the ship *De Sterre* in the Chesapeake "in the name of an English skipper," and sent her to the Island of Jersey. Virginia officials must have aided this transaction. Weeden quotes from the Massachusetts archives the story of another Dutch skipper whose ship was seized because he "broake his word to the Governor in not clearing his ship to belong to the English." Governor Andros, who tried to enforce the laws, complained because there were "noe Custom houses," and because the "Governor of Massachusetts gives clearings, certificates and passes for every particular thing from thence to New York" without inquiring whether these things had been lawfully imported into Massachusetts.

The king's instructions to Governor Dongan tell him how "to prevent the acceptance of forged Cockets (which hath been practiced to our great prejudice)." A cocket is a document given by a customs officer to a merchant as a certificate that the goods have been entered according to law. Randolph reported (April, 1698) that he had asked the Governor of Pennsylvania "to appoint an Attorney Generall to prosecute" certain men who had aided in an evasion of the laws, "but he did nothing in it." In the same year Randolph was arrested in New York by aggrieved merchants because he had, as he alleges, seized a smuggler in Virginia, and although his case seems now to have been according to law, Governor Bellomont had much difficulty in getting him out of jail. No one sympathized with a revenue official.

Before Bellomont's time no official except Governor Andros had tried to enforce the navigation acts. When Bellomont took office, he found all New York opposing him in his efforts to enforce them. When the ship *Fortune*, Captain Thomas Moston, came to port, bringing cargo worth £20,000 direct from Madagascar (where it had been purchased of a gang of pirates), and Bellomont asked Collector of Customs Chidley Brooks to seize her, he replied that "it was none of his business, but belonged to a Man of Warr; that he had no boat; and other excuses; and when I gave him positive commands to do it, which he could not avoid, yet his delay of four days" gave the smugglers time to unload and conceal all of the cargo except a part estimated to be worth £1000. Thus runs one of Bellomont's letters. He also acknowledged that several cargoes had already been smuggled in without his learning the fact until it was too late to intercept them.

In Boston, as Bellomont learned, there were various ways of smuggling. "When ships come in the masters swear to their manifests; that is, they swear to the number of parcels they bring, but the contents unknown; then the merchant comes and produces an invoice, and whether true or false is left to his ingenuity."

"If the merchants of Boston be minded to run their goods," he continues, "there's nothing to hinder them. Mr. Brenton, the Collector is absent and has been these two years; his deputy is a merchant; the two waiters keep public houses, and besides that, that coast is naturall shap'd and cut out to favour unlawful trade." It was a "common thing to unload their ships at Cape Ann and bring their goods to Boston in wood boats." If that were thought too expensive the goods could be "run" within the city, where there were "63 wharfs," or in Charlestown, where there were fourteen more, all unguarded. French and Spanish ships were bringing many goods to Newfoundland and the ports of Canada, where they met New England ships ready to "swap" cargoes. There was lively trade carried directly to the ports of Canada and to the French and Spanish ports of the West Indies.

After returning to New York from Boston, Bellomont wrote that "Nassaw alias Long Island" was notorious for smugglers and pirates. "There are four towns that make it their daily practice to receive ships and sloops with all sorts of merchandise, tho' they be not allowed ports." They were "so lawless and desperate a people" that the governor could "get no honest man" to go among them to collect the revenue. From Long Island the goods were brought to New York by wagons and small boats. "There is a town called Stamford in Connecticut colony" where "one Major Selleck lives who has a warehouse close to the Sound.... That man does us great mischief with his warehouse for he receives abundance of goods, and the merchants afterwards take their opportunity of running them into this town." During Bellomont's time Selleck's warehouse was the favorite resort of the merchants doing business with the Madagascar pirates. Selleck had £10,000 worth of the goods which Captain Kidd brought from the East.

Turning now to the stories of the pirates, we read that when one Captain Cromwell, a pirate with three ships, manned by eighty men, came to Plymouth in 1646, and remained five or six weeks with the Pilgrims, Governor Bradley referred to the visit in these words:—

"They spente and scattered a great deal of money among ye people, and yet more, sine, than money."

The statement that the Pilgrims (of all others!) entertained the pirates so well as to detain them for weeks in the harbor is somewhat shocking to one not fully acquainted with the conditions of commerce in that period. The facts regarding the pirates seem worth, therefore, some consideration.

While pirates were found upon the ocean as soon as other ships in the early history of the world, some of the piracy affecting the early commerce of the colonies grew out of a curious system of private reprisals that was previously countenanced by European governments. Thus, when the Inquisition in the Canary Islands seized the property of Andrew Barker, an

Englishman, in 1576, and he was unable to obtain redress from any Spanish authority, he, with the permission of his government, "fitted out two barks to revenge himself." He captured enough Spanish merchantmen to recoup his loss with interest. His commission was called a letter of marque and reprisal.

Then recall the system of forcing trade that was practised in the West Indies. Sir John Hawkins sold slaves to the Spanish at the muzzles of his guns. Eventually Sir John's fleet was "bottled up" in Vera Cruz by a Spanish squadron and destroyed. Drake was one of the men ruined by this act of Spanish "perfidy," and to recoup his losses he began the series of raids by which he acquired fortune and a title.

Reprisals led to wanton aggressions, like those of the buccaneers, and wanton aggressions produced reprisals again. All governments encouraged their merchantmen to rob those of rival peoples as a means of promoting commerce, just as the warring fur traders on the American frontier were encouraged in their fights waged to the same end.

The encouragement of reprisals was at all times more or less covert. In war times the armed merchantmen were openly commissioned and sent afloat not only to prey upon the ships of the enemy but upon those of neutral powers as well. It was the theory of all statesmen that the best way to encourage the shipping of one nation was to injure as much as possible, and by all means, the shipping of all rivals. As late as the end of the eighteenth century the Barbary pirates were subsidized by some governments to encourage them to prey upon the shipping of rivals.

At one time the privateer captain was the judge of the offending of the neutral. Later, when privateers were obliged to carry captured ships before a court of admiralty, the difference between the robbery as committed by the privateer and the confiscation ordered by the court was found only in the course of procedure.

A theorist here and there denounced the systems of reprisals and privateering. Governor Bradford was worried somewhat by the doings of Cromwell's men. Government officials denounced as pirates the privateers who smuggled in goods instead of bringing them in openly and paying the usual fees and duties. But the state of civilization warranted the Pilgrims in the warmth of the reception they gave to the pirates.

How far the piratical cruisers influenced the American merchant marine is not definitely told in the documents, but it is certain that damage was inflicted. We get a glimpse of a vicious raid in the story of a French pirate (perhaps he had a commission, however) named Picor, who landed on Block Island in July, 1689. The pirates "remained in possession of the island, plundering the houses, and despoiling it of every moveable thing," for a week. Two of the islanders were tortured to make them reveal the hiding-place of valuables, and two negroes were killed.

From the island the pirates went to New London, but they were driven away. On sailing toward the open sea once more, they were intercepted by two armed sloops that had been sent out from Newport under one Captain Paine. *A Naval History of Rhode Island* says that Paine had "followed the privateering design" in former years as a lieutenant under Picor, and that the Frenchman, on recognizing him, fled, saying he "would as soon fight the devil as Paine."

In the *Canadian Archives* (1894) are two stories of raids upon French possessions, made in one case by "Englishmen" (they took Quebec), and in the other by "the people of Massachusetts."

Many letters charging various colonies with encouraging pirates are found in the old documents. Rhode Island, New York, and the two Carolinas were accused in this way more frequently than the others, and New York was the chief offender in the days of Governor Benjamin Fletcher (1692-1697). While the buccaneers were ravaging the Spanish mainland, another horde found opportunity in the conditions prevailing on the coast of Asia. These latter pirates formed a settlement upon Madagascar Island, wherein gold and jewels were abundant, but such products of civilization as rum and weapons were scarce and much wanted. New York merchants usually supplied these wants, but New Englanders sent them at least one cargo of masts and yards for their ships. The merchant captains engaged in this supply trade also took a turn at piracy whenever opportunity offered. Governor Fletcher did a thriving business in supplying captains with commissions when they sailed, and "protections" when they returned. Captain Edward Coates, of the ship *Jacob*, said that he paid £1300 for "his share" of the price of the commission with which the ship sailed. At the end of the voyage the crew "shared the value of 1800 pieces of eight, a man." Fletcher took the ship, valued at £800, for his bribe when he allowed Coates to land the cargo. The sailors had to pay the governor from seventy-five to one hundred pieces of eight for "protections."

Captain Giles Shelly, of the ship *Nassau*, carried rum which cost two shillings a gallon to Madagascar, and sold it for from fifty shillings to three pounds a gallon. "A pipe of Madeira wine which cost him £19 he sold for £300."

Captain William Kidd was the most notorious of the captains engaged in the Madagascar trade, but the story of his career is interesting chiefly because of the light it throws upon the state of civilization then prevailing. His troubles began when Lord Bellomont and some other noble lords of

England fitted out a private armed ship to go to Madagascar and rob the pirates. Bellomont describes this venture as "very honest." Kidd was chosen to command the ship—*The Adventure Galley*. On arriving at Madagascar, he found that the pirates had a stronger ship than his, and he was afraid to attack them. The crew had been shipped on the usual privateer plan of no prize, no pay, and on finding they were to get no prize they became mutinous. Many of them deserted to the pirates of the island. In a half-hearted effort to maintain discipline among those remaining, Kidd hit a man with a bucket and happened to kill him. Then he went cruising, pirate fashion, and captured a ship belonging to "the Moors," which was valued at £30,000. In this ship Kidd sailed for home. He learned, on the way, that he had been proclaimed as a pirate. Bellomont had been accused by political enemies in Parliament of fitting out a piratical cruiser, and being unwilling to face the charge by telling the facts frankly, he shuffled, told falsehoods, and eventually made a scapegoat of Kidd, who was hanged (May 12, 1701).

That this man, who at worst had killed one man in a sea brawl, and had taken one ship, should have had ballads written about him in which he was described as "bloody" is one of the most remarkable facts in the history of the sea. But that he should have been referred to ever since in all literature as a typical pirate is still more remarkable.

A book, Hughson's *Carolina Pirates and Colonial Commerce*, has been written to tell about the deeds of such men as Bane, Stede Bonnet, Moody, and Edward Thatch, or Blackbeard, but it has little to say about the influence of the pirates upon commerce, because there is little to say. The pirates mentioned captured a few ships, American as well as English, and for brief periods interrupted the trade of various ports. On the other hand, some of them supplied the colonists with low-priced goods, and at times the only coin in circulation was that brought in by the freebooters.

On the whole, in a financial point of view, the pirates benefited the young merchant marine more than they damaged it. In anticipation of attacks by pirates, all ships in deep-water trade carried cannon, and some coasters did so, especially in the longer voyages. In the trade with Spain and Portugal and the Canary Islands the American vessels were often chased, and sometimes captured, by Barbary pirates who had learned their trade from European renegades. New England ships in the West Indies were always obliged to keep a sharp lookout for piratical cruisers under French and Spanish flags. But these aggressions were not an unmixed evil. For such conditions increased freight rates and the profits on cargoes carried on owners' account. Thus the freight rate from Boston to Barbados, in 1762, was "14 per ton or four times former rates," and all because of pirates. Sure fortune came to the ship captain who was equal to the emergencies of the trade. Dangers cultivated the courage and enterprise of the crews. In a still broader view the habits of a people soon to become an independent nation were forming, and it was well worth while for some of them to learn how to swim in rough water.

CHAPTER IV
BEFORE THE WAR OF THE REVOLUTION

TWO of the trades in which the ships of the American colonies were largely engaged during the seventeenth century are of special interest here—the whale fishery and the slave trade. It was in 1712 that Captain Christopher Hussey, while off Nantucket, in an open boat, looking for whales, was blown away to sea, where he killed a sperm whale, the profitable sale of which led the people of his famous home island to go cruising in deep water for more whales of the kind. The growth of the fishery that followed was swift. In 1730 Nantucket alone had twenty-five deep-water whalers, and they brought home oil and bone that sold for £3200. In the meantime the islanders had begun sending their products directly to London, thus establishing a new line of trade. With the increase of profits came an extension of the territory where the search for whales was made. In 1751 they went to Disco Island in the mouth of Baffin's Bay. In 1763 they were found on the coast of Guinea (looking for whales and ignoring the slave trade), and that, too, in spite of the wars that had covered the seas with pirates. In 1767 no less than fifty whalers crossed the equator "by way of experiment." That statement is perhaps the most significant of any that can be made of the fishery. Nantucket alone owned 125 whalers in 1770; they were, on the average, 93 tons' burden in size, and in the course of the year they brought home 14,331 barrels of oil worth $358,200 as soon as landed.

These facts are of special interest to the story of the American merchant marine for several reasons. The oil and bone formed an important part of what a farmer might call the cash crops of the nation. Then the whalers were producers whose work added to the comfort and prosperity of the world. Travellers from Europe were astonished to learn that America was a land where "no one begged." Nantucket was a community not only where no one begged but where every man was a capitalist, or at worst had capital within reach. For every man went whaling, or might do so, and a "greasy" voyage made every member of the ship's crew rich enough to buy shares in a whale ship. The "lay" of the whale ship was like the private venture of the freighter. Further than that the whaler carried a number of petty officers found on no other kind of a ship—the "boatsteerers." The ambitious youth before the mast found promotion nearer at hand. Many a youth who went afloat as a "greenhorn" returned proudly wearing the badge of the boatsteerer. It was a matter of no small importance in a country wherein were many bond-servants looking forward to freedom and an opportunity to rise in the world.

More important still was the influence of the adventures enjoyed and dangers risked by the whalers. Wherever whale-oil was burned, men were found telling the tales of the sea. The people who listened were peculiarly susceptible, for they had come across the sea, looking for new lands and opportunities, or they were the immediate descendants of those who had done so. When Captain Shields led the way around Cape Horn, he not only aroused a spirit of emulation in all other whalers, but he inspired a whole people. As they listened to the story the people of the interior were reminded that the streams before their doors were dimpling highways to the sea and the wonder world beyond its borders; and there were no other highways worth mention in the country in those days.[2]

In every story of the slave trade one must remember that modern readers are able only with great difficulty to obtain the right point of view.

We err greatly in judging the people of the seventeenth century by the standards of the twentieth. There was work to do—the world's work—and many of the workers, though they saw dimly, or not at all, the task in hand, were so eager to do their share of it that they voluntarily sold themselves into bondage in order to go about it. Were such men as these, or their contemporaries, likely to see anything wrong in compelling the less developed but strong-armed Africans to take hold and "keep the ball rolling"? Manifestly, slavery was an unavoidable feature of the evolution of the race, and the slave-owners of yesterday were as well justified in their belief that slavery was just, as we are in our belief that the able financier— the good business man—is entitled to a much greater share of the good things of life than a man of different mental caliber—say a college professor, for example.

The traffic in slaves followed immediately upon demand. Says Winthrop's *Journal:*—

"One of our ships which went to the Canaries with pipe-staves in the beginning of November last, [1644] returned now and brought wine, and sugar and salt and some tobacco which she had at Barbadoes in exchange for Africans which she carried from the Isle of Maio."

The *Desire*, with her slaves from Providence, was the first American slaver, but long before the end of the seventeenth century the colonial ships trading to the Madeiras and Canaries made a regular practice of slaving. For the wine and salt which were obtained in the islands were not of sufficient bulk to fill the holds of their ships. The enterprising captains wanted to make use of the vacant space between cargo and deck, and nothing they could find for that purpose would yield as much profit as negro slaves bought on the coast of Africa, and carried to the one-crop colonies like Barbados and Virginia.

It is true that when the captain of a Massachusetts ship helped to raid an African village, and thus, by assault, captured two slaves, the General Court ordered them returned to Africa. But in deciding the questions arising in this case the Court distinctly, if indirectly, affirmed the doctrine that slaves were property: "For the negroes, (they being none of his *but stolen*), we think meete to alowe nothing." If he had obtained them by purchase, the Court would have allowed him full value.

Between 1585 and 1672 inclusive, six monopolistic companies were organized in England to control the African trade. Because of the monopolistic work of the last one, the people of Barbados declared, at first, that it was "killing the provision trade from New England." That is to say, that for a time New England ships were driven from the island trade; but the smugglers soon circumvented the monopoly. "Interlopers" attempting to leave England for the slave trade were easily detained at the request of the company, but American ships were not to be so detained. Then the company appointed agents to intercept the cargoes brought to the Barbados ports, but all in vain. "Armed multitudes on foot and on horseback" attacked the unfortunate agents who tried to do their duty. Cargoes of slaves were landed on the beach between ports while agents slept. The work of the company simply increased the profits of the "interlopers."

When, in 1698, Parliament opened the trade to all merchantmen, the increase of the trade was considered "so Highly Beneficial and Advantageous to this Kingdom" that efforts were made to secure the slave traffic of the Spanish islands also, and with success. The most valued feature of the Peace of Utrecht (March 13, 1713) was the Assiento by which Spain agreed to permit England to send not less than 4800 slaves every year thereafter to the Spanish colonies.

With Spanish as well as all English West India islands open to the trade of the New England slavers, it is interesting to note that one port soon forged ahead of all others in the number of ships engaged in the traffic. Rhode Island merchants secured a much greater share of it than those of other parts of the coast. Their success appears to have been due in part to geographical conditions. Thus the people of Massachusetts led those of Rhode Island in the fisheries because they lived nearer the Banks, but they had no advantage in carrying forest and farm products to the West Indies. In fact, Newport was measurably nearer to Barbados than Boston was; her ships did not have to risk the dangers of Cape Cod. This was a small advantage, but all the more interesting on that account. Boston gave her attention chiefly to fish; Newport perforce made a specialty of something else, and of all the products of the soil used in trade, within her reach, there was nothing that gave so large a profit as molasses, when it was the raw material for the manufacture of rum. Newport thought to fish, at one time; a bounty was paid on whale-oil taken by ships of the colony. But the production of rum needed no artificial stimulation. Molasses cost thirteen or fourteen pennies a gallon, and Rhode Island distillers became so expert that some of them made a gallon of rum from one of molasses, though the ordinary product was 96 gallons in 100. Rum was not only cheap, it was satisfying. Even the French Canadians bought rum, instead of brandy from their native land.

Gaining the lead in the manufacture of rum gave the Newport merchants the lead in the slave trade, for of all goods carried by enlightened and civilized white men to the degraded heathen of Africa nothing proved so tempting as this deadly stupefier.

Many stories of the early slave trade remain, but none shows the conditions as they were better than that of a voyage made by Captain David Lindsay, in the 40-ton brigantine *Sanderson*, belonging to William Johnson & Co., of Newport, in 1752. She sailed for the black coast on August 22, at 11.32 o'clock, the exact minute being noted on an astrologer's chart which the captain had obtained as a guide. The chief part of her cargo consisted of "80 hhds. six bbs. and 3 tierces of rum, containing 8220 gals." Lumber and staves for sale at Barbados, as well as for use in making the slave deck, were also carried, but in small quantities. A partial description of the vessel before sailing says she was "tite as yet." In a letter dated "Anamaboe 28th Feb. 1753," Captain Lindsay reports progress:—

"I have got 13 or 14 hhds of Rum yet left a board & God noes when I shall get clear of it. Ye traid is so dull it is actually a noof to make a man Creasy." Officers and men had been sick, one was likely to die, "and wors than yt have wore out my small cable & have been obliged to buy one heare.... I beg you not blaime me in so doeing. I should be glad I could come rite home with my slaves for my vesiel will not last to proceed farr. *We can see day Lite al round her bow under deck.*"

In his next report (Barbadoes, June 17, 1759), the captain says:—

"These are to acqt you of my arivel heare ye day before yesterday from anamaboe. I met on my passage 22 days of very squaly winds & continued Rains so that it beat my sails alto piceses.... My slaves is not landed as yet: they are 56 in number for owners all in helth & fatt.... I've got 40 ounces gould dust & eight or nine hundred weight maligabar pepper for owners."

As we see it the trade was horrible, but consider the courage and fortitude of the captain and crew who, after seeing "day Lite al round her bow under deck," headed away across the ocean on a passage lasting ten weeks, during which, for twenty-two days, they faced storms which beat the sails to pieces and poured floods of water through the open seams.

A report of the consignee shows that forty-seven of the slaves sold for £1432 12s. 6d. The usual price of a slave on the African coast was 110 gallons of rum. After deducting expenses, the consignees credited the owners of the ship with £1324. After adding the gold dust, the pepper, and the small sums received for the lumber and staves, one sees that the dividend on the cost of the *Sanderson* (£450) was large. Of the price received for the remaining negroes, and the profit on the molasses which was probably carried home, nothing is said in the record. (See *Am. Hist. Record*, August and September, 1872).

The income of the slaver captain was large for that day. In addition to the ordinary monthly wages, he received several commissions. "You are to have four out of 104 for your coast commission," wrote the owner of the schooner *Sierra Leone*, in which Captain Lindsay made a voyage in 1754, "& five per cent for the sale of your cargo in the West Indies & five per cent for the goods you purchase for return cargo. You are to have five slaves Privilege, your cheafe mate Two, if he can purchase them, & your second mate two."

The "Privilege" was the "private venture" of the trade. The foremast hands had no "privilege." Their pay was about £3 per month.

As a matter of record, to show something of the way business was done by the ship-owners of the day, here is a copy of a bill of lading, followed by a letter of instructions to a captain about to sail in the slave trade:—

"Shipped by the Grace of God in good order and well conditioned, by William Johnson & Co., owners of the Sierra Leone, in & upon the said Schooner Sierra Leone, where of is master under God for this present voyage David Lindsay, & now riding at Anchor in Harbour of Newport, and by God's Grace bound for the Coast of Africa: To say, Thirty-four hogsheads, Tenn Tierces, Eight barrels & six half barrels Rum, one barrel Sugar, sixty Musketts, six half barrels Powder, one box beads, Three boxes Snuff, Two barrels Tallow, Twenty-one barrels Beef, Pork and Mutton, 14 cwt. 1 qr. 22 lbs. bread, one barrel mackerel, six shirts, five Jacketts, one piece blue Calico, one piece Chex, one mill, shackles, handcuffs &c.

"Being marked and numbered as in the Margent; & are to be delivered in like good Order & well conditioned, at the aforesaid port of the coast of Affrica (the Dangers of the Seas only excepted) unto the said David

Lindsay or to his assigns, he or they paying Freight for the said Goods, nothing, with Primage and Average accustomed. In Witness whereof, the master or purser of the said Schooner hath affirmed unto three Bills of Lading: all of this Tenor and date: one of which Three Bills of Lading being accomplished the other two stand void. And so God send the good Schooner to her desired Port in Safety: Amen."

The enormous profits of the slave trade were made in spite of active competition. In 1750 there were 101 Liverpool merchants in it, while London had 135, and Bristol 157. The English slavers were much larger than the American, on the average, being able to carry 300. Nevertheless, New Rhode Island held her own well. In 1740 she had, according to *The American Slave Trade*, 120 vessels in the trade, and in 1770 the number was 150.

An interesting view of the seafaring people of New England in the seventeenth century is found in the autobiography of the Rev. John Barnard, who served Marblehead well, beginning in 1714. He says that upon his arrival in the place "there was not so much as one proper carpenter nor mason nor tailor nor butcher in the town. The people contented themselves to be the slaves that digged in the mines [figuratively speaking] and left the merchants of Boston, Salem and Europe to carry away the gains; by which means the town was always in dismally poor circumstances, involved in debt to the merchants more than they were worth; ... and they were generally as rude, swearing, drunken and fighting a crew as they were poor.

"I soon saw that the town had a price in its hands, and it was a pity they had not a heart to improve it. I therefore laid myself out to get acquainted with the English masters of vessels that I might by them be let into the mystery of the *fish trade*; and in a little time I gained a pretty thorough understanding of it. When I saw the advantages of it I thought it my duty to stir up my people ... that they might reap the benefit of it.... But alas! I could inspire no man with courage and resolution enough to engage in it, till I met with Mr. Joseph Swet, a young man of strick justice, great industry, enterprising genius, quick apprehension and firm resolution, but of small fortune. To him I opened myself fully, laid the scheme clearly before him, and he hearkened unto me.... He first sent a small cargo to Barbadoes.

"He soon found he increased his stock, built vessels and sent the fish to Europe, and prospered in the trade.... The more promising young men of the town soon followed his example," and "now, [1766] we have between thirty and forty ships, brigs, snows and topsail schooners engaged in foreign trade."

Moreover (and it is an important matter in that it shows one influence of shipping in that day), foreign trade had improved the manners of the people. "We have many gentlemanlike and polite families."

CAPTAIN KIDD'S HOUSE AT PEARL AND HANOVER STREETS, NEW YORK, 1691

Copyright, 1900, by Title Guarantee and Trust Company

One finds in the documents many glimpses and not a few detailed stories of life in what may be called the ordinary trades of the American merchant marine during the eighteenth century. Here, for example, are some extracts from a diary kept by a Salem youth, who had recently graduated from Harvard and was making a voyage to Gibraltar with Captain Richard Derby, in 1759. The diary is to be found in the possession of the East India Marine Society of Salem:—

"Nov. 12.—Saw a sail standing to the S. W. I am stationed at the aftermost gun and its opposite with Captain Clifford. We fired a shot at her and she hoisted Dutch colors.

"15.—Between 2 and 3 this morning we saw two sail which chased us, the ship fired three shots at us which we returned. They came up with us by reason of a breeze which she took before we did. She proved to be the ship Cornwall from Bristol.

"23.—We now begin to approach to land. At eight o'clock two Teriffa (Barbary) boats came out after us, they fired at us which we returned as merrily. They were glad to get away as well as they could. We stood after one, but it is almost impossible to come up with the piratical dogs.

"Dec.—10.... In the morning we heard a firing and looked out in the Gut and there was a snow attacked by 3 of the piratical Teriffa boats. Two cutters in the Government service soon got under sail, 3 men-of-war that lay in the road manned their barges and sent them out, as did a privateer. We could now perceive her (the snow) to have struck, but they soon retook her. She had only four swivels and six or eight men.... They got some prisoners (of the pirates) but how many I cannot learn, which it is to be hoped will meet with their just reward which I think would be nothing short of hanging."

Tales of the resourcefulness of the foremast hands on the colonial vessels are of special interest here. As an example, consider that of the brig *Sally*, which turned bottom up while on her way from Philadelphia to Santo Domingo, on August 8, 1765. Six of the crew who were on deck saved themselves at first by clinging to such wreckage as floated beside the hull, and then, when the squall was over, climbed to the upturned keel. Then, to procure food and drink, they cut the wreath (a flat bar of iron encircling the mainmast head) from its place, using their jackknives, it may be supposed, and with that as a tool made a hole through the bottom of the hulk. It took six days of continuous labor, watch and watch, of course, but they succeeded, and got out a barrel of bottled beer and another of salt pork. During the six days of work they subsisted without water, and with no other food than the barnacles on the planking. Moreover, they built a platform of staves and shingles upon the sloping bottom of the hull, upon which they could sleep without danger of rolling into the sea. In this fashion they lived until September 1, twenty-three days, when they were rescued.

Of the lost rudders that were replaced with pieces of spare spars bound together with rope, and the small boats made by castaways who had nothing but barrel hoops and staves with canvas for planking, no more than mention need be made.

In the log of the sloop *Adventure*, Captain Francis Boardman, during a West India voyage, in 1774, are found the following entries:—

"This Morning I Drempt that 2 of my upper teeth and one Lower Dropt out and another Next the Lower one wore away as thin as a wafer and Sundry other fritful Dreams. What will be the Event of it I can't tell."

"this Blot I found the 17th. I can't tell, but Something Very bad is going to hapen me this Voyage. I am afeard but God onley Noes What may hapen on board the Sloop Adventure—the first Voyage of being Master."

There were terrors of the sea of which the masters were more "afeard" than they were of the "Teriffa" pirates, but, in spite of all, they held fast tack and sheet, continued on the course, and finally told in the log-book—

at least Captain Boardman did—just what came after the dire portents. On arriving off Boston, Boardman wrote:—

"The End of this Voyage for wich I am very thankful on Acct. of a Grate Deal of Trouble by a bad mate. His name is William Robson of Salem. He was drunk most part of the voyage."

The Captain Richard Derby mentioned above was one of several generations of Salem Derbys that followed the sea with success. A letter written by him while at Gibraltar, in 1758, gives a good idea of the state of trade at that time:—

"I wrote you the 1st instant by way of Cadiz and Lisbon; since which I have landed my white sugar and sold it for $17½ per cwt., and my tar I have sold at $8½ per bbl. I have not as yet sold any of my fish, nor at present does there appear to be any buyer for it; but as it is in very good order, and no fear of its spoiling, I intend to keep it a little longer. I am in hopes that this Levanter will bring down a buyer for it. I hope to get $12 for my brown sugar. We have this day had the Sallie delivered up to us, and intend to sell her for the most she will fetch; as to sending her to the West Indies, I am sure if she was loaded for St. Eustia, she would be seized by the privateers before she got out of the road, and having no papers but a pass, would be sufficient to condemn her in the West Indies, if she should be taken by an English cruiser. I have bought 140 casks of claret, at $10 per cask, which I intend to bring home with me. I have written Alicant for 500 dozen handkerchiefs, if they can be delivered for $4 current per dozen. My cargo home I intend shall be 140 casks of claret, 20 butts of Mercil wine, 500 casks of raisins, some soap, and all the small handkerchiefs I can get."

By way of illustrating the dangers of losses from assaults by armed vessels under the English flag, it should be told that in 1759 a Salem schooner named the *Three Brothers* was overhauled by an English privateer that took away such specie from her as was found on board, and then sent her to one of the West India Islands "to be robbed again by a court of admiralty," as the senior Derby, her owner, wrote. In 1672 another Derby vessel was captured by a Frenchman who took a bond of, and released, her. The old captain sent a cartel in due course to redeem the bond, but a British warship seized her on the charge that she was bound to a port of the enemy. The court in England acquitted the cartel, but in the meantime the owner of the vessel had been put to a great expense unnecessarily, and he had no redress.

Richard Derby mentioned above bought a French prize of 300 tons at Gibraltar, loaded her with wine, and sent her under Captain George Crowninshield to the West Indies, where her cargo was sold to good advantage, and sugar purchased. With this she headed away for Leghorn, but was taken by an English privateer on the plea that she had no register. As a matter of fact the voyage was entirely lawful; she had no register, but being a purchased prize, she did not need one until she should be able to go to an English port. Nevertheless, when the vessel was taken before the court in the Bahamas, she was at once condemned. It was sheer robbery. The records of that court showed that, of 200 ships that had been brought in, the only ones escaping condemnation were a few belonging to owners who had been willing to pay the judge a higher price than the privateers were. The governor of the colony as well as this judge had gone to their posts poor, but in a few years they retired worth fortunes of £30,000 each.

The Derby vessels were seized in each case on the charge that they had violated one or another section of the navigation laws. The navigation laws had at last begun to injure the shipping of the colonial owners. A remarkable change had taken place in the condition of affairs. What had happened, and through what agencies had the change come?

A small space only is needed for a statement of the important facts, but the reader is reminded that here, as in the case of slavery, it is difficult to get the right point of view. The eighteenth-century state of morality, not that of the twentieth, prevailed.

From the beginning of the eighteenth century until well past the middle, England was constantly at war with France and Spain in spite of treaties that were made from time to time to provide for peace. There was never a day from 1700 to 1763 when the ships of either nation were free to sail the seas unmolested. It was the period during which Lord Clive fought the battles of his country in the East Indies, and when, in America, the frontiersman never saw the sun set without a well-grounded fear that the night would bring bloodthirsty and fiendishly cruel enemies prowling around his cabin. According to the documents that remain, these long wars were seemingly no more than disputes over boundaries (neighborhood quarrels over line fences), or efforts to avenge some such personal injury as that when Captain Jenkins had his ear cut off by the Spaniards while sailing near the coast of Cuba. But as seen now, each seemingly petty quarrel was but a feature of a prolonged struggle between races for the commercial control of the New World.

"Shall half the World be England's for industrial purposes, ... or shall it be Spain's for arrogant-torpid, sham-devotional purposes contrary to every Law?" is the way Carlyle put the question in his history of Frederick the Great, and he adds: "The incalculable Yankee Nation itself, biggest Phenomenon (once thought beautifullest) of these Ages,—this too ... lay involved."

In the middle of the century, while the prolonged struggle was culminating, privateering as a method of warfare reached its zenith. The Thurots and De Cocks of France and the Wrights of England swarmed over the seas, gathering fortune and a sort of fame not soon to be forgotten. They captured thousands of ships—literally, and if the truth be told, the French got more ships than the Wrights did. But during the period preceding the declaration of open war in 1756 the English privateers were alone especially active and successful. They brought in 300 ships manned by 10,000 men, and the ships were confiscated and the men imprisoned.

Still more important to this story, however, is the fact that many Dutch as well as French ships were looted by the English. While the assaults upon the French were justified because they avenged similar assaults made by French privateers, and because enough French sailors to man a fleet of battleships were thereby sequestered, there was no such excuse for looting the Dutch. Nevertheless, by the real standards of international law of that century (not the avowed standards), these captures were justified on the ground of necessity in connection with the end for which the war was waged with such "fierce, deep-breathed doggedness"—commercial supremacy. For when war was raging, the ships of neutral nations were permitted by ordinary international usage to carry on their commercial operations unmolested. The Dutch, being neutrals, gained rapidly in the carrying trade of the world. They even had hope that they might attain the proud position they had occupied in the early part of the seventeenth century. The situation looked ominous to the English. If they were to retain the supremacy which good fighting in Cromwell's time had given them, it was absolutely necessary to destroy, or at least check, in some way, the growing prosperity of the Dutch. It was to this end that English privateers (even fishermen in open boats, armed with clubs) were encouraged in looting Dutch merchantmen. To give color of law to this form of piracy, the "Rule of 1756" was provided. Under this rule, which was merely a dictum of the English crown, neutral ships were forbidden to enter any trade in time of war from which they were commonly excluded in time of peace. For example, the Dutch were excluded from the trade between France and the French colonies in time of peace; when war was declared, the French were glad to have Dutch ships in the trade, but England declared she would confiscate every Dutch ship found in it.

With these facts in mind,—remembering especially that in the state of civilization then prevailing, some forms of piracy were justified by expediency,—recall the feeling with which an influential part of the people of England were coming to regard the colonies.

"How much I despise them!" wrote Lord Bellomont, in 1700, when some New England merchants objected to his seizure, confessedly contrary to law, of a cargo of timber. In 1724 the master ship-builders of the Thames united in a formal complaint to the king, in which they said, truthfully, that their trade was depressed and their workmen were emigrating because of the competition of the New England yards. Nor were the ship-builders the only ones in England who were depressed by American competition. The books of Sir Josiah Child were, perhaps, no longer read, but his warnings were coming to be heeded more and more, and the contempt which Lord Bellomont had expressed was well-nigh universal among the nobility.

As the reader remembers, the petition of the Thames ship-builders was not granted. As late as 1739 Walpole said:—

"It has been a maxim with me to *encourage* the trade of the American colonies *in the utmost latitude*. Nay, it has been necessary to pass over some irregularities."

That was a most important statement. In 1739 Walpole encouraged the trade of the Americans in the utmost latitude. With inconsiderable exceptions as to time and conditions, the Americans had been, in fact, encouraged in the utmost latitude during nearly 100 years. Even a tax laid on foreign molasses, at the request of the English West Indies, in 1733, had been as dead as the navigation laws of Charles II.

But when the privateers of England were loosed to prey upon neutral ships as well as on those of the enemy, the navigation laws were suddenly revived. The privateers found, in the colonial evasions of these laws, golden opportunities to secure plunder, for colonial ships were constantly evading the laws, and the penalty for doing so was confiscation in favor of the informer. Naturally the English privateers seized the colony ships all the more eagerly because of England's growing jealousy of American shipping. The rôle of these piratical privateers as guardians of the law was supported by courts of admiralty which were composed of judges who received fees that were increased by every condemnation.

For the sake of emphasis let the facts be repeated. After a period of nearly 100 years, during which such leaders as Walpole had "encouraged" American ship-owners "in the utmost latitude," a horde of pirates and corrupt judges resurrected the law; and when a valuable prize was in question, they even disregarded the law they pleaded, as well as justice, to condemn her. And there was no redress.

Of the acts of the British government in connection with the Stamp Act, the duty on tea, and the other efforts to tax the American colonists contrary to their constitutional rights as British citizens, nothing need be said here except to remind the reader that ships of the royal navy were commissioned as revenue cutters and stationed on the American coast (1764), from Casco Bay to Cape Henlopen.

To illustrate the conditions that prevailed thereafter until the War of the Revolution, here is a brief account of the events in Rhode Island waters that led to the destruction of the British naval revenue cutter *Gaspé*.

The schooner *St. John*, Lieutenant Hill commanding, was the first of the naval fleet stationed in Rhode Island waters. It was the duty of Lieutenant Hill to examine every vessel trading in those waters to learn whether she were violating the laws. A brig that had discharged cargo at Howland's Ferry was suspected of being a smuggler, but she was not molested until she had gone to sea. Then she was followed, brought back, and found to be entirely innocent. If examined before sailing, no injury to her owners would have resulted, but to bring her back when well under way, and that, too, at the whim of a supercilious naval officer, not only caused loss but roused indignation. A mob of Newport people gathered to attack the schooner, but they were prevented doing so by the arrival of another man-o'-war in the harbor.

While the people were yet fretted by the needless interference with the brig, the man-o'-war *Maidstone* came to port, and began impressing seamen from the merchant ships in the bay, and finally took the entire crew from a ship just home from the year-long voyage to the coast of Africa. It seems impossible, now, that a naval officer should be guilty of such needless cruelty as taking men under such circumstances, but the truth is that the naval officers of that period found pleasure in cruelty. It was because of inhumanity—the harshness with which men were treated in the navy—that impressment was necessary. The friends and relatives of the impressed seamen were unable to obtain redress, but they expressed their feelings by burning one of the *Maidstone's* small boats.

In 1769 Captain William Reid, commanding the war-sloop *Liberty*, seized a merchant brig on Long Island Sound and brought her to Newport, where, although it was found that she was not, and had not been, violating the law in any way, she was held for several days. And when the captain of the brig went to the *Liberty* in an effort to secure release, and, on failing, expressed his indignation in sailor language, a number of muskets were fired at him. To avenge this indignity, a mob boarded the *Liberty* that night, cut away her mast, threw her guns overboard, and when she drifted ashore on Goat Island, burned her.

Finally the *Gaspé*, commanded by Lieutenant William Dudingston, came to the bay. Dudingston thought that every innocent colonial vessel in those waters ought to be subjected to every inconvenience rather than let one smuggler escape. In fact, the naval officers on the coast had all come to the opinion that all colonists were criminals, as well as of the lowest class of people in the social scale, and that it was a duty to inflict punishment upon them whenever possible.

In this frame of mind Dudingston stopped everything afloat, including the open boats carrying farm produce across the bay; threw here and there the cargoes, regardless of the losses thus created; looted some of the produce, and finally seized a sloop (*Fortune*), carrying twelve hogsheads of rum, and sent her to the Court of Admiralty at Boston, although the law expressly provided that vessels seized in Rhode Island waters should be tried by the Rhode Island court.

"I was not ignorant of the statute to the contrary," wrote Dudingston to Admiral Montegue. He violated the law because he supposed the Massachusetts court would be more likely to condemn the sloop. The zeal of the lieutenant was highly commended by the admiral.

Having thus roused the indignation of every American living in the region, Dudingston went in chase of the packet sloop *Hannah*, in her passage from Newport to Providence, on the memorable 8th of June, 1772. The *Hannah* was called a packet because she plied regularly on one route. She had fully complied with the laws before leaving Newport, but Dudingston stopped everything, as said, and he now tried to bring-to the *Hannah*, but Captain Lindsey, commanding her, held his course. She had sailed at noon with a fair tide, but Lindsey knew that she would have the tide against her for two hours, at best, and he was not going to spoil the passage by stopping, and thus losing what tide was coming his way. Indignant at this lack of respect for one of the king's naval officers, Lieutenant Dudingston made all sail in chase, and followed the *Hannah* until she tacked across what was called Namquit (now Gaspee) point, when, in trying to follow her, the *Gaspé* grounded.

When Captain Lindsey told his story in Providence, a drummer paraded the streets, gathering recruits, and enough men assembled to fill eight "long boats," the largest size of boat carried by merchant ships. Though these men were going to attack a naval vessel armed with cannon, they were armed with but few weapons better than clubs and paving-stones. Having disguised themselves in the garb of Indians, they rowed with muffled oars to the stranded schooner, shot down the lieutenant with one of the few muskets carried, clubbed the rest of the crew into submission, and then burned the schooner.

The owner of the *Hannah*, who instigated this attack upon the king's vessel, was Captain John Brown, the wealthiest merchant in Providence. The leader of the expedition was Captain Abraham Whipple, who, as a privateer, had taken a million dollars' worth of prizes during the wars with

France and Spain. The whole mob, for a mob it was in the eyes of the law, were representative citizens not only of Rhode Island but of all the seafaring people of the colonies. The time had come when Americans would, in defence of Justice, do more than evade an unjust law; in burning the *Gaspé* they were, as Lord Dartmouth declared, "*levying war* against the king."

CHAPTER V
MERCHANTMEN IN BATTLE ARRAY

SOME of the most stirring tales in the history of the American merchant marine are those of the battles of men who, like Captain Jonathan Haraden, of Salem, commanded armed merchantmen during the War of the Revolution. These stories are of special interest here because they portray one side of the character of the American sailors as developed by the peculiar conditions where forest life and sea life met at the surf-line. But before giving any of these tales, it seems necessary to describe briefly the peculiarities of the ships in use in the colonies during the eighteenth century.

While the dictionaries define, fairly well, all sorts of sea terms, it seems worth noting here that a ship, in the earliest days of the colonies, had three masts, two of which were fitted with yards to spread four-sided sails across the hull, while the third carried a long, slender yard that spread a lateen sail fore and aft. Moreover, a square sail was spread by a yard that hung beneath the end of the bowsprit. Because the lateen sail was difficult to handle, and the one on the spritsail-yard dipped into the water, both were soon abolished on the American ships. American sailors were high-priced, economy was necessary, and rigs that reduced the number of men needed were adopted perforce.

The ketch was another rig that did not last long. A ketch had one mast amidships, with yards crossed upon it, and another smaller mast well aft, upon which yards were also crossed, though sometimes a fore-and-aft sail was found there. It was, doubtless, the worst rig ever seen in American waters.

The snow was a modified brig. She had two masts with yards crossed as in a ship, and in addition had a slender mast close abaft the main—a sort of spencer-mast upon which a fore-and-aft sail was set. This style of rig lasted much longer than its name, though that persisted until the nineteenth century.

The most popular rig, during the first hundred years of the colonies, was the sloop, and it can still be seen on oyster boats, brick carriers, and yachts. No other rig will give a hull as great speed, in proportion to the canvas, as this one, and yet the rig can be managed by few men, provided they know their work, and are vigilant. Long coasting voyages were made with sloops carrying forty tons of cargo, and no more than four men. Voyages to the

West Indies were made in larger sloops with six men, while oversea voyages were accomplished with one or two more.

In 1713 a contemplation of the advantages of the sloop rig led Captain Andrew Robinson, of Gloucester, Mass., to build a hull, somewhat larger than the ordinary sloop of the day, and place in it two masts, each of which carried the sloop rig. If rigged as a sloop, the one sail would need to be so large that it would be difficult to handle. By dividing the canvas between two sails *of the same form*, a great enough spread for speed would be obtained, and yet neither sail would be larger than the single one on a smaller hull. The sails were probably stretched before this vessel was launched, and one may believe that the novelty of the rig drew a large crowd to the launching. Beyond doubt, too, everybody cheered as the hull took the water, and one enthusiast shouted,—

"Oh, how she scoons!"

"Scoon" referred to the light and swift motion of the hull as it seemed to glide over, rather than plough through, the water, but Captain Robinson, who had been wondering what he would name the curious rig, seized upon the word "scoon" and said, "A scooner let her be!"

Perhaps the most important event in the shipyards of America, previous to the launching of Fulton's steamer, was the invention of the schooner. For under this rig a hull of twice the capacity of an ordinary sloop could be handled with no, or but a small, increase in the number of men. Moreover, the cost of the rig was less than that of any other for a hull of similar size. In short, a schooner gave her owner more ton-miles of work than any other kind of vessel for each dollar of expense. Schooners were soon used almost exclusively in the cod-fishery on the banks. They rapidly made their way into the coasting trade, where they gathered cargoes for the ships used in the export trade, and served to strengthen the slender cords binding one part of the country to the other. They even went on foreign voyages with great success—as they might do now, if only American owners would take what lies before them.

With the growth of American shipping it was inevitable that American sailors should go privateering. The love of adventure was born into the people who lived where salt spray gave a tang to the odors of a pine forest. Armed ships from Boston hunted Dutch merchantmen as long as the Hudson region was called New Amsterdam. American sailors ate broiled rawhide with Morgan on the banks of the Chagres River. Kidd came from London to New York seeking sailors born in the Highlands of the Hudson, because they were, of all men in the world, best fitted by experience and natural inclination for the work he had in hand. Franklin at one time expressed the hope that the American coast would never shelter such hosts as were found in Algiers and Tripoli, and the thought was founded on his knowledge of the eager determination to get on in life, at all hazards, which the conditions of life in America had generated.

The most important era in the apprenticeship of the colonial merchantmen was that passed in fighting the French and Spanish during England's long struggle for commercial supremacy in the eighteenth century, a period during which New York alone commissioned 48 vessels, carrying 675 guns and 5530 men. As affording interesting views of the work done by the American seamen at that time, consider some of the incidents of the siege of Louisburg, for while the siege was a land contest, it was carried on by men the majority of whom, perhaps, were sailors, and the incidents to be recalled were, at any rate, peculiarly characteristic of the New England foremast hand.

The armed ships numbered thirteen, and ninety merchantmen were chartered to carry the men. The number of ships then owned in the colonies at that time is nowhere stated, but it was not difficult to gather this fleet in New England.

Although the heavy masonry forts at Louisburg mounted 42-pounders, the heaviest guns the fleet carried were 22-pounders; but 42-pounder shot were cast for the expedition, and taken along, because every man in the fleet was entirely confident that 42-pounders would soon be captured from the enemy.

Having landed about two miles from the main fortification (April 30, 1745), one William Vaughan, "a youth of restless and impetuous activity," led 400 men "to the hills near the town and saluted it with three cheers." On May 2 this same impetuous youth, while wandering around with a squad of twelve men and boys, reached a number of unguarded storehouses belonging to the enemy. They were so far from the main scene of activity of the colonists that the French, apparently, had not thought it worth while to guard them. Vaughan set them on fire, and the conflagration frightened the soldiers in a large detached fort so much that they fled. A little later Vaughan and his gang took possession of the abandoned fort, and while a boy of eighteen years climbed the flagstaff and spread a red coat to the breeze in place of a flag, another one ran to the colonial general (Pepperrell) with this message from Vaughan:—

"May it please your Honour to be informed that by the grace of God and the courage of thirteen men, I entered the Royal Battery about 9 o'clock, and am waiting for a reinforcement and a flag."

The 42-pounders for which shot had been cast in Boston were secured—twenty-eight of them, besides two 18-pounders.

When the siege guns were landed from the transports, and an effort was made to take them forward across a wide swamp, in order to mount them where they would reach the town, they sank out of sight in the mud. Thereupon the men made a broad-runner sled for each gun, harnessed themselves to the sleds, and waded across the swamp, dragging the guns after them. That feat has excited the admiration of all historians who have written about it. But these men had built ships a mile from the water—back in the woods—and, when each was ready for the sea had dragged it to the beach with many yoke of oxen; dragging cannon across the swamp was a small matter in their estimation.

A trained engineer wanted them to advance upon the big fort of the enemy in the usual scientific manner—by digging parallels, one after another, and covering every step of the advance with earthworks. The proposal made them laugh. Taking advantage of a foggy night, they went forward, rolling sugar hogsheads, brought for the purpose, before them, until they arrived at the most advanced point desirable, and there they up-ended the hogsheads, filled them with dirt, mounted their siege guns (including 42-pounders taken from the royal fort), and opened fire.

Meanwhile they were without tents; their clothing and shoes wore out under the excessive abrading of their work; they were soaked by cold rains, but shelters of evergreen boughs were erected, and "while the cannon bellowed in front ... the men raced, wrestled, pitched quoits, fired at marks," and "ran after the French cannon balls that sometimes fell in the camp" where "frolic and confusion reigned" perpetually.

The capture of Louisburg had small effect upon the country, but the work of the besiegers, rightly seen, was of the most important ever done in the colonies. Throughout the siege they were inspired by the idea that "the All of Things is an infinite conjugation of the verb *To Do*"; they took hold of each task with hearty good-will, and were irrepressible; their rude disregard for convention gave opportunity to their resourcefulness, and contributed to the evolution of military science. And lessons learned before Louisburg were applied at Bunker Hill, and elsewhere, during the Revolution.

Among the heroes of the privateer ships of the Revolution we may well recall Captain Jonathan Haraden, as a type. In 1780 he sailed from Salem in the 180-ton ship *Pickering*, armed with fourteen 6-pounders, manned by about fifty men, all told, bound to Bilboa with a cargo of sugar. At this period of the war the British, taught by experience, had sent out fleets of frigates and sloops of war, besides many brigs, cutters, and privateers of large size in order to suppress the armed ships of the "rebels." On the way across, Haraden met a heavy cutter and beat her off. While reaching across the Bay of Biscay, one night, he overhauled a ship the lookouts of which appeared to be asleep; for there was no stir upon her deck until Haraden hailed and ordered her to surrender, saying that his ship was an American frigate and he intended firing a broadside immediately. The sleepy captain obeyed the order. It was then learned that she was a privateer much superior to the *Pickering* in the number of guns and of men. On arriving off Bilboa a big armed ship was seen coming out, and the captured captain told Haraden she was the privateer *Achilles*, mounting forty-two guns and manned by 140 men.

"I shan't run from her," said Haraden, quietly.

The *Achilles* took possession of the privateer captured in the Bay of Biscay, but because it was a calm night, and the *Pickering* would be unable to escape, the captain of the *Achilles* determined to wait until morning before attacking. On seeing this, Haraden arranged a proper lookout and then went to sleep.

At dawn, when the *Achilles* came down ready for battle, the *Pickering* was lying so far inshore that a throng of people, supposed to number 100,000, gathered on the hills to watch the contest, and they found the spectacle worth the trouble taken. Calling his men to the mast, Haraden assured them that they would win in spite of the greater force of the enemy, and then ordered them to "Take particular aim at the white boot top."

Inspired by the air of confidence with which the captain had addressed them, the men returned to quarters. Their ship was loaded down so far in the water that she "appeared little larger than a long boat" when the *Achilles* ranged alongside, but, as *Captain Haraden had foreseen*, the difference in height gave him a decisive advantage.

The *Achilles*, with her great battery and numerous crew, opened a fire that seemed overwhelming. But at that time (and for years afterward) English sailors relied upon speed of fire only to win their battles; the guns of the *Achilles* were discharged without aiming, and because the gun deck was far above the water, nearly every shot passed over the *Pickering*. But the American gunners were half sailor, half backwoodsmen; they took particular aim at the white boot top of the *Achilles*, and drove so many shot through her side near the water-line that, after about three hours of fighting, the British captain found that he would have to haul off or sink. He decided to fly. Then, on seeing the British sailors running to the braces to swing the yards, Haraden ordered his gunners to load with crowbars, hoping to cut the rigging of the *Achilles* with these curious projectiles, and thus keep her from running away; but "she had a mainsail as large as a ship of the line," and when that sail began to draw she escaped.

As the *Pickering* and her recaptured prize came to anchor in the bay, the enthusiastic spectators of the battle flocked off in such numbers that at one time it would have been possible to build with the boats around her a pontoon bridge reaching from ship to shore.

When Captain William Gray was a lieutenant on the privateer *Jack*, she was attacked by one of the enemy of such superior force that she was soon disabled. Thereupon the enemy came alongside and tried to board. In heading his men in repelling the attack, Gray was struck by a bayoneted musket which had been pitchpoled at him. The bayonet pinned him fast to a gun carriage so that he was unable to get away, but after one of his men had withdrawn the bayonet, he again attacked the boarders and they were repelled.

When Captain John Manly commanded the privateer *Jason*, of Boston, he was chased by a British frigate into a roadstead near the Isle of Shoals. He would have been captured there but for a friendly squall which, while it dismasted him, drove away the frigate. At this, however, Manly's troubles began. He had previously lost the privateer *Cumberland*, and his crew decided that the dismasting was clear proof that he was unlucky. A mutiny followed, but Manly, snatching a cutlass from one of the crew, attacked the mutineers single-handed, and after cutting down two of them, set the remainder at work rerigging the ship; and he kept them at it until she was ready for sea thirty-six hours later. Finally, he went to Sandy Hook and captured two big privateers fresh from that port and very valuable.

As noted in the *Story of the New England Whalers*, there is abundant reason for saying that "out of the 1700 men who had manned Nantucket whalers before the war, some hundreds shipped on the privateers. They took kindly to a calling in which there was such a strong element of chance. The hope of good luck was strong within them." When an American privateer was captured by the enemy, they separated the Nantucket men from the remainder of the crew, and then by bribery on the one hand, and starvation and other kinds of ill treatment, on the other, they forced as many as possible into the English whaleships.

Many more tales might be related, but the facts here given show well enough that the men who were at once woodsmen, ship-builders, fishermen, and sailors could also fight. It is especially notable that they could usually think calmly and decide swiftly, as Haraden did. The conditions under which the American seamen of the period had been reared had made them, as so frequently pointed out herein, at once resourceful, enterprising, persistent, and unafraid.

The records of the privateers are so few in number that only imperfect estimates can be made of the number and force of the fleet. The

Continental Congress bonded 1699 privateers during the war, but since many ships were bonded more than once, some under different names, it is not possible to say how many individual ships were thus represented. Further than that the colonies commissioned many vessels that had no commission from the Congress. Hale, in Winsor's *History of America*, says that Massachusetts owned 600 privateers. Salem alone owned 158. More than 200 were owned in Connecticut, Rhode Island, and New Hampshire. The fleets of the Delaware, the Chesapeake, and of Charleston were considerable. Certainly more than 1000 armed ships were sent to sea by American owners to seize the merchantmen of the enemy. The fishing smack *Wasp*, carrying 9 men and no cannon, was, perhaps, the weakest;[3] the *Deane*, carrying 30 cannon and 210 men, was the most powerful. There were 40 American privateers of the force of 20 guns and 100 men or larger.

American histories have, almost without exception, glorified these privateers. They note that Dodsley's *Register* for 1778 recorded the capture of 733 British ships by American cruisers, of which 559 were brought into port. What these prizes sold for is not recorded, but it appears that the British loss was estimated at £2,600,000. Gomer Williams, in his history of the Liverpool privateers, says that the War of the Revolution put an entire stop to the commercial progress of that port. It was the venturesome American privateer who haunted the Irish channel until the Dublin linen fleet sailed under convoy to Chester, that thus injured Liverpool. According to Troughton, another Liverpool historian, "the manners of the common people" of the town "made a retrogression towards barbarism." Mr. Hale estimates that 3000 British ships were captured, and that the losses crippled the commercial prosperity of England severely.

On the other hand, however, while the American cruisers were capturing the 773 British ships, the British cruisers captured and sent into port 904 American ships, which brought the captors £2000 each on the average. The losses of the American owners were, of course, much larger. Worse yet, the American ships were all eventually driven from the seas, save only as a few of the largest and most powerful were able to dodge and outsail the frigates and sloops-of-war which the British sent in pursuit of them. Haraden himself, though he captured more than a thousand guns from the enemy, was at last caught at St. Eustatia by Admiral Rodney's fleet.

If the accounts of gains and losses could be posted ledger fashion, the struck balance would show that while the captured goods[4] were at times almost the only resource of the colonists needing goods of foreign manufacture, and while, too, a few individuals were enriched, the losses of the ship merchants as a class, and of the country, far outweighed the gains. American independence was not won, as so often claimed, by the privateers; it was not even forwarded.

There was a further loss, which, though it cannot be measured, was real. There is abundant evidence to show that the successes of the few made gamblers, and even thieves, of many merchants. While two frigates were on the stocks in Rhode Island, the timber belonging to the government was stolen for use in privateers. Still another evil influence is found in the fact that the magnified stories of privateer work made the people believe that the greed of the merchants would serve to defend the new-born nation from foreign aggression better than a navy could do it. And not until after the War of 1812 was brought upon us was the miserable delusion dispelled.

In two respects only did the privateers serve the American merchant marine well: they gave some thousands of individual seamen increased ability to handle ships under difficult conditions, and they improved the speed of the whole fleet.

Captain Elias Hasket Derby, of Salem, was perhaps the first American to make a systematic study of ship models with a view of increasing speed. He established a shipyard near his wharf at Salem; with untrammelled mind he made experiments, and eventually he built 4 ships of from 300 to 360 tons' burden, each of which became noted for strength and speed. One of them (the *Astræ*, a vessel less than 100 feet long), while on her way to the Baltic, made the run from Salem to the Irish coast in eleven days. In 1783 this vessel crossed from Salem to France in 18 days, and she made the passage home in 19.

Only a few ships remained in commission to float the flag of the "new constellation" at the end of the War of the Revolution, but it was a matter of no small significance that these ships were, on the average, far superior to those that had formed the American merchant marine in colonial days. Indeed, they were literally the best merchantmen in the world. And the conditions under which they were to sail, though harrowing to the owners and to all patriotic Americans, were to maintain the standard of the fleet for many years to come.

CHAPTER VI
EARLY ENTERPRISE OF THE UNITED STATES MERCHANT MARINE

WHEN the War of the Revolution came to an end, the territory of the United States extended along the Atlantic coast from Maine to Georgia, and westward over the Appalachian Mountains as far as the Mississippi River. The population, including slaves, numbered no more than 3,500,000. The settlements have usually been considered in groups—those of New England, of the Middle states, of the Southern states, and, last of all, that most interesting group west of the mountains. Virginia, Massachusetts, and Pennsylvania were the most populous states. Philadelphia, the largest city, boasted a population of 42,520 in the first census year (1790). New York was second, Boston third, Charleston fourth, and Baltimore fifth. Newport and Portsmouth, though small, were yet ports of importance, and so, too, was Salem.

The interests of the different groups of population of the country were then supposed to be in some ways antagonistic. The Southern states produced tobacco, rice, and indigo for export, and had relatively few ships; wanting low freight rates, they expressed, at times later, the fear of combinations between owners of ships living elsewhere, by which rates would be raised. The seeming antagonisms were magnified by the lack of means of intercourse between them. While roads wide enough for vehicles had been cut from town to town near the coast as far south as Virginia, and a few had been opened into the interior along the routes of armies during the war, the most comfortable way of travelling was by water, and ships were the only means for transporting freight, save only as some goods were carried on mules and wagons into the interior—on one route as far as Pittsburg.

CUSTOM HOUSE, SALEM

From a print in the possession of the Lenox Library

On the whole, a bird's-eye view of the United States showed a wilderness, 820,680 square miles in extent, that had a line of settlements along the coast. The political condition of the country was not unlike its physical—chaotic. The thirteen colonies, having thrown off allegiance to the mother-country, had essayed the formation of a ship of state, but had created only a raft of thirteen logs, if such a simile may be permitted, which chafed each other with growing friction. Congress was nominally the executive, the legislative, and the judicial head of a nation, but the money it issued ceased to circulate, and the bonds, representing borrowed coin and war material, were little better. As a body, the Congress consisted of a score or so of respectable gentlemen who met in a hall hired for the purpose, where they expressed their opinions on matters of international as well as local concern, and then begged the sovereign states to take action. They had no power *to do* anything—not even to raise the money with which to pay the rent of the hall in which they met.

An examination of the American merchant marine at this time shows that it had fallen far below that of the colonies. In a communication to Congress, 19 ship-builders of Philadelphia said (1789) that while they had launched 4500 tons of shipping per year before the war, "it appears from an average of three years past that we have built only to the amount of 1500 tons annually." Similar complaints were made by the shipwrights of Charleston, Baltimore, and Boston. The Charleston communication was especial interesting. It said:—

"From the diminished state of ship building in America, and the *ruinous restrictions* to which our vessels are subject in *foreign ports*; from the distressed condition of our commerce, languishing under the *most disgraceful inequalities*, its benefits transferred to strangers ... who *neither have treaties with us* ... nor are friendly to our commerce," it therefore seemed necessary to ask Congress to consider what ought to be done in the matter (*Am. State Papers*, VII, 9; X, 5-6).

It will help to a comprehension of the condition of our merchant marine if we recall once more the feeling of the English public towards the colonists before the war. While statesmen like Robert Peel fostered the growth of American shipping and commerce by encouraging them in evading the navigation laws, the growth thus fostered roused a strong feeling of ill-will on the part of many patriotic Englishmen. This feeling was entirely natural and unavoidable. It was not alone that the Americans were well able to compete with the mother-country for the carrying trade of the world. Under the influence of environment the Americans were developing into a distinct people. The successful colonial was often and perhaps usually self-assertive and boastful; he was necessarily aggressive. Then, too, he showed a lack of deference in the presence of rank that seemed shocking to the nobility. Men who were doing the world's work in the American wilderness made no efforts to conceal their contempt for royal governors, and the influential part of the people of England accepted the complaining letters of these baffled governors as accurate characterizations of the American people. Because of a sort of race prejudice thus produced, the measures of the king, when coercion was attempted, were heartily approved by the majority of the English people.

Then, during the war, the expelled American loyalists had *ex parte* stories to tell that added indignation to animosity. The successful American cruisers added to the ill feeling. At the same time the British authorities observed a tendency among the foremost hands in the British navy that was not a little alarming. While their navy lost, in the years from 1776 to 1780, 19,788 men through disease and battle, no less than 42,069 deserted. Some of these deserters were, of course, Americans who had been impressed, but many a good British tar learned about the opportunities in the new land and made haste to go to meet them.

In short, it was through natural and unavoidable causes that the influential Britons came to regard their "American cousins" with a feeling of, say, intense animosity not wholly unmingled with apprehension.

Keeping in mind this mental attitude, recall the fact that a command of the sea was then absolutely essential to the well-being of the British people, and further, that the supremacy which the British then boasted had been obtained, and maintained for a century, by good hard fighting; and further still, that many British thinkers had been alarmed at such American progress as had been manifested even a hundred years before the Declaration of Independence. Bluntly stated, while the British people had learned to hate the American, they suddenly saw that he alone had shown an ability to dispute that supremacy upon the sea which seemed absolutely necessary for the preservation of their national existence. And as an independent citizen of the world he was in a position to force the issue. It follows, therefore, that the British were naturally led to do all they could to oppose all progress in the United States. The "ruinous restrictions" of which the Charleston ship-builders made mention were a natural sequence of the success of the Revolution.

While the British were thus hostile upon the sea (they were also holding American territory in the West, and inciting the Indians to war), the French and the Spanish were united in an effort to cut off all that part of the United States west of the Appalachians. For civilization was then in the primitive state where men, though they talked about international law, were guided only by unenlightened selfishness, and acknowledged no other court of appeal than that afforded by the sword.

The story of foreign aggressions upon American shipping and commerce will be told in the next chapter, but by way of illustrating conditions in the years following the Revolution, consider one fact regarding the British work of opposition. All American trade with the British West Indies was forbidden, and so strictly was this regulation enforced that thousands of slaves starved to death in those islands for want of the "refuse fish" and other food which the planters had been accustomed to obtain from America; and even some of the poorer white people died for the same reason.

Because of ruined industries, and of a chaotic government at home, and of the ruthless opposition of the nations of Europe, the condition of the people of the United States seemed almost hopeless. So great was the depression of the seafaring part of the population, indeed, that even the optimistic whalers of Nantucket thought about removing their industry to France, and many of them did migrate.

And yet it was in this period of deepest gloom that the American merchant marine first reached out for the trade of the Far East. In the *Journals of Congress* for 1784 (p. 333) is a paragraph referring to "a letter of the 23d December, 1783, from Daniel Parker, stating, that a ship called the '*Empress of China*' will shortly sail from New York for Canton in China, under the command of Captain John Green, and requesting sea-letters."[5]

No commercial ventures to the East Indies were made in colonial days because, in part, of the monopoly of the East India Company, but chiefly because abundant profitable employment for all available capital was found in various trades nearer home. The fact that ships in the China trade very often made cent per cent was, of course, very well known in the colonies, and colonial merchants had a general knowledge of the cargoes suitable for that trade. They knew, for instance, that ginseng, a root growing wild in American forests, was highly valued in China for its supposed medicinal qualities. Accordingly, when the war ended, and American ships were excluded from such a large part of the trade which they had enjoyed in former days, the ship-owners naturally thought of the trade to the Far East. New York and Philadelphia merchants united in fitting out a vessel which they renamed the *Empress of China*. She measured 360 tons, and the chief part of her cargo was ginseng. Sailing from New York on February 22, 1784, with the sea letter noted above for a passport, she arrived at Canton Roads (Macao) on August 23, and she reached home on May 11, 1785. The profit on the venture was $30,000, which, being only a little more than 25 per cent on the investment, was considered small. Other voyages of the period are worth consideration, if only to illustrate the spirit of the ship-owners of the day.

The most interesting of the China voyages, in this point of view, was that of the sloop *Experiment*, a vessel with one mast and a capacity for eighty tons of cargo, that was built at Albany for the trade of the Hudson River. Captain Stewart Dean, her master, had served in two privateers during the Revolution. She carried six cannon, with a liberal supply of small arms, and her crew numbered fifteen (one account says twenty), men and boys. "Martial music and the boatswain's whistle were heard on board with all the pomp and circumstance of war." She carried out ginseng and brought back tea and silks, with profit; and what is of more importance, perhaps, in this story is the fact that she made the return voyage in four months and twelve days. The record shows what a fore-and-aft rig can do in a round-the-world voyage.

In the same year a Hingham sloop of only forty tons, commanded by a Captain Hallett, sailed from Boston, bound for Canton, but got as far only as the Cape of Good Hope. At that point English ship captains offered Captain Hallett two pounds of good tea for each pound of ginseng he carried, and he was willing to take the profit thus insured rather than risk a longer voyage in the hope of a larger one.

The story of the entrance of Elias Hasket Derby, of Salem, into the China trade is of interest because of the view it affords of a peculiarity of most of the successful ship-owners of the day. Derby considered the possibilities of the trade as early as any one, but while the *Empress of China* was on her way to Canton, Derby sent his *Grand Turk* as far as the Cape of Good Hope only. By trading ginseng and provisions to the English captains who were found at the Cape, Captain Ingersoll, commanding the *Grand Turk*, was able to make a fair profit on the voyage; but the main object in view was to learn all about the demands of the Canton trade; and in this he was entirely successful. It may be worth mentioning that Captain Ingersoll also went up the coast of Africa to complete his cargo with gold-dust, ivory, etc., and that he was under orders not to take on slaves, even though he should thereby be able to make a paying voyage out of a losing one. Elias Hasket Derby was one of the few individuals who were far enough ahead of their age to see the iniquity of the trade, but the important feature of the story of the voyage is this, that Derby would take the risks of the voyage to the Cape to obtain information. In the meantime, too, he sent one of his sons to Europe, where he spent several months in a study of the India trade of England and France.

Elias Hasket Derby

From a print in the possession of the Lenox Library

With the knowledge thus gained, Captain Derby despatched the *Grand Turk* (December 5, 1785) on a voyage to the Far East, but instead of sailing direct to Canton she called at the Isle of France (Mauritius); then she went to the coast of India, and thence to Canton. The trade at Mauritius and on the Indian coast added greatly to the profits of the voyage without increasing the length of time required to a serious extent.

The trade to China thus initiated was so profitable that in 1789 no less than fifteen American ships were in the Canton roads, of which four belonged to Captain Derby. One of the four is worth especial notice. She was the swift *Astræ*, Captain James Magee, Jr., commanding, and Thomas Handyside Perkins, supercargo. More than twenty individual ventures were made in this voyage of the *Astræ*, and a few notes from her outward manifest (list of cargo) will serve well to show the course of trade in those days. Thus Tenney and Brown, of Newbury, sent "9 kegs snuff," and a note in the margin of the manifest tells Captain Magee that "⅓ the net proceeds you are to credit E. H. D.'s account for freight—the other ⅔ to lay out on account of T. & B. in light goods." Opposite the item "1 phaeton and harness complete, with saddles and bridles &c., cased up" is a note saying: "This belongs to Folger Pope ... the net proceeds is to be credited to E. H. D.'s account, as friend Derby is to have the use of the money for freight." David Seas sent "Boxes containing $15,000, 16 casks ginseng, 5570 lbs. This at one-fifth for freight." William Cabot sent a box "containing 21 pieces plate, weight 255 oz. 16 dwts. 12 gr." Rum, wines, beer, fish, flour, "598 firkins butter 32,055 lbs," and spermaceti candles were conspicuous items in the manifest.

Some quotations from Derby's letter of instructions to the captain and supercargo are also interesting. "Make the best of your way for Batavia, and on your arrival there you will dispose of such a part of the cargo as you think may be most for my interest. I think you had best sell a few casks of the most ordinary ginseng if you can get one dollar a pound for it. If you find the price of sugar to be low you will then take into the ship as much of the best white kind as will floor her, and fifty thousand weight of coffee, if it is low as we have heard, ... and fifteen thousand of salt petre, if it is very low, some nutmegs, and fifty thousand weight of pepper; this you will store in the fore peak for fear of injuring the teas. The sugars will save the expense of any stone ballast, and it will make a floor for the teas &c. at Canton. At Batavia you must, if possible, get as much freight for Canton as will pay half or more of your charges.... You must endeavor to be the first ship with ginseng, for be assured you will do better alone than you will if there are three or four ships at Canton at the same time with you." As another of the Derby ships was to be at Batavia on the arrival of the *Astræ*, directions were given for the loading or the sale of that vessel, according as circumstances seemed to require, but special stress is laid upon the necessity of making careful calculations before selling the vessel, in order to be sure that that course would pay better than bringing her home full of cargo. It is manifest that Derby did not care to sell her. "Captain Magee and Mr. Perkins are to have 5 per cent commission for the sales of the present cargo, and 2½ per cent on the cargo home, and also 5 per cent on the profit made on goods that may be purchased at Batavia and sold at Canton, or in any other similar case that may arise on the voyage. They are to have one-half the passage money—the other half belongs to the ship. The privilege of Capt. Magee is 5 percent of what the ship carries on cargo exclusive of adventures. The property of Mr. Perkins, it is understood, is to be on freight, which is to be paid for like other freighters. It is orders that the ship's books shall be open to the inspection of the mates and doctor of the ship, so they may know the whole business" in case of the death of captain or supercargo. "The Philadelphia beer is put up so strong that it will not be approved until it is made weaker; you had best try some of it.... The iron is English weight; ... there is four percent you will gain if sold Dutch weight.... You are not to pay any moneys to the crew while absent from home, unless in case of real necessity, and then they must allow an advance for the money.... It is likewise my order that in case of your sickness that you write a clause at the foot of these orders putting the command of the ship into the person's hands that you think the most equal to it, not having any regard to the station he at present has in the ship.... Lay out for my account fifteen or twenty pounds sterling in curiosities."

The sale of the *Astræ* is forbidden for this voyage, but "if at Batavia or Canton you can agree to deliver her the next season for $20,000 or $25,000 you may do it." The final paragraph says that while the orders are "a little particular" "you have leave to break them in any part where you *by calculation* think it for my interest."

As there were fifteen American ships at Canton when the *Astræ* was there, the market was flooded with American goods. Her ginseng sold for $20,000 less than prime cost. Two of Derby's ships were sold; the other two brought home 728,871 pounds of tea. Although the consumption of the country at that time was only about a million pounds a year, the total imports of the year amounted to 2,601,852 pounds. In the meantime the government had been organized under the Constitution and a duty levied on imports which, in the case of the *Astræ*, amounted to about $27,000. On the face of the documents the voyage of the Astræ was disastrous. But Derby, by petition, obtained the privilege of putting his goods in the warehouse and paying the duty as they were sold and removed. The system of bonded warehouses became common later. And according to the biography of Captain Derby, published in *Hunt's Merchants' Magazine*, his capital was not impaired seriously, if at all, by the voyage.

Another merchant who reached out for trade in strange seas was Captain Ebenezer Parsons, who sent ships to the Red Sea, took on cargoes of coffee for Smyrna, and cleared, in some voyages, from 300 to 400 per cent. A still larger profit was made by Captain Jonathan Carnes, of Salem, in a number of ventures to Sumatra. While at Bencoolen, on that island, he learned by accident that pepper grew wild on its uncivilized northwest coast. Returning to Salem, Carnes imparted his information to Jonathan Peele, who at once furnished the money with which a schooner named the *Rajah* was built. Carnes armed the *Rajah* with four guns, shipped a crew of ten men, loaded her with brandy, gin, tobacco, bar iron, and dried fish, and then, in November, 1795, cleared out for the East Indies. These proceedings aroused the greatest curiosity in Boston as well as Salem; for neither owner nor captain would say a word about the destination of the schooner; and this curiosity grew, as the months passed and nothing was heard from the *Rajah*. Accordingly, when, after eighteen months, the schooner came sailing into port loaded to the hatch coamings with pepper, she created more excitement in Salem than any other vessel that entered the port that year. The profit on this voyage amounted to 700 per cent. When the *Rajah* was fitted for a second voyage in the same secret manner, a number of merchants sent other vessels in chase, hoping to find where she obtained her pepper; but Captain Carnes eluded them all, and once more brought home a cargo at an immense profit. In the third voyage, however, his secret buying place was discovered, and thereafter he had to be contented with the ordinary cent per cent.

One of the most celebrated voyages of the period was that of the ship *Columbia*, Captain John Kendrick, with the sloop *Washington*, Captain Robert Gray, as a tender, to the northwest coast of the continent to trade for furs.

The *Columbia* was a ship of 240 tons' burden. She could just carry the cargo of an Erie canal boat of the size in use in 1909. The expedition was fitted out by Joseph Barrell and four others. It sailed on October 1, 1787, and arrived at Nootka Sound in September, 1788. On July 3, 1789, Captain Gray sailed for home in the Columbia; and, returning by the way of China and the Cape of Good Hope, was the first to sail around the world under the American flag. The work done by these two captains is chiefly of interest here, however, because of the discoveries made on the coast and of the use the nation made of the discoveries later. For the Strait of Juan de Fuca and adjoining waters were thoroughly explored, the Columbia River was discovered, and its navigable waters were explored. Land was purchased of the Indians, forts were built, and a vessel called the *Adventurer* (of 40 tons' burden) was launched. The claim thus established by American citizens was used with effect, when it had been made good by subsequent occupation of the land, in settling the boundary between the United States and the British possessions to the north thereof.

The trade on the northwest coast was continued by Boston people with varying results until after the War of 1812, and many interesting stories have been related by those engaged in it. John Ledyard, the American traveller, was first to suggest engaging in it. He was with Captain Cook, when that celebrated explorer was on the northwest coast, and learned that the sea-otter skins, which the Indians had in abundance, could be sold for $120 each in China. On returning home, he almost succeeded in getting Robert Morris to enter the trade, but nothing was done in it until the *Columbia* sailed.

The voyage of the *Columbia* did not pay her owners, but those who followed her often made large profits. Perhaps the most interesting venture was one made by William Sturgis. While trading with the Indians (blankets, cutlery, firearms, molasses, and trinkets were then in demand), he learned that the Indians used the skin of the ermine in its winter coat as a currency, and that it was highly valued. Accordingly, Sturgis sent home a fine specimen of the ermine skin, and ordered as many as could be obtained. His correspondent secured 5000 at the Leipsic fair, and on the next voyage Sturgis carried them to the coast, where he traded five, which had been purchased for thirty cents each, for a sea-otter skin. He thus obtained a thousand sea-otter skins, which he sold in China for $50 each, or $50,000 for that part of the venture alone. Mr. Sturgis, in a lecture delivered in Boston, on January 21, 1846, said that he had known of a capital of $40,000 yielding a return of $150,000 in that trade, and in one voyage "an outfit not exceeding $50,000 gave a gross return of $284,000."

In the meantime Captain Derby's young supercargo on the *Astræ*, Thomas H. Perkins, had established a trading house in Canton. He entered the northwest coast trade with success, and in the course of twenty-two years his ships made thirty round-the-world voyages from Boston, by the way of the Horn, the northwest coast, Canton, and the Cape of Good Hope. It is an interesting fact that in the years immediately following the War of 1812 "all the supplies for the British [fur-buying] establishments, west of the Rocky Mountains, were brought from London to Boston, and carried thence to the mouth of the Columbia in American ships; and all their collections of furs were sent to Canton consigned to an American house, and the proceeds shipped to England or the United States in the same vessels." (*Hunt's Magazine*, XIV, 538.)

In connection with the stories that have been told of these voyages to the Far East, consider the following facts in the biography of Captain Nathaniel Silsbee:—

"Among the officers who rose most rapidly to distinction in the service of Mr. Derby, none is more prominent than the Hon. Nathaniel Silsbee, late Senator from Massachusetts. His father had enjoyed the entire confidence of Mr. Derby, and after his death Mr. Derby transferred that confidence to his son.

"In 1790 he appears as the mate and captain's clerk of a small vessel bound to Madeira. In 1792 [when but nineteen years old] he is master of a sloop in the trade to the West Indies, which Mr. Derby impowers him to sell for $350. In 1793, at the early age of twenty years, he is on a voyage to the Isle of France in command of the new ship *Benjamin*, of 142 tons. From the Isle of France he proceeds to the Cape of Good Hope, returns to the Isle of France, and brings his ship home with large profits.

"In 1796 Mr. Derby dispatches him in the ship *Benjamin* to Amsterdam and thence to the Isle of France, with a credit of $10,000 for his own private adventure. After selling his ship and cargo at a great profit he purchases a new ship of 450 tons for his owner and returns to Salem with a full cargo of East India goods for his owner, and such favorable results for himself as to enable him to commence business on his own account, in which he soon achieved fortune."

When Silsbee, at the age of twenty, was master of the *Benjamin*, on the way to the Isle of France, his first mate, Charles Derby, was nineteen years old, and his second mate, Richard J. Cleveland, was only eighteen. In 1799 this Cleveland made a voyage in a fifty-foot sloop from Canton to the northwest coast of America, and, though hampered by a mutinous crew, he secured there a cargo of furs which sold, on his return to Canton, for $60,000. The outfit had cost him $9000.

Although all ships of the day were, by modern standards, dangerous in size and rig; though scurvy was the plague of crews in long voyages; though vast breadths of the sea had never been explored, and the wild coasts visited had never been charted; although the first voyages were made when the American people were financially prostrate and the symbol of the American government was utterly powerless, not only in home affairs but in the face of the open and covert enmity of the leading commercial nations of the world,—in spite of all this, the American ship-owners reached out for the commerce of all the earth, and *young men having ambition and ability worked their way to the command of ships before they were old enough to vote.*

The picture of one of those boyish sea-captains flinging the Stars and Stripes to the breeze on the far side of the earth portrays, better than anything ever said, written, or done, the spirit of America.

CHAPTER VII
FRENCH AND OTHER SPOLIATIONS

ON July 25, 1785, while the schooner *Maria*, Captain Isaac Stevens, of Boston, was sailing past Cape St. Vincent, on the southwest corner of Spain, she was captured by an armed ship from Algiers, and carried to that port. Five days later the ship *Dauphin*, Captain Richard O'Brien, of Philadelphia, when fifty leagues west of Lisbon, suffered a similar fate. These vessels with their cargoes were confiscated, and the crews, numbering twenty-one men all told, were sold into slavery.

In connection with these facts consider a quotation from Lord Sheffield's *Observations on the Commerce of the United States*, published in 1784;—

"It is not probable that the American States will have a very free trade in the Mediterranean; it will not be the interest of any of the great maritime powers to protect them from the Barbary states. They cannot protect themselves from the latter; they cannot pretend to a navy."

It will now be instructive to recall a letter written by Edward Church, American consul at Lisbon, on October 12, 1793, in regard to the Algerine pirates. Portugal had been protecting her trade from the Algerines by means of war-ships, and had incidentally afforded convoy to such American merchantmen as needed it in those waters. Having learned that a number of Algerine corsairs had gone cruising in the Atlantic, Consul Church went to the Portuguese Minister of Foreign Affairs to learn why the Portuguese war-ships had allowed them to leave the Mediterranean. The minister replied that Charles Logie, British consul at Algiers, acting under orders from the British government, had *concluded* a treaty of peace between Algiers and Portugal. Portugal, he said, had not authorized such a treaty, nor had she been consulted as to the terms. The British government had guaranteed the execution of the treaty, and the payment of the tribute that it called for, however, and with the British to aid them the pirates had gone forth to prey on commerce. Church, with more attention to accuracy than diplomatic language, termed the arrangement thus made a "hellish conspiracy" against American shipping.

A brief account of the Algerine pirates will now prove interesting. For time out of mind the people of the north coast of Africa lived by piracy, but it was not until the seafaring outlaws of Europe taught them to build and handle large ships that they became really menacing to commerce. While the English were fighting the Dutch in the middle of the seventeenth century, they were obliged to send Blake with twenty-five well-armed ships to overawe these pirates. In 1672 another squadron was sent for the same purpose. These two squadrons proved that it was easy and inexpensive to crush the power of the pirates; but instead of continuing to use their navy to protect their merchantmen, the British made no further attacks upon the pirates until 1816. Indeed, instead of crushing their power, the British government adopted the policy of adding to their means of destroying commerce. And in this policy several European powers soon joined.

Secretary of State Jefferson, in a report on "Mediterranean Trade," dated December 30, 1790, said that Spain paid "from three to five million dollars to Algiers" in one lump to induce the Dey to make "peace." France in 1788 had paid an unknown sum in hand, and had since paid an annual subsidy of $100,000 for immunity from attack. Great Britain paid an annual subsidy of 60,000 guineas to the four Barbary powers. Portugal alone of the European maritime powers used her fleet to protect her trade. In addition to the regular subsidies, the powers named made presents to the Barbary chiefs, and these presents included usually, if not always, armed ships and other war material.

The reason for paying subsidies instead of fighting is most interesting. It was done to encourage the pirates to ravage the shipping belonging to the rivals of the subsidy payers.

In 1793 England was at war with France. America was the leading neutral maritime nation. The British statesmen saw that the American shipping would secure much of the trade in the Mediterranean which English ships had been doing, unless checked promptly by some extraordinary means, and it was to administer this check that the pirates were loosed upon the Atlantic.

The injury done to our shipping in the raid mentioned above was insignificant, save only as the story gives emphasis to the other facts given—facts which show the state of civilization among the most enlightened nations of Europe. The state of American civilization, at the time, is shown by the treaty made with the pirates, under which we agreed to pay them tribute; for it was tribute and not subsidy as in our case. We paid it in war material, too, as shown by the following extract from the *Life of General William Eaton*, who, in 1798, was American consul at Tunis:—

"On the 22d of December Mr. Eaton ... went on board the U. S. brig *Sophia*, Capt. Henry Geddes, commander, bound to Algiers; in company with the *Hero*, a ship of 350 tons burden, loaded with naval stores for the Dey of Algiers; the *Hassan Bashaw*, an armed brig of 275 tons, mounting eight 6-pounders, destined to Algiers; the *Skjoldabrand*, a schooner of 250 tons, 16 double fortified 4-pounders, destined to Algiers; and the *La Eisha*, of 150 tons, 14 4-pounders, also destined to Algiers. All these vessels excepting the *Sophia* were to be delivered to the Dey of Algiers, for arrearages of stipulation and present dues."

With these facts in mind we shall be able to comprehend why American shipping was subjected to ruthless spoliations during the entire period between the end of the War of the Revolution and our second war for liberty, which we began in 1812. The sole criterion of right in international affairs was might.

AN EARLY TYPE OF CLIPPER SHIP: *MARIA*, OF NEW BEDFORD, BUILT 1782

As the reader remembers, the French spoliations grew out of the anarchy prevailing during the French Revolution. To appreciate the facts, one needs to put himself in the place of the French people and feel not only their aspirations but their blinding indignation. A well-meaning, most energetic, and (more or less) hysterical National Convention displaced an impotent monarchy. "Of the 11,210 decrees passed by the Convention one-third have a political aim, two-thirds have a humanitarian aim." (Hugo, in *Ninety-Three*.) The surrounding nations, alarmed lest republican principles gain headway among the "common people," formed a coalition to avenge the death of the French king and destroy the French Republic. England, without declaring war, held in her ports all merchantmen (including neutrals) bound for France, and then began to capture and send into port all neutral ships found at sea with cargoes of food for French consignees. It was then that France began to strike back in a way that affected American shipping. In March and April, 1793, our Minister at Paris had to complain of several ships captured by French privateers, and in one of his letters to the French Minister of Foreign Affairs he said:—

"I avoid troubling you with the afflicting recital of the violences committed on those different occasions, and which were so much the less excusable inasmuch as they took place after the prizes were taken possession of, and when no resistance was met with."

On May 9, 1793, the French government authorized the seizure of "all neutral vessels which shall be laden wholly or in part" with food products and "destined for an enemy's port."

The decree was contrary to the treaties made between France and the United States in 1778, but it was confirmed on the 27th of July.

This decree was avowedly made because food was scarce in France and because England was trying to starve the French into submission by stopping all food-laden ships bound for France. In the French view it was justified as a measure of necessity.

On July 2, 1796, however, it was decreed that "the flag of the French Republic will treat neutral vessels either as to confiscation, as to searches or capture in the same manner as they shall suffer the English to treat them."

In the meantime the United States had made, under duress, a treaty with England (Jay's, 1794), which gave the English advantages of which the French, though by treaty our allies, were deprived; and this treaty was ratified in spite of the fact that the British aggressions had exceeded the French not only in extent, but in their aggravating character. Moreover, this treaty was not promulgated until May 9, 1796, and France justly complained of the concealment as disingenuous. It was partly because of the resentment thus created that the decree of July 2, 1796 was made, and it was wholly because of resentment that, on March 2, 1797, a decree was issued declaring that "every American vessel shall be a good prize which has not on board a list of the crew in proper form, such as is presented by the model annexed to the treaty of the 6th February, 1778."

No American vessel had carried this *rôle d'equipage* since the end of the War of the Revolution; the decree was passed with the intention of driving all American ships from the sea. Then, as a final thrust at America, it was decreed that, October 29, 1799, American sailors found serving on the ships of enemies should be treated as pirates, and that they should not be allowed to plead in extenuation that they had been impressed.

The following stories of French aggressions illustrate well the usual course of life at sea in American ships during the period under consideration:—

In 1796 the French privateer *Flying Fish* came to Philadelphia, purchased supplies, and made repairs. In the meantime her captain, aided by the French consul, obtained information about all the ships then loading with valuable cargoes for foreign ports. With these facts in hand the captain then went to the Capes of the Delaware, waited until one of the most valuable of the American ships passed out to sea, and then captured her and turned her crew adrift in a small boat.

In the same year, while the American ship *Hare* was lying in London, with a valuable cargo on board, her captain went to Paris and arranged with the French Minister of Marine to bring her into French waters and have her condemned as a prize to him as captor. And this bargain was carried out.

Some Philadelphia merchants fitted out a vessel named *Les Jumeaux* as a French privateer. When going to sea she drove off a revenue cutter that tried to stop her, and she finally made a prize of a vessel belonging to neighbors of her owner.

The brigantine *Patty*, Captain Josiah Hempsted, belonging to Justus Riley, of Wethersfield, Connecticut, was captured while on her way to St. Bartholomew, on July 31, 1796. When Captain Hempsted appeared before the "special agent" (a sort of governor and judge in admiralty) ruling at Guadaloupe, that official shook his fist under the captain's nose, and said:—

"I have confiscated your vessel and cargo, you damned rascal."

The French frigate *Thetis*, having captured the brigantine *Eliza*, of New York, a seaman named Henry Doughty, a native-born citizen of Boston, was placed with a number of English sailors who had been captured, and was then delivered to the British in exchange for French sailors. Using American sailors in effecting exchanges became a common practice with the French naval commanders.

The crews of American vessels taken to the West Indies were commonly turned ashore without clothing (except what they were wearing), or food, or means of procuring either. On November 10, 1797, seven captured American vessels were lying at Petit Guave, three-fourths of the crews of which had died because of the hardships they had suffered when thus turned ashore. In some cases the crews were imprisoned. Captain Breard, of the schooner *Zephyr*, of Portsmouth, who ventured to go on board the privateer that had captured him and there beg for a little of the food of which he had been robbed, was thrown over the rail. Captain Codwise, of the brig *Glasgow*, was thrown into prison at Leogane and kept for thirty-six hours without food.

A more cheerful picture of the life at sea in American ships at that time is found in a letter (written in 1799) from Captain Elias Hasket Derby, Jr., to his father. The young man was in command of the Salem ship *Mount*

Vernon, and he had arrived at Gibraltar after a passage of seventeen and a half days.

"The first of our passage was quite agreeable; the latter, light winds, calm, and Frenchmen constantly in sight for the last four days. The first Frenchmen we saw was off Tercira—a lugger to the southward. Being uncertain of his force we stood by him to leeward on our course and soon left him. July 28th, in the afternoon, we found ourselves approaching a fleet of upwards of fifty sail, steering nearly N. E. We run directly for their center; at 4 o'clock found ourselves in their half-moon; concluding it impossible that it could be any other than the English fleet, continued our course for their center to avoid any apprehension of a want of confidence in them. They soon dispatched an 18-gun ship from their center, and two frigates, one from their van and another from their rear, to beat towards us—we being to windward. On approaching the center ship under easy sail I fortunately bethought myself that it would be but common prudence to steer so far to windward of him as to be a grapeshot's distance from him, to observe his force and maneuvering. When we were abreast of him he fired a gun to leeward and hoisted English colors. We immediately bore away and meant to pass under his quarter, between him and the fleet showing our American colors. This movement disconcerted him, and it appeared to me he either conceived we were either an American sloop of war, or an English one in disguise, attempting to cut him off from the fleet; for while we were in the act of wearing on his beam he hoisted French colors and gave us a broadside. We immediately brought our ship to the wind, and stood on about a mile—wore towards the center of the fleet—hove about and crossed him on the other tack, about half grapeshot distance, and received his broadside; several shot fell on board of us without much damage. All hands were active in clearing ship for action, for our surprise had been complete. In about ten minutes we began firing our stern chasers and in a quarter of an hour gave him our broadside in such style as evidently sickened him, for he immediately luffed in the wind, gave us his broadside, went in stays in great confusion, wore ship afterwards in a large circle, and renewed the chase at a mile and a half distance—a maneuver calculated to keep up appearances with the fleet and escape our shot.

"At midnight we had distanced them; the chasing rocket signals being almost out of sight. We have been in constant brushes ever since. The day after we left the fleet we were chased till night by two frigates, whom we lost sight of when it was dark. The next morning off Cape St. Vincent, were chased by a French lateen-rigged vessel, apparently 10 or 12 guns, one of them an 18-pounder. We brought to for him, [but] his metal was too heavy for ours, and his position to windward.... [As] it was not in my power to cut him off we of course bore away and saluted him with our long nines. He continued his chase till dark, and when we were nearly by Cadiz, at sunset, he made a signal to a consort whom we had just discovered ahead. Having a strong breeze I was determined to pass my stern over him if he did not make way for me. He thought prudent to do so. At midnight we made the lights in Cadiz city, but found no English fleet. After lying to till daylight concluded that the French must have gained the ascendancy in Cadiz and thought prudent to proceed to this place, where we arrived at 12 o'clock, popping at Frenchmen all the forenoon. At 10 A.M., off Algesiras Point, were seriously attacked by a large lateener who had on board more than 100 men. He came so near our broadside as to allow our 6-pound grape to do execution handsomely. We then bore away and gave him our stern guns in a cool and deliberate manner, doing apparently great execution. Our bars having cut his sails considerably, he was thrown into confusion, struck both his ensign and his pennant. I was then puzzled to know what to do with so many men. Our ship was running large, with all her steering sails out, so that we could not immediately bring her to the wind; and we were immediately off Algesiras Point, from which I had reason to fear she might receive assistance, and my port, (Gibraltar) in full view. These circumstances induced me to give up the gratification of bringing him in. It was, however, a satisfaction to flog the rascal in full view of the English fleet who were to leeward. The risk of sending here is great indeed for any ship short of our force in men and guns—but particularly [when short of] heavy guns. Two nines are better than six or eight sixes, and two long twelves do better than twenty sixes.... I have now, while writing to you, two of our countrymen in full view who are prizes to these villains. Lord St. Vincent, in a 50-gun ship, is in the act of retaking one of them. The other goes into Algesiras without molestation."

Spain took scores of American ships, and when the French privateers carried an American ship into a Spanish port, the Spanish officials invariably assisted in the robbery. The other nations robbed in proportion to their power and opportunity. The third volume of our *Foreign Relations* contains a list of fifty-one American ships that were carried into the ports of Denmark and Sweden. The French aggressors were inspired primarily, as said, by indignation; the English were acting in defence of their maritime supremacy, as shall appear further on, but these smaller powers of Europe were animated by no other motive than that of the Algerine pirates.

As to the total of the damages suffered from the French republicans, it must be said that no complete calculation was ever made. But documents written under oath show that more than 600 ships were despoiled before the year 1800, and that losses amounting to more than $20,000,000 were sustained. These losses included ships and cargoes only; incidental losses due to the conditions at sea could not be measured.

Though really a part of our naval history, perhaps it may be worth adding that when, at last, our naval ships, though few in numbers and small in size, were ordered to sea to protect our trade, no more than three or four well-fought actions were needed to bring the French Republic spoliations to an end. It was, and, unhappily, it is yet, in human nature to despise any appeal to altruistic notions of right in an effort to secure justice, but all accord hearty respect to him who is able and willing to fight for his rights. We were amused by the antics of the Japanese as a nation of artists; we took off our hats and stood erect with our heels together in the presence of the heroes of the Battle of the Yellow Sea.

CHAPTER VIII
THE BRITISH AGGRESSIONS

BEFORE considering the aggressions of the British government upon our shipping during the period between the Revolution and the War of 1812, it seems still more necessary than it was in the case of the French to try to get the point of view of the aggressor. The men who governed England were placed in power not only to guard but to promote English interests against those of all other nations. Patriotism and natural ambition inspired them to do this as fully as possible. The welfare of the nation being in their charge, it was their duty to consider first of all entire safety from invasion, as everybody believed then, and believes now, that safety depended upon the supremacy of the nation upon the high seas. To maintain that supremacy every Briton felt obliged to make every needed sacrifice. Small wonder, then, that in maintaining that supremacy the rulers of England should have felt obliged to hamper all possible rivals for that supremacy. The state of public mind at the end of a century wherein England had been at war four years for every three of peace demanded that the British supremacy at sea be maintained at *any* cost; and the morality of the world has not even yet reached a condition where an English patriot can feel sentiments differing greatly from those of the end of the eighteenth century.

At the beginning of the twentieth century, civilized nations acknowledge certain rules of national conduct called international law, but at the end of the eighteenth nothing of the kind had any real weight in regulating international affairs. Men quoted Vattel in their correspondence, but the one recognized rule contained three words only, "Might makes right." Practical, not altruistic, considerations controlled all negotiations, *and no nation had, or could expect to maintain, any "right" which it was unwilling to support by force.* It was the duty of neutral powers to build ships of the line, or meekly suffer the consequences. The facts of history support no statement more fully than this, that American shipping suffered from spoliations, between 1783 and 1812, solely because they begged, instead of fighting, for that freedom of the sea which they claimed as a natural right.

As an introduction to the story of the British aggressions, here are a few extracts from letters written by one Phineas Bond, a native-born American who served England as consul at Philadelphia, beginning in 1787. The letters were written either to the British Secretary of State for Foreign Affairs, or to one of the under secretaries. (See *An. Rep. Am. Hist. Asso.,* 1894.)

On February 21, 1787, in referring to an act of Parliament relating to the registry of English ships, Bond said that "if properly pointed it must inevitably cramp the remnant of commerce now enjoyed by this country." He is confident that the "alarm and perplexity" which the act occasioned in America, prove that it will be beneficial to British shipping.

On May 17 Bond said that the American ships from China were bringing home more goods than the country could use, and that the surplus was shipped to Europe, where it would undersell the goods of the British East India Company. By the use of bribes (he speaks plainly of bribing officials), he obtained copies of the manifests of all American ships from China, and forwarded them to England. Then on July 2 he wrote:—

"This country is so restricted by the regulations of trade of other nations ... and so weak are the resources of the merchants *here*, that if an early check or restraint can be thrown in their way, either by thwarting their credit or by withholding the articles suitable to their commerce, they would never rally; and then, my Lord, they would be confined to their coasting trade and to illicit communication with the Spaniards: These come in a secret manner into the ports of America and bring specie to a large amount ... the amount of specie is enormous ... at least 500,000 dollars were brought into this port last year." To take away this trade with the Spaniards Bond advised the "establishing of a free port in the Bahamas ... from which the Spaniards could draw the supplies they want."

In a letter dated September 29 Bond took a look ahead: "The rumor of war has inspired the Americans with new spirits: they anticipate the benefits of a free trade, and already calculate upon the profits of being the carriers to all the belligerent powers."

In a letter dated November 20 Bond tells "of two persons, natives of England who with great resolution and no small personal risque purchased here and reshipped to Liverpool three machines for spinning cotton and a machine for carding cotton for spinning." The machines had been brought from Liverpool "clandestinely ... packed in queensware crates." They were bought by the "natives of England" and reshipped to Liverpool in order to hinder the establishment of a cotton-spinning industry in the United States.

Bond said he did not "apprehend" that any such factories would be "speedily brought to a state of Rivalship with those of Gt. Britain," but it was "fit to guard against an evil which tho' at present in its infancy," might grow in time.

In several letters Bond urged that restrictions be placed upon passenger-carrying ships leaving England for the United States, "Under color of a humane provision for the comfort of" emigrants, in order to stop or at least "discourage" all emigrants, and especially mechanics, likely to be of value in developing the industries of the United States.

Of especial interest is the warning which Bond sent when he learned that the British government considered the propriety of admitting American vessels of limited size, (seventy tons was offered later), into the trade of the British West Indies. He said:—

"Any indulgence of this sort would certainly divert the trade out of its present channel—the people of New England are an enterprising people, the number of their ports and the locality of their situation favor the increase of seamen. They navigate their vessels frugally and their outfits are infinitely less expensive than the outfits of Brit. vessels. When once admitted to trade with the W. India Islands, ship building which has lain dormant, almost, and which was formerly a source of great profit to this country, would instantly be revived—*America would soon monopolize* the advantages of carrying; limited as to size the numbers of her vessels would be increased, and by increasing the numbers would supply the means of conveying all the produce of America which is consumed in our islands, and that, too, at a much cheaper rate than any other nation could afford. But the enterprising spirit of the people of New England would, as soon as they found the channels of profit open, be exerted to the raising a maritime force which in case of future war might operate very detrimentally to the interests of England."

That Bond was encouraged in this kind of work appears from the fact that he was promoted later. There was no detail of American business too small to escape the careful attention of the British government in its efforts to throw what Bond called an "early check or restraint" upon all American progress, and especially upon the prosperity of American shipping.

A comparison, briefly made, of the laws and regulations of England and the United States follows:—

The British prohibited American vessels from entering the ports of their West India Islands, Canada, and other American possessions, and their East India spice market. We admitted British vessels into all our ports on payment of a tonnage tax of fifty cents per ton (our ships paid six cents per ton), and goods brought in British ships paid a revenue duty of 10 per cent more than goods in ours.

In the treaty made in 1794 the British offered to let our vessels of no more than seventy tons enter their West Indies on condition that we would admit British ships of any size on payment of the same tax and duty as our own.

The British imposed double lighthouse taxes on American vessels bound to any port in England except London. We imposed no extra lighthouse dues.

British merchants were prohibited from using American-built vessels in a number of trades. We allowed our merchants to use British-built vessels in any trade on payment of the extra dues mentioned above.

The British prohibited the importation of goods by American vessels from every country except the United States. We permitted the British vessels to bring us goods from all countries.

The British prohibited the importation of some of our agricultural products during specified periods of time, and of some at all times. We admitted the importation of all British agricultural products at all times.

An American citizen was not allowed to import some goods into some ports of the British domain, even in British ships. In other ports an extra tax was laid on the American. We permitted the British citizen to import all goods into all our ports, and we laid no extra tax upon him.

The British prohibited the consumption of certain American articles the importation of which they permitted. We did not prohibit the consumption of any British article.

The British prohibited the importation of American goods from all countries except the United States. We permitted the importation of British goods from all countries.

Consul Bond, in a letter (April 19, 1789), to Lord Carmarthen, berated Mr. Madison because "he by no means adverts to that important consideration, that so great indulgence has been granted by Gt. Britain to the United States."

Omitting for want of space any account of many previous attacks upon American shipping, it may be said that the first made in connection with the war upon the French Republic was the order to British warships on June 8, 1793, to "detain all vessels laden wholly or in part with corn, flour or meal" bound to any French port. It was provided that each ship so captured should be restored, but the cargo was to be confiscated for the account of the British government, which was to pay for it the invoice cost with 10 per cent added. This order was issued ostensibly to starve the French republicans into submission to the old monarchy, but it was well known that no such result could follow because France had never depended upon the United States for any part of its bread worth mention. Thus, in 1792, when we exported 546,913 bushels of wheat to Great Britain and her possessions, France took only 54 bushels. The order, therefore, had some other object in view, and the brief story of the ship *Neptune*, Captain Jeffries, is instructive at this point. When the *Neptune* was captured under this order, she was restored as soon as convenient to do so, and an order was issued for the payment of the invoice price of her cargo with 10 per cent added. The addition of 10 per cent for profit seemed at first glance to be an effort to act with some degree of fairness, but as a matter of fact the owners were deliberately robbed; the market price of wheat in England, at that time, was very much higher than the invoice price with 10 per cent added, and Captain Jeffries pleaded for permission, not to go on to the port for which he had been sailing (where the price was still higher), but for permission to sell the grain to merchants there in London, who were anxious to give the market price; but the government insisted on taking it at the mere advance of 10 per cent.

We may suppose that Captain Jeffries's failure to be satisfied with a profit of 10 per cent was considered a plain illustration of American avarice.

On November 6, 1793, British cruisers were ordered to capture all neutral ships laden with the produce of the French West Indies. American ships were carrying immense quantities of those goods, and all the larger because they were excluded from the British West Indies. To make certain of a clean sweep of these American ships, the order in council was kept secret for several weeks in order to give the British cruisers time enough to get on the ground and take everything unawares. (H. Adams, II, 322.)

On January 8, 1794, this order was changed so as to permit American ships to carry the French colonial produce to American ports, but the direct trade to Europe was still forbidden. In the meantime more than 200 American vessels had been captured and confiscated under the original order.

While American ships were forbidden to carry French colonial goods from the colonies direct to France, they were, as said, yet allowed to carry the produce to the United States and then reëxport it to Europe, provided it was entered in the American port, landed, and all duties, etc., paid before the voyage was continued. In the case of the *Polly*, decided April 29, 1800, Sir William Scott (Lord Stowell), confirmed this right of American ships, and the American minister "succeeded in obtaining from Pitt an express acceptance of this rule." One may note that this concession was obtained immediately after our warships had been sent to protect our merchantmen from the aggressions of the French; the guns of the *Constellation* had been heard in London, so to speak.

When, on April 29, 1803, England declared war upon Napoleon, however, a new administration had been inaugurated in the United States, and all Europe knew that no use would be made of such American war-ships as remained in commission. Accordingly, as a first measure to hamper the American ships in their effort to become carriers for the beleaguered French, two British frigates were sent to Sandy Hook to detain and search all ships for property belonging to the French. American waters were occupied for the purpose of hampering American trade. In the course of the blockade thus established, a British gunner, just for a joke, fired a shot at a coaster, aiming so as to frighten the crew. The man at the coaster's helm was killed.

This invasion of American waters was a fair notice of the British determination to compel the United States to abide by all English laws and orders in council made for the protection of British shipping. By refusing to declare war, the American administration justified the aggressors.

Then the British government, still further to promote British trade and shipping, adopted Phineas Bond's advice, and established free ports in the West Indies, to which small unarmed traders from the colonies of the enemy were invited to come and buy British goods. These free ports were supplied by British ships under convoy.

In the meantime preparations were made to deprive the Americans of the indirect trade from the French colonies by way of the United States to Europe. On July 23, 1805, Sir William Scott, reversing his decision in the case of the *Polly*, decided that a ship called the *Essex* was a good prize, although in a voyage from Bordeaux she had called at Salem, discharged cargo, made repairs, and reloaded before heading away for a West India port.

The all-influential British navy had joined in with the British ship-owner to demand that the American ships should be excluded from all trade between the colonies of the enemy and Europe. The ship-owners demanded it because the American ship, in spite of the great expense of the indirect voyage, was yet able to take the trade from the British, even though they were supported by free ports and other aids. The demand made by or for the British naval officers was unique. When voiced by one James Stephens (*War in Disguise; or the Frauds of the Neutral Flags*), he pictured a British admiral grown old and full of honors in the service, who, in spite of his honors, had been unable "to wrest [from the enemy] the means of comfortably sustaining those honors." As long as American ships were allowed to engage in the indirect trade, the naval officer would have to "look in vain for any subject of *safe* and uncontested capture." If American ships were excluded, they would still take chances, and they would then be captured without danger and condemned without contest.

Mere mention need be made of the British practice of taking American sailors from American ships and compelling them to serve in British warships. Many American merchantmen were left short-handed upon the high seas, and there is no doubt that some of them were, for this reason, lost with all hands. The practice was maintained as one method of depressing our navigation, but the subject seems to belong to our naval histories.

Brief space will serve for a consideration of the various orders in council and paper blockades issued and laid in 1806 and 1807. In May, 1806, the British declared that the European coast "from the river Elbe to the port of Brest inclusive ... must be considered as blockaded." No blockading fleet was maintained. In reply to this Napoleon issued his Berlin decree declaring the British islands "in a state of blockade," and that "all commerce and correspondence with the British Islands is prohibited."

The French navy was unable to go to sea; Napoleon had only a few privateers with which to enforce his decree, but the British used it as an excuse for the order in council of January 7, 1807, by which no vessel was "permitted to trade from one port to another both which ports shall" be so far under the control of the enemy "*that British vessels may not trade freely thereat.*"

"If we may not no one else shall." The chief influence of this order upon American vessels was to interdict their trade as coasters in Europe, and to prevent their seeking a cargo in another port when they failed to find one in the first port entered.

The order in council of November 11, 1807, was issued partly because, as it stated, that the one of January 7 had failed to induce Napoleon to withdraw his Berlin decree, and because no neutral power had declared war upon him because of that failure. The chief reason for issuing it however (and this was also plainly declared), was "for *supporting that maritime power* which the exertions and valor of his [the British king's] people have, under the blessing of Providence enabled him to establish and maintain." To this end all the ports from which "the British flag is excluded" were declared in a state of blockade. "Maritime power" meant "merchant marine."

The principal ports of the world to which American vessels had been accustomed to trade, having thus been closed with a paper blockade, they were all reopened again on condition that the trade to them be carried on by way of England. On the 25th of the month it was further provided that the ships thus trading by way of England were to land their cargoes in the English port visited.

This placed the ships of the United States in the condition endured by American vessels in colonial days when goods purchased in Europe had to be carried to an English port and "laid on shore" before they were taken to America. Some writers have supposed that this was done as a step toward returning the United States once more to the position of colonies. The fact is that the rulers of England had found that they could not exclude American ships altogether from the sea, and they had determined, therefore, to make them serve British interests as far as possible—first by carrying *British goods* to the ports from which British ships were excluded, and second, by making them pay a tribute by landing their cargoes in English ports. Practically the United States was thus made a vassal of England.

In reply to this order Napoleon decreed that any ship that should in any way submit to or take advantage of it should be good prize.

The dates of the several orders in council and decrees are of some interest because these show that the British began the series by the paper blockade from the Elbe to Brest. But the chief interest is in the fact that the orders were all issued for the benefit of British *trade*. The talk found in various histories about "retaliation" and England's "death struggle with tyranny" was all sham. Said Spencer Percival, in a frank speech in Parliament, (March 3, 1812):—

"The object of the orders in council was not to destroy the trade of the continent but to force the continent to trade with us."

"I am of the opinion," said Lord Hawkesbury, "that *some decisive measure* in support of our own commerce ... is become indispensable, not merely as a measure of commercial policy, *but in order to put the contest in which we are engaged upon its true grounds*." (Quoted by H. Adams, IV, 90.)

But while England strove by every means to preserve her trade and shipping at the expense of her American rival, and Napoleon, with motives no higher than those of a highwayman, confiscated American ships and cargoes to the value of $10,000,000, the American merchant marine prospered.

On December 31, 1789, ships of an aggregate capacity of 123,893 tons were registered under the American flag for foreign trade. In 1792 the tonnage registered was 411,438. In 1793, the first year of extensive spoliations, the tonnage was reduced to 367,734, but thereafter, in spite of the fact that Americans were obliged to fight their way through swarming enemies, our shipping grew until in 1800 we made boast of the possession of 667,107 tons in the foreign trade. Further than that, British shipping aggregating 115,000 tons entered and cleared out of American ports in 1790, but in 1800, only 40,000 tons. From 1790 to 1792 the American tonnage that entered and cleared averaged 54,000 tons a year; in 1800 the tonnage that entered and cleared was 236,000.

Even when the stupidity of the administration added the embargo to all other ills afflicting our shipping, its vigor was not destroyed. The registered tonnage fell from 840,163 in 1807 to 765,252 in 1808 under the embargo, but after the embargo was removed (March 1, 1809), the figures grew within the year to 906,855, and in 1810 we had 981,019 tons registered for foreign trade. Moreover, 127,000 tons of new ships were built during that year, and in that year, too, our ships carried 91.5 per cent of all American imports and exports.

The reasons for this prosperity are readily found. American enterprise was, in those days, irrepressible. When Salem merchants heard that dried sea slugs (*bêche de mer*) were highly prized as food in China, and that the waters of the Fiji Islands swarmed with the worms, they despatched the bark *Active* (July 26, 1811), under Captain William P. Richardson, to collect and dry enough of the slugs to freight the ship for the Canton market. A more remarkable illustration of the enterprise of the day is found, perhaps, in the fact that when a colony of New Englanders settled at Marietta, Ohio (Captain Abraham Whipple was of the number), they began to build ships there for the deep-water trade. The brig *St. Clair*, of 110 tons, was launched in 1800. In 1801 a ship of 230 tons and a brig of 126 were built. Three ships of 300 or more tons were completed in 1806 besides a number of smaller ones. A similar record was made the next year. The largest ship built there was the *Francis*, of 350 tons, built by Whitney for B. J. Gilman. She was of the largest size of her day. In all, seven ships, eleven brigs, six schooners, and two gunboats (for the navy), were built at Marietta before the War of 1812. Imagine a full-rigged ship, with all sails set, plunging down over the Falls of the Ohio!

To enterprise was added unequalled opportunity. The wars of Europe drove the ships of European nations from the sea, save only as voyages were made under convoy. The Americans took the risks because the pay was adequate. Captain George Coggeshall, in *American Privateers* (p. 200), says he received $45 per ton freight from Bordeaux to Boston. In the voyage of Captain Elias Hasket Derby, described in the last chapter, his cargo carried to Gibraltar cost him $43,275. The net profit made upon it was more than $100,000.

How the perils of trade affected the quality of American ships, especially their speed, must have mention. Hundreds of our vessels were captured by the enemy, but many more were chased in vain. It was at this time that the Baltimore clippers gained world-wide fame. The narrow and shoal waters of the Chesapeake had compelled Baltimore designers to make shallow models that could beat to windward swiftly in all winds. The peculiarity of these vessels was the great breadth of beam and a consequent ability to carry large areas of sail. No models equalled those of Baltimore, and when speed was the price of safety at sea, the Baltimore model was copied everywhere in America.

A Virginia Pilot-boat, with a Distant View of Cape Henry, at the Entrance of the Chesapeake

When our tonnage in the foreign trade almost reached the million mark in 1810, the most efficient ships in the world were those under the American flag. And the character of our merchant seamen is shown by the fact that when the British confiscated one of our ships, they were obliged to cut down her spars before they could handle her. And yet some of our nautical writers would have us believe that American ships increased in number in those days because, they say, a discriminating duty laid on imports brought to the country in foreign ships afforded "protection" to ships under the American flag!

CHAPTER IX
THE BEGINNINGS OF STEAM NAVIGATION

IT will help us to appreciate the work of the men who first experimented with steam-driven ships if we recall the fact that James Watt, working at Soho, near Birmingham, England, invented the engine which used steam on both sides of the piston in 1782, and that it was for many years after that date an enormously heavy and cumbersome machine. From this fact we see the state of the mechanic arts in England at the end of the eighteenth century, when practical experiments in steam navigation were first begun. That the state of those arts was still lower in the United States would be naturally inferred from the story of Bond's efforts to restrain progress by reëxporting the machinery that had been imported at Philadelphia. As a matter of fact, when one American inventor began to make experiments in steam navigation, he was obliged first of all to train men in the work of building engines; he was unable to find, anywhere in the country, men with the necessary skill.

One of the most curious of the early experiments was that made by James Rumsey, who was a bath tender at a pleasure resort in Virginia. He first planned to mount an old-style, single-acting engine in a boat, connect it with a pump, draw in water through a pipe at the bow, and then force it out astern. When this plan was explained to Washington, he wrote a testimonial, saying, "the discovery is of great importance." A boat built on this plan was eventually driven at a speed of four miles an hour. Rumsey also experimented with a screw propeller, but he was poor, and could not carry the experiment to a conclusion. Finally he went to England to get capital (a fact to be remembered), and there he died before he could accomplish anything of real moment.

Another interesting experimenter was John Fitch, of Pennsylvania, a man who was handy in the use of tools, and who was also a surveyor and mapmaker. On December 2, 1785, he presented to the American Philosophical Society of Philadelphia a model, with drawings, of a steamboat. The New Jersey legislature then gave him the exclusive right to navigate the waters of the State with steamboats, and a company was organized to develop the invention. The first engine built had a 3-inch cylinder. It was mounted in a skiff and was connected at one time with a screw propeller, at another with an endless chain dragging alongside, and with a "screw and paddles," but neither device would drive the boat at a practical speed. Then Fitch conceived the idea of driving with paddles somewhat after the fashion of canoe men. This plan worked so well that a boat forty feet long was built and furnished with an engine having a 12-inch cylinder. In spite of the fact that the cylinder of this engine had wooden ends that leaked, and a piston that did not fit the bore, the boat was driven at a speed of four knots an hour.

In 1788 Fitch built a boat sixty feet long with a larger engine, and in October she carried thirty passengers to Burlington, New Jersey, a distance of twenty miles, in three hours and ten minutes. The speed of this boat being unsatisfactory, still another was built, and in May, 1790, she covered a measured mile in seven and a half minutes, or at the rate of eight miles an hour. She was then put on the river as a packet plying between Philadelphia and Trenton, and made more than thirty trips of which records remain. She was operated by paddles at the stern.

Though Fitch's plan was not the best conceivable, it is now admitted that his boat was a mechanical success. He built a workable boat, but, unhappily, he was far ahead of his day in his hopes and work. The people were not yet ready for steam navigation, and the company failed to pay dividends. Meantime another boat that he had built to run on the Mississippi was wrecked, and that loss ended the enterprise. Fitch finally went to the banks of the Ohio, where he continued his efforts without success.

"The day will come," he wrote, "when some more powerful man will get fame and fortune from *my* invention, but nobody will believe that poor John Fitch can do anything worthy of attention." Then he killed himself.

In 1786, Oliver Evans, a Philadelphia millwright, asked the legislature of the State to give him the exclusive right to build steam gristmills and road-wagons,—automobiles, in other words,—but his plans were not treated seriously. In 1801, however, he built a steam plaster mill, and in 1804 he demonstrated, in a way that yet astonishes the reader, the entire feasibility of steam navigation.

Having obtained a contract for dredging some of the slips along the Philadelphia water front, he built a scow, 30 × 12 feet large, to carry the dredge. The scow was put together at his shop, which was located a mile from the Schuylkill. When done, he mounted a steam engine, (5 × 19 inches large), on its deck, placed temporary wooden axles with temporary wooden wheels underneath, connected the axles and engine shaft, and then steamed away to the river. There he removed the wheels and put a paddle wheel at the stern for use afloat. Then he launched his scow, steamed down the Schuylkill and up to the slips he was to dredge. The engine was thereafter used in the work of dredging. Although that was in 1804, the people were not yet ready for steam navigation. The only practical result of the work of Evans was the adoption of the high-pressure engine, so called. His engine had no condenser. It exhausted its steam into the open air, and this style of engine was found to be best adapted for use on the steamboats of the Western rivers, later on.

In the meantime Robert Fulton, who was to succeed, had been at work. Fulton was a Pennsylvania artist who had shown so much talent that he went to England to study under Benjamin West. In the meantime, however, he had been greatly interested in mechanics, and had dreamed of steamboats. In London his thoughts turned more and more to mechanics, and in 1793 he abandoned art to take up his life-work.

In the popular view the most interesting chapter in Fulton's life is that relating the story of the first voyage of his first steamship; but for the encouragement of struggling inventors the most important facts in his life are those showing how he went about his task. For Fulton made a thorough study of his subject; while experimenting for himself he took care to learn as much as possible about what others had already done in the same line. In modern days, when every important invention is known to be a development from crude ideas and appliances into a perfect design, it seems not a little curious to read that in Fulton's time his method of work—his determination to learn his subject thoroughly before building—was considered not quite creditable. Invention, it was thought, consisted in working out an inspiration in the dark!

Fulton's first effort to build a steamship was made in 1794, when he went to Paris and tried to induce the National Convention to take up the invention, and thus "deliver France and the whole world from British oppression." Of course the chaotic conditions in Paris prevented the realization of his hopes.

Returning to England, Fulton published a pamphlet on steam navigation (1796), but failed to interest the people. Then he became interested in marine torpedoes and submarine navigation. With these ideas he went again to Paris (1802), where he made experiments in working a boat under water, but failed to convince Napoleon, who was then the despotic ruler of France. While thus engaged, however, he met Robert R. Livingston, the American minister to France. In connection with John Stevens and Nicholas J. Roosevelt, of New Jersey, Livingston had already made experiments looking toward steam navigation on the Hudson, and in aid of his enterprise had secured from the legislature of New York the exclusive privilege of navigating New York waters with steamboats. This privilege had expired by limitation, and the experiments had come to an end, so far as he was concerned, but on meeting the enthusiastic Fulton he at once became interested again, and furnished money for further experiments.

Thereupon Fulton built a steamboat that, when launched upon the Seine, in 1803, instantly broke in two and sank. The frames were not strong enough. Fishing up the engine, Fulton built a stronger hull, and this time the engine worked, though the speed was so slow that only Fulton and Livingston believed the experiment to be a success.

With the optimism that breeds success, Fulton, backed by Livingston, now made drawings of an engine to be used in a boat which he purposed building upon the Hudson, and these plans he carried to England, where he ordered his engine of Watt, who was building the most efficient engines in use.

In the meantime, William Symington, a Scotch engine builder, had been experimenting with steamboats. In 1789 he had installed an engine upon a double-hulled yacht, with which one Patrick Millar navigated Lake Dalwinston, in Scotland. Although Millar spent $150,000 in experiments with steam, nothing came of them. In 1801 Symington induced Lord Dundas, president of the Forth & Clyde Canal Company, to build a steam-tug for towing barges.

This tug, named the *Charlotte Dundas*, had an engine with a 22-inch cylinder (stroke four feet), and the piston was connected directly with the shaft of a stern paddle-wheel by means of a piston rod and a connecting rod—a plan of such simplicity that it came into universal use later on. The rudder of the boat was handled by means of a wheel placed near the bow, and this plan, too, received universal approval. In March, 1802, this tug towed two 70-ton barges nineteen miles and a half, against a strong wind, in six hours. As a demonstration of the feasibility of steam navigation on smooth water, that passage should have been entirely convincing, but the fear that the wash from the wheel, or wheels (for Symington thought to try side-wheels), would injure the banks of the canal, prevented the adoption of the tug.

Fulton had learned about the experiments with this tug, and while in England contracting for the engine mentioned, he went to Scotland and visited Symington, who fired up the boat and showed Fulton how it worked.

In December, 1806, Fulton came to New York, where he contracted with Charles Brown, who had a shipyard on East River, between Stanton and Third streets, for the hull of a new boat. The model of this hull is memorable. In planning ships in those days it was customary to make them approximately three and a half times as long as they were broad, and at least half as deep as they were broad. But Fulton's plans called for a keelless hull 140 feet long over all, by 13 feet wide, and only 7 feet deep. One feels a certain sympathy, even now, for the sailors of that day who, on learning the facts about this ship, named it *Fulton's Folly*.

The boiler for supplying the engine with steam was 20 feet long, 8 wide, and 7 feet deep. It was set in masonry. The fuel used was dry pine. The engine had a cylinder 24 inches in diameter with a 4-foot stroke. It was not a typical Watt engine, however, for Watt's piston rods were kept in line by a combination of levers and rods known as a "parallel motion," while Fulton had called for a cross-head on the end of the piston rod, and the cross-head worked in guides in an A-frame. From each end of the cross-head hung a connecting rod. These connecting rods were joined to a "bell-crank," which was not unlike a "walking beam" in the modern river-boat, but it was located down in the hull. Connecting rods led from the bell-crank to cog-wheels on the inner ends of the two main shafts. The cog-wheels served as cranks which turned with the vibrations of the bell-crank. The paddle-wheels were on the outboard ends of the main shafts, of course. Then cog-wheels on the inner ends of these shafts geared into pinions on a smaller shaft which carried two fly-wheels, placed outside the hull, which were provided to carry the engine over the "dead centre" at each end of the stroke. The paddle-wheels were 14 feet in diameter. The main shafts were each of cast iron, and 4½ inches in diameter. The A-frame and guides, the cross-head, the bell-crank and connecting rods to the cross-head, and crank cog-wheels, the crank-wheels, paddle-wheels, and shafts, and the fly-wheels and their driving gear were all of Fulton's design.

According to Fulton's diary, he paid Watt £548 for the engine. The boiler, built by Cave & Son, of London, cost "at 2*s* 2*d* the pound, £476 11*s* 2*d*." This was the first engine of the kind that Watt was allowed to build for export, and Fulton writes on March 22, 1805:—

"Fee at the treasury on receiving permission to ship the engine to America, £2 14*s* 6*d*."

Fulton had no little trouble in raising the money for his boat. Livingston contributed the larger share, while Joel Barlow and David Dunham gave the next larger shares. The remainder of the sum was collected among personal friends by personal solicitation, and that was work that tried the soul of the man. The fact that the engine lay on the pier where it was landed for a period of six months because Fulton could not raise the money to pay the freight is significant.

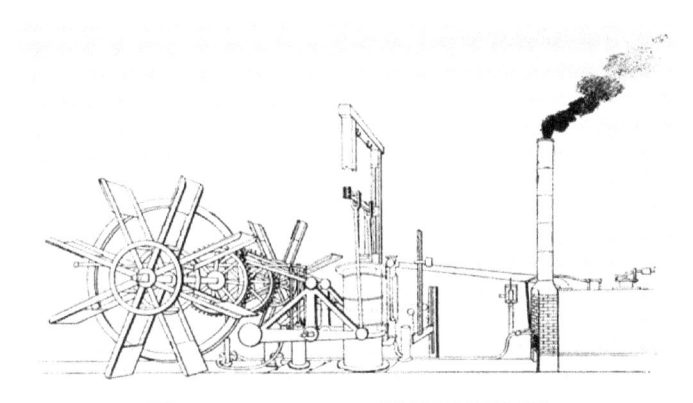

ENGINES OF THE *CLERMONT*

By courtesy of *American Industries*

The new ship was named *Clermont*, the name of Livingston's home on the Hudson. At noon on Monday, August 17, 1807, she was lying near the old State prison which stood on land now bounded by Washington, West Tenth, West and Charles streets, and thousands of people gathered to gaze at the remarkable vessel because it had been announced that she was to make a trial trip some time during the day. They observed that Brown, the builder, was working at some sails stretched to a mast standing at each end of the hull, although the sails were not set. A man named Maxwell (he had been brought from the shop of the London makers) was tinkering around the boiler—stopping leaks with melted lead, very likely, as he did, at any rate, later. Another man, Van Lea, was adjusting what is called a harpoon gun in the records. Harpoon guns, as the American whalers know them, were not yet invented, but swivels had previously been used for throwing harpoons, and this was, perhaps, such a gun. What it was to be used for is not recorded. The spectators were naturally cynical, and the humorists of the class that in modern days write the jokes for newspapers, shouted to Fulton: "God help you, Bobby!" "Bring us back a chip of the north pole!" "A fool and his money are soon parted!" The small boys whistled, and also yowled like cats. Fulton's correspondence shows that his sensitive soul was cut to the quick.

At 1 o'clock, as the start was described by the *Evening Post*, everything seemed ready, and Fulton told Captain Moses Rogers[6] to cast off the lines. The order was given to the engineer, Stevens Rogers, a relative of the captain, to start the machinery. A long blast was blown on a big tin horn as a warning to near-by boats, and then there was a "strange creaking, whirring, churning sound, a hiss of the escaping steam; the awkward-looking wheels, towering full seven feet above the deck on either side, began to turn, and we were really started on the first steamboat voyage on the Hudson." The next moment, however, the spectators saw the machine come to a sudden stop, and, supposing it had failed, they gave a derisive shout. The captain of a passing river-sailing packet sheered his boat close in to the pier line, and "made a sarcastic offer" to "throw us a line and tow us to Albany."

Perhaps the jeering at this time did not hurt Fulton so much as that previously mentioned, for he had ordered the engine stopped in order to readjust the boards or floats on the paddle-wheels. He had noted that they dipped too far into the water. An hour or more passed while the crew did this work. When it was done and the throttle was again opened, there was less strain on the machinery, and the *Clermont* moved smoothly away from the landing.

"The jeers of the ignorant, who had neither sense nor feeling enough to suppress their contemptuous ridicule and rude jokes, were silenced for a moment by a vulgar astonishment which deprived them of the power of utterance till the triumph of genius extorted from the incredulous multitude which crowded the shores shouts and acclamations of congratulation and applause." (Colden's *Life of Robert Fulton*.)

Heading across to the west side of the river to escape the main current of the tide, the *Clermont* passed the sloop whose captain had jeered her (the passengers on the *Clermont* yelled ecstatically at him when they saw his look of wonder), and then steamed along under the shadows of the Palisades. Night came on as she entered the Tappan Zee, and because it was a dark night the crews of a number of river-sloops saw a vision that they remembered vividly the remainder of their lives. For while they gazed down the river, knowing nothing of an experiment in steam navigation, they saw far away through the darkness the flame and sparks that poured from the smokestack of the *Clermont*—a cloud of fire moving along between heaven and earth like that which had guided the Children of Israel in the desert. Then, as it drew near, a hoarse growling was heard and a frightful form was seen coming up the river directly against the tide. In abject terror many crews jumped into small boats and fled ashore. Others sought shelter in the holds of their boats and drew the hatches tight, while others still fell upon their knees "and besought Providence to protect them from the horrible monster."

In the meantime the guests on the *Clermont* (she carried invited guests only on this trip), finding the river air somewhat chilly, gathered in the cabin, where, by the flickering light of a "candle in its high protecting glass," they discussed "the popular Salmagundi papers," speculated "on Mr. Irving's forthcoming Knickerbocker's *History of New York*," and finally "began to ply

Mr. Fulton with questions about the steamboat and what had led up to it." They also sang "Ye Banks and Braes o' Bonny Doon," a favorite song with Fulton.

Twice on the way up the river the *Clermont* stopped for fuel, one of the deck hands awakening the echoes with the big tin horn on each occasion to let the wood-yard men know that she was about to land. Then, just twenty-four hours after leaving New York, she cast anchor before the home of Livingston. The distance she had covered was 110 miles. She remained here until the next day, and it is noted in the histories that during the evening Livingston and a party of friends boarded the *Clermont*, where, in a congratulatory speech, he announced the engagement of his niece, Miss Harriet Livingston, to Robert Fulton.

Leaving the next morning at 9 o'clock, the *Clermont* reached Albany at five in the afternoon. In her run to that city the *Clermont* had averaged just under five miles an hour, regardless of wind and tide.

While neither freight nor paying passengers had been carried on the trip up, the boat was now advertised as a packet. Thereupon a number of men came on board for a passage to New York, and when one of these tendered the money for the trip, tears came into Fulton's eyes. For more than twenty years he had hoped against hope, and now he saw the fruition of his work.

"Although the prospect of personal emolument has been some inducement to me," he wrote to an intimate friend, "yet I feel infinitely more pleasure in reflecting on the immense advantages my country will derive from the invention."

On her return to New York the *Clermont* began her career as an Albany packet, with regular dates for leaving each end of the route. She was advertised in the *Evening Post*, of New York, on September 2, 1807, as follows:—

"The North River steamboat will leave Paulus Hook Ferry on Friday the fourth of September, at six in the morning, and arrive at Albany on Saturday at six in the afternoon.

"Provisions, good berths, and accommodations are provided.

"The charge to each passenger is as follows:—

		Time
To Newburgh	$3	14 hours
To Poughkeepsie	4	17 "

To Esopus	4½	20	"
To Hudson	5	30	"
To Albany	7	36	"

"For places, apply to Wm. Vandervoort, No. 48 Cortlandt Street, on the corner of Greenwich Street."

"Way passengers to Tarry Town, etc., will apply to the captain on board.

"The steamboat will leave Albany on Monday the seventh of September at six in the morning, and arrive at New York on Tuesday at six in the evening."

Meals were served without extra charge, and baggage weighing sixty pounds was carried free with each adult passenger. The freight rate to Albany was three cents a pound. The *Clermont* left New York on her first trip as packet at 6 o'clock in the morning on September 4, 1807, carrying twelve through and three way passengers. It was noted in the papers of the period that people were very much incensed because the steamer left her pier promptly at the hour advertised. They had been accustomed to having the river-sloops wait for them.

Morrison points out, in his *American Steam Navigation*, that no single detail of the *Clermont* was invented by Fulton. As the *North American Review* of July, 1838, says, the "great and surpassing merit of Fulton consisted not so much in absolute originality as in the skill with which he availed himself of all the theoretic knowledge of the day, and applied it to practical purposes." His choice of location for the inauguration of steam navigation is to be noted, for New York and the Hudson afforded an amount of traffic perhaps more valuable than could have been found elsewhere for such a vessel. Moreover, he was fortunate in making the trial at a time when the public were sufficiently enlightened to appreciate the value of steam.

The number of passengers and the amount of freight carried by the *Clermont* in the fall of 1807 led Fulton to rebuild her during the winter, in order to give her greater capacity. Having a monopoly of the waters by act of the legislature (the monopoly was contrary to the Constitution of the United States, but the courts did not decide the matter until 1824), Fulton had no trouble in raising capital, and with the growth of traffic a new steamer, the *Car of Neptune*, was placed on the river in 1808. The *Paragon* was built in 1811, and in 1812 the *Fire Fly* was built for way traffic. On the whole, however, the evolution of steam navigation on the Hudson was slow, at least so far as improvement in the vessels employed was concerned, until the monopoly was broken. For Fulton died in 1815, and his associates were not progressive. In 1825 an opposition line put on two steamers that were much superior to those of the old line, and in 1827 they added a third. In this year Robert L. Stevens, a son of John Stevens, put a third line of steamers on the river, and in 1828 some Albany capitalists sought a share of the traffic with a steamer called the *De Witt Clinton* that made a record of more than fourteen miles an hour between Albany and New York.

In 1832 the companies on the river consolidated, and used the superfluous boats in a night line that was successful from the first.

Two notable improvements were made in the engines in the meantime. Robert L. Stevens designed a light wrought-iron "walking beam" to replace the heavy cast-iron beam that was previously used. Then in 1824 James P. Allaire, who had made a reputation as an engine builder, brought out a "compound" engine. A compound engine has two or more cylinders of different diameters coupled to the one shaft. In the Watt engines the steam was conducted from the boiler to one end of the cylinder and allowed to flow in until the piston was driven almost to the opposite end. Then it was shut off and the way to the condenser was opened. Later it was found that if the flow of steam was cut off at half the length of stroke and the steam already in the cylinder was allowed to work by expansion, the total power of the engine was reduced only a little, while the saving of coal was very great. While thinking of this fact, it occurred to Allaire that the principle involved might be used to better advantage if the steam was taken at full pressure into a small cylinder and exhausted thence into a second and larger one to work by its expansive power. The *Henry Eckford*, the *Sun*, and a number of others were supplied with engines on this principle. The *Eckford* had a small cylinder 12 inches in diameter and a large one of 24. Both had the same stroke, of course. But, curiously enough, it was not until about 1870 that compound engines became the fashion.

The racing era, as one may call it, began on the Hudson about 1835, the year that Daniel Drew became interested in the Hudson River steamers. Racing had been done before the consolidation of 1832, but it was mild in comparison with that under Drew's initiation. An unreasoning mania for speed took possession of the public as well as of the owners of steamers. Though no practical end was to be served by the saving of an hour in the time required in the trip from New York to Albany, every sacrifice was made and every risk was taken to secure it. Instead of going to a pier or dock to land way-passengers at the towns along the river, the unfortunates were dumped into a small skiff that was towed at the end of a long rope. Then, as the steamer ran in close, but not too close, to the landing, the man in charge of the skiff, using a steering oar, sheered it within a few feet of the landing, and the passengers were told to jump. And jump they did. Of course a few fell into the water at every trip; perhaps some were drowned thereby. But the steamer's reputation for making quick passages was maintained, and for a long time the public protested in vain. When legislation was invoked (1842) the act was opposed as an unwarranted attempt to interfere with private business which could much better regulate itself!

It is an interesting fact that while the racing on the Mississippi resulted in the explosion of many boilers and the consequent loss of hundreds of lives, no such disasters occurred on the Hudson. The Hudson immunity was due to a difference in machinery. On the Mississippi "high-pressure" engines were used—there was no condenser, and the steam, which was sometimes carried at a pressure of 150 pounds to the square inch, was exhausted, after use, into the open air. When the safety-valve on such a boiler was tied down and the fire was urged until an explosion followed, the whole boat was ripped to pieces. On the Hudson condensers were used because the water was deeper and the extra weight was not of quite so much importance. Moreover, fuel was more expensive, and the low-pressure engine was more economical. Hudson River boats often reached the end of the run with boiler-plates bulging and ruined, but the heartrending disasters of the Mississippi were unknown in the East.

From the Hudson the use of steam spread first to the Delaware. John Stevens, who had been associated with Livingston and Roosevelt at the end of the eighteenth century, continued his experiments after Livingston went to France as American minister. He could not find any mechanics fit to help him carry out his ideas, but he built a machine shop and trained young men for the work. In 1804 he made a number of trips on the Hudson with a 25-foot boat that was propelled by screws. He also invented the tubular boiler "which at least has been the means of working wonders, for in a boiler six feet long, four feet wide and two feet deep he exposed four hundred feet of surface, in the most advantageous manner, to the action of fire." (Macfarlane, *History of Propellers.*)

In 1807, while Fulton was bringing out the *Clermont*, Stevens had a smaller, but none the less practical, boat, almost ready. He missed the honor of leading by no more than two weeks. Being unable to use her on the Hudson, Stevens, in June, 1808, sent her to the Delaware, under the command of Captain Moses Rogers, who had commanded the *Clermont* on her first voyages, and his son, Robert L., served as engineer. Thus this vessel—she was named the *Phœ nix*—was the first steamer that ever went to sea. On the Delaware the *Phœ nix* proved a commercial success.

The next step in the expansion of steam navigation was taken when Nicholas J. Roosevelt built the steamer *New Orleans* at Pittsburg (1811), and demonstrated to the incredulous frontiersmen of the region—especially to the "half horse, half alligator" keel boatmen—that a steam-driven boat could overcome the current of the swiftest part of the Mississippi.

In 1813 Fulton and his associates reached out for alongshore trade by building the *Fulton* for use between New York and New Haven, but because of the activity of the British war-ships on the blockade, she did not make her first trip until March 21, 1815, when she carried thirty passengers to New Haven in eleven hours.

The *Massachusetts* was the first steamer in use at Boston. She began plying to Salem in 1817. In the same year the *Fire Fly* was sent from New York to Rhode Island, where she was used between Providence and Newport. Rounding Point Judith in this vessel was considered a feat showing extraordinary courage, and this, too, among sailors who thought nothing of a voyage around the world in a ship less than a hundred feet long.

In 1818 the *Walk-in-the-water* was built at Black Rock, (now a part of Buffalo), on the Niagara River, for use on the Great Lakes. When ready for her trial trip, she was unable to stem the river current until eight yoke of oxen were brought to her assistance, but once on the lake she did well. She made her first trip to Detroit, starting on August 20, 1818, and covered the distance in about forty hours, using a cord of wood an hour.

By the annual report of the Commissioner of Navigation it appears that four steamboats, aggregation 457 tons, were built in the United States in 1812, the first year for which there is a record. In 1813 seven of an aggregate tonnage of 1430 were built, and in 1819 the number was twenty-eight, with a tonnage of 7291. More than a hundred had been built in all. This expansion was almost but not quite all made upon inland or sheltered waters. Fulton had looked toward the high seas. He had built a steamship, which he named the *Emperor Alexander*, to sell to the Russian government, but the War of 1812 prevented his trying to navigate her across the ocean, and she was eventually worn out at home. During the war he built the huge war steamer *Demologos*, a vessel fit to go along the coast, and crude as she was, she would have changed the manner of war at sea had she been set afloat a year sooner.

The year 1819 is especially memorable because a transatlantic steam passage was then made. It appears that Captain Moses Rogers was the originator of the venture. In 1818 Francis Fickett built a common sailing ship at New York that was 100 feet long by 28 broad and 14 deep. Rogers had had the honor of first navigating the sea with a steamer, and he had been selected in 1816, because of his reputation for courage and skill, to take the steamer *New Jersey* from New York to the Chesapeake, a voyage thought to be full of danger for such a vessel. He was now inspired with the ambition to be the first to drive a steamship across the Atlantic, and after a look at the ship that Fickett was building, he persuaded Scarborough & Isaacs, ship merchants of Savannah, to buy and fit her with a steam engine for use between Savannah and Liverpool.

The engine for this ship was built by Stephen Vail, of Speedwell, New Jersey, and the boiler by David Dod, of Elizabethtown, New Jersey. It is worth while to interrupt the narrative to consider these two facts. At the beginning of the century mechanics had been so scarce in the nation that Stevens had to train men for his work. But in 1819 mechanics and shops fitted for engine building were found not only in the larger cities but in some of the smaller towns close to navigable waters. That these shops had been brought into existence through the mechanical progress—perhaps it may be called the mechanical awakening—that was due to the success of steam navigation is beyond question. Many machine shops had been built, and were profitably employed. They not only built engines, but other tools for many kinds of work. The day when a British consul like Bond could hamper the progress of American manufactures by reëxporting tools made in England was passing.

The paddle-wheels fitted to the new ship for use on the Atlantic were made of iron. They had eight radial arms, each so arranged (according to Preble) that they could be folded up like a fan and laid inboard when the ship was under sail; for her sailing rig was retained.

Leaving New York on March 28, 1819, under Captain Rogers, this ship (she was named *Savannah*) ran to her home port in eight days and fifteen hours, during which she used steam for forty-one and a half hours. On May 24 she sailed for Liverpool, and made the passage in twenty-seven days, during which she used steam for eighty hours. While off the coast of Ireland the crew of a revenue cutter that saw her supposed she was on fire, and made haste to go to her assistance. In a trip from Liverpool to St. Petersburg, Russia, occupying, with stops at ports on the way, thirty-three days, she was under steam ten days. She finally arrived back at Savannah on November 30, and then went to New York, where her machinery was removed and sold.

The Savannah was what would now be called an auxiliary steamer; steam was used when the wind did not serve. She failed to inaugurate steam traffic across the Atlantic chiefly because of the space occupied by fuel—wood.

Although Captain R. B. Forbes, one of the ablest seamen the nation ever produced, built an auxiliary steamer (the *Massachusetts*) in 1845, that made profitable voyages, and there were features of the system that make it seem very attractive for certain trades, few vessels of the class have ever been used.

The year 1819 is also memorable because of an effort to establish a line of steamers running from New York to New Orleans, with stops at Charleston, South Carolina, and Havana, Cuba, on the way. The line was maintained for five years, and then withdrawn because it could not be made to pay.

In 1819, too, a ship was put on the route between Mobile and New Orleans, but this was also a failure.

In 1822 the steamer *New York* began to ply between New York and Norfolk, but she was unable to compete with the sailing packets. The steamer *Patent*, that began making regular voyages between Boston and Maine ports in 1823, also failed to pay dividends.

Not to add details of this kind, it may be said that while fortunes were made in steamboats plying on inland waters of the United States, almost every venture made with American steamers upon the ocean during the thirty years following the *Clermont's* first trip on the Hudson proved unprofitable. In connection with this dismal record the story of the steamer *Home*, built for the trade between New York and Charleston, South Carolina, is instructive. Keeping in mind the fact that this steamer was designed to round Cape Hatteras, where the worst storms on the coast were known to rage, consider these facts: the *Home* was 212 feet long by 22 wide and 12 deep. She was nearly 18 times as long as she was deep, and she was built of wood, at that. The engine, which was placed near the centre, as usual, had a cylinder 56 inches in diameter, with a stroke of 9 feet, and that is to say it was enormously heavy for a hull of such proportions. A set of iron braces was provided on each side to strengthen the hull, but on the first trip they "broke loose from their sockets on deck at their forward ends, by the elastic movement of the vessel in a heavy sea," as W. C. Redfield, a New York engineer, said in describing the vessel.

Two voyages were made with no greater visible injury than the breaking, on each voyage, of the worthless braces. On November 9, 1837, as the *Home* was bound on her third voyage, she was overtaken by a northeast gale, and shortly after passing the Hatteras shoals, it was found that the "elastic movement" of the hull, which, according to Engineer Redfield, was "necessarily and properly manifested," had opened an uncontrollable leak. The *Home* was then driven on the beach, where she at once went to pieces. About a hundred lives were lost.

It is important to note here that Engineer Redfield, in writing his defence of the *Home* (1842), was entirely sincere. Further than that, the owners of the vessel were so confident that she was of a proper model in all respects that the only insurance they carried upon her was for a small sum to secure a creditor.

From this story, and others of the kind to be found in the records, it appears that, while American designers were then building sailing ships and inland-water steamers that were highly profitable, they were astonishingly ignorant of the requirements of a steamship for deep-sea navigation.

In a search for the reasons for this curious condition of affairs it is found that the success of the inland-water steamers was the primary cause of the American failure at sea. The men who designed the sea-going steamers had been trained in their art by designing, first of all, steamers for inland waters. Because these inland-water steamers succeeded so well, it was entirely natural that similar proportions should be given to the engines that were to be used upon deep water. It was also natural to model the hulls as nearly as possible like the hulls on smooth waters. At the same time it was believed, incredible as the statement may seem now, that an "elastic" hull—one that bends to the lift of the waves as a rope does—was not only swifter but safer than a stiff one.

A paragraph as to the durability of the inland-water steamers will now prove instructive. In the report of Israel D. Andrews on "Colonial and Lake Trade" (Sen. Ex. Doc. 112, 32 Cong. 1 Sess.), it is said (p. 665) that "the period of the natural life of a steamboat" in use on the inland waters of the United States at that time (1851) was only "three and a half to four years." This statement included the steamers in use on the Great Lakes, which had much longer lives than those on the rivers.

With all these facts in mind, one sees why the deep-water American steamers failed. Led on by the success of the river steamers, the designers turned out engines of the lightest possible weight consistent with the greatest power, and then bolted them fast to the frames of hulls that were "elastic"—would yield to the waves like a rope. Not many of these steamers went to pieces as the *Home* did; good seamanship saved them from that fate; but neither good seamanship nor any economy practised afloat or ashore could make them pay dividends in the face of the enormous expense due to the wear and tear of machinery. Machinery built for speed could pay dividends on the inland waters because the steamers had no competition except that which they created among themselves, and that lasted for short periods only. The only competitors on the river-banks were stage-coaches and big wagons that were driven over the worst roads in the civilized world. The inland-water steamers charged what prices they pleased. At sea the steamers with their unfit machinery had to compete with the swiftest, most comfortable, and in every way the most economical sailing packets in the world. And until the designers had learned the requirements of a sea-going steamship, the sailing packets won.

CHAPTER X
PRIVATEERS, PIRATES, AND SLAVERS OF THE NINETEENTH CENTURY

WHEN seen in its true light, one of the most curious and interesting chapters in the history of the American merchant marine is that relating to the men who, having the might, used it to take from those who were weaker not only property but liberty and life; but the reader who supposes that superior ability, natural or acquired, gives him the *right* to take more of the good things of life than his less-favored neighbor receives, will scarcely comprehend the facts.

The fighting done by the American merchantmen who were commissioned as privateers during the War of 1812 has been well described by our histories of the navy, but the story of one battle is worth recalling briefly because it may well stand in some respects for the story of the entire fleet. On March 26, 1815, the privateer schooner *General Armstrong*, Captain Samuel Chester Reid, anchored in Fayal Roads, in the Azores. As night came on, a British squadron, bound for New Orleans, came into the roads, and on seeing the *Armstrong*, sent four boats full of men to capture her. A well-directed broadside from the privateer sent them in haste back to their ships, but a little after midnight the enemy came again in twelve boats, carrying more than 400 men. Each boat was armed with a cannon. The *Armstrong* had 90 men, and she mounted a long 24-pounder on a pivot with four 9-pounders in each broadside.

When the flotilla came within point-blank range, Captain Reid opened a fire that would have beaten back any other civilized enemy, but this veteran host pulled steadily in until the boats were alongside from stem to stern, and then they rose up, as one man, and strove to board the low-lying schooner. But with sword and pike and battle-axe the privateersmen fought not only for life but to avenge the wrongs that had been suffered by American seamen at the hands of press-gangs, and even British valor could not face them. One of the defeated wrote that the "Americans fought more like blood-thirsty savages than anything else." We may believe that they were thrilled with the joy of battle, and if a modern, peace-loving American is ever permitted to envy any of his countrymen who have had part in any battle described in the histories of the nation, the men of the *General Armstrong* will come to his mind first of all. But a liner, a frigate, and a brig were at hand to back the boats, and at last Reid had to burn his ship.

The gallant fight and the ultimate loss stand for much good fighting without profit in the work of our private armed ships during the War of

1812. Our histories, almost without exception, have overstated the success of the privateers and their influence upon the course of the war. A few of these ships—a very few—made enormous profits; the others made insignificant gains or actual losses. Our histories laud the work of the few that really succeeded; they ignore all that failed, save only as the reader is left to infer that all, or nearly all, did well. Thus the fact that the *Rossie*, of Baltimore, Captain Joshua Barney, in a single cruise, captured vessels supposed to be worth more than $1,500,000 is told in every history; the equally well-authenticated fact that Barney's share of the plunder amounted to only $1000 (see Mary Barney's *Memoir*), because the much-vaunted prizes were either destroyed at sea, or were sold for little or nothing in port,—this fact is deliberately omitted.

In the matter of net gains the *Rossie* stands as a type of the successful privateers, with a few exceptions. On November 23, 1812, less than six months after war was declared, and while the successful privateers were securing the best of their prizes, the privateer owners of Boston, New York, and Norfolk united in a petition to Congress, begging help through legislation because captured goods sold for such low prices that no profit was made by even the successful privateers. The captured ships, it was said, could not be sold at any price, even when fit for use as privateers. In short, "the profits of private naval warfare are by no means equivalent to the hazard." (Rep. Com. Ways and Means, December 12, p. 3.)

In Guernsey's *New York City During the War of 1812* is a list of the privateers sailing from that city—120 in all. Of these, 57 took not one prize. It is to be presumed that 21 of them made some money, because they took at least 5 prizes, while 7 took at least 15, and it may be supposed that they did well. But when it is remembered that in those days a ship commonly paid for herself in one voyage in ordinary trade, it cannot be said that privateering was of any special benefit except to three or four that took many prizes.

The total number of merchant ships that were used for privateers during this war was 515, and the total number of prizes was 1345. The British admiralty reported the capture of 1328 American merchantmen, of which 228 were privateers. The unrecorded disasters to privateers through storms certainly brought the number of total losses of these vessels up to a half of all that were commissioned. It is notable, too, that the number of American merchantmen captured by the enemy was only thirteen less than the number taken from the enemy, and it follows that the American losses were greater, in this respect, than those of the British; for the American ships were, on the average, worth much more than the British. On the whole it appears that, if the predatory part of the War of 1812 had any influence upon the result, the Americans were the greater losers.

Then, too, the losses of property were only one part of the injury inflicted upon the country by this kind of war. A consideration of the effect of the prevailing greed for a "subject of safe and uncontested capture" is of special interest here because some of the owners of our privateers, influenced solely by this greed, became pirates after the war ended. The Spanish colonists in America had revolted, beginning in 1810. The insurgent armies were scattered in small bands, here and there, in the vast territory between Texas and the Rio de la Plata, and the leader of every band was a law unto himself. But in every revolted province some aggregation of patriots—some *junta*—was recognized by foreign powers as enough of a government to be entitled to belligerent rights. When the War of 1812 came to an end, the privateers that were loath to give up their predatory career looked away to the Spanish main. The insurgent leaders were competent to commission armed cruisers for war upon Spanish commerce, and rich Spanish ships were afloat.

Some of the work done by American ships sailing under Spanish-American commissions is memorable. Two that were owned in Baltimore brought to Norfolk, in March, 1817, coin and cochineal valued at $290,000, and there is reason to suppose that Captain James Chaytor, who was senior officer of the two, and one of the best known of the men so engaged, brought to port property worth half a million of dollars in the course of that year. One of Chaytor's prizes was a galleon from the Philippines, and it was taken within sight of Cadiz.

Captain Joseph Almeda, of Baltimore, was another noted commander of this class of cruisers. In a vessel named the *Congress* he blockaded the port of Havana for weeks at a stretch, and took prizes almost within range of the Morro.

For a time the American people applauded the success of these cruisers, because it was supposed that they were aiding struggling patriots to gain liberty. The story of one of the cruisers, as told in court, however, in time changed public opinion. Captain James Barnes, commanding a Baltimore cruiser named the *Puerrydon*, with a commission from Buenos Ayres, captured on March 21, 1818, the Spanish brig *Corrunes*, while she was carrying general merchandise from Tarragona, Spain, to Vera Cruz, Mexico. A prize crew of seven men was placed upon the prize, and five of her Spanish crew were left on board to help work ship. On May 8 a storm separated the two vessels, whereupon the foremast hands upon the prize mutinied, put their officers upon a passing merchantman, and then went cruising along the coast of the United States. They were not bound for any particular port; they were just enjoying life while they might. Eventually they ran ashore on Block Island, and when the inhabitants came to the beach to look at the stranded brig, the mutineers began trading the cargo of the vessel for fresh provisions, and later for coin. The islanders made such good bargains that they sent for friends in Newport to come over and share in the good fortune, but that was an error of judgment, because the revenue officers thereby learned about the trading, and brig, crew, and some of the traders were haled before the United States court.

The trials that followed were among the most remarkable ever reported in the annals of the Supreme Court. Although held in jail on the charge of piracy, the crew libelled the vessel on the ground that they had rescued her from Barnes, whom they denounced as a pirate. Captain Barnes and the other owners sued for the property on the ground that Barnes had captured it while he was a citizen of Buenos Ayres, and in command of a lawful Buenos Ayres cruiser. A Spanish consul sued for it in behalf of the original owners. In the court of last resort it was held, in spite of much perjury, that the naturalization of Barnes in Buenos Ayres was "altogether in fraud of the laws of his own country," and that the owners of the cruiser were asking for the possession of a vessel that they had captured "in violation of the most solemn stipulation of a treaty, and provision of a law of their own country, and of which they had been dispossessed by their own associates in guilt."

"It is a melancholy truth," continued the court, "too well known to this court, that the instruments used in these predatory voyages, carried on under the colors of the South American states, are among the most abandoned and profligate of men."

Under the treaty mentioned, these American-owned cruisers were pirates. How many cruisers of the kind were fitted out from American ports (there were some European ships in the business also) cannot be learned now, but a list of twenty-eight is printed in the Annals of the Fifteenth Congress. The list is incomplete. Most of them were owned in Baltimore, and in 1823 the Columbia, South Carolina, *Telescope* denounced that city as "the home port of a fleet of Spanish-American pirates." In reply to this, *Niles's Register*, dated May 24, 1823, said:—

"Perhaps it may afford the editor of the *Telescope* some satisfaction to learn that *every* person who was fully regarded as being engaged in whatever could have given rise to his censure for piracy has become a bankrupt as well in character as in property."

It is to be noted, further, that these cruisers were not pirates merely by the existence of a treaty with Spain. They captured the ships of all nations when it could be done safely, and sometimes they did this openly. When Almeda was blockading Havana, he seized a British vessel at the mouth of the harbor because she happened to have some Spanish property on board. But the most deplorable cases were those in which the ships were seized by cruisers that had been unlucky. For in such cases the prizes were robbed and then sunk with all hands.

Still another result of the work of these pirates was the establishment of two remarkable communities, one in Texas and the other in Florida, both of which territories were then under the Spanish crown. Both settlements were made to provide a market for the goods which these cruisers captured; for after the decision of the courts noted above, the prizes could be no longer sent to the United States.

The Texas community was established by Jean Lafitte, who had had much experience as a smuggler at Barataria Bay, Louisiana, both before and during the War of 1812. He had also made several cruises on pirate ships—enough to learn that more money could be made buying prizes from the cruisers than in cruising.

Lafitte went to the island where the thriving city of Galveston now stands, late in 1816, and found there a number of shanties which had been built by one Luis de Aury, a pirate who had intended to establish such a nautical "fence" as Lafitte had in mind. But Aury thought the distance from the United States too great, and left the place to Lafitte, who at once sent word to all the ports of the warm seas that he was at the head of "an asylum to the armed vessels of the party of independence." The asylum included facilities for repairing vessels, stores for the sale of supplies, and numerous taverns and other places of resort for the crews. In short, a town—seaport—was built there by capitalists and mechanics, but all paid tribute to Lafitte. As at Barataria, slave-ships were more highly prized than any others because of the ease with which the "goods" could be smuggled into the United States. When General James Long, a noted Texas filibuster, visited the settlement, he found that "doubloons were as plentiful as biscuit," while the harbor was strewn with the wrecks of prizes.

After a time Lafitte went through with the forms of organizing the "Republic of Texas," and elected a governor, who appointed a justice to preside over the court of admiralty that the constitution of the "Republic" had provided. Then cruisers were commissioned and prizes were condemned, but when these condemned prizes were sent to New Orleans, they were seized by the United States authorities, and some of the pirate crews were hanged. Nevertheless, it was not until 1821—after nearly five years of unmolested prosperity—that Lafitte was driven away, and even then he was allowed to carry away all of his portable plunder. To add to the interest of the story, when Lafitte left the island he disappeared forever. Rumor said he was seen in Mexico, and in the thick of a fight at sea, and in France, but the truth is that he had gone to the port of missing ships. When the Luis de Aury mentioned above left Galveston Island, he cruised around for a while, and then, on September 2, 1817, landed on Amelia Island, Florida, where Fernandina now stands. A Scotch adventurer named MacGregor had been trying to build a town there and organize the "Republic of the Two Floridas," but without success. He sailed away when Aury came, and Aury continued the work of nation-building, combined with smuggling goods captured by "the party of independence." He thought the location admirable because of the proximity to the United States, but he soon learned that the convenience due to distance was more than counterbalanced by the attention attracted. Many speculators came to the camp and bought his goods, but the customs officials pressed them closely. Moreover, while Aury supplied the planters with cheap slaves, he was so short-sighted as to encourage Georgia slaves to leave their masters to join his forces. The Georgia planters who suffered losses in this way had no difficulty in persuading the Washington authorities to invade Spanish Florida and drive the pirate away—December 23, 1817. But Aury, like Lafitte, was allowed to carry away his plunder.

The effect of the piracies upon American commerce can be traced in the annual reports of exports and imports. Thus the exports of American products to the Spanish West Indies amounted to $3,606,588 in the fiscal year 1816-1817, while American exports of foreign goods to the same ports reached the sum of $3,477,511. The corresponding figures for 1819-1820 were $3,439,365 of American products and $2,545,717 of American exports of foreign goods. American tonnage fell off, also, of course. The common saying that there is no friendship in business is untrue. American commerce and the use of American ships were increasing in that period at an astonishing rate in all other trades, but Spanish resentment produced a "boycott" that is shown by the official returns.

But this boycott was the mildest form of expression of Spanish resentment. Within a short time after the American-owned cruisers under the Spanish-American flags began ravaging Spanish commerce, the Spaniards retaliated by making reprisals after the fashion common in the sixteenth century. Encouraged by the island authorities, the ship-owners of Cuba fitted out armed vessels to prey upon American commerce. The Cuban pirates were in no case commissioned, but the Porto Rico authorities gave commissions to half a dozen or more. The Cuban pirates, however, worked openly. Regla, a village on the east side of Havana Bay, was the chief pirate port. In November, 1821, eleven Spanish pirate vessels were cruising between Cape Maisi and Santiago, five were working as a squadron at Cape San Antonio, and at least five more were cruising on the north coast east of Matanzas. Between Havana and Matanzas was a flotilla of small boats the crews of which kept constant watch for vessels becalmed in the offing. All such vessels were attacked as soon as night came. Another gang of small-boat pirates operated at Cape Cruz, where they lived in the caves for which the region is noted.

The extent of the depredations of these pirates was never completely known, of course, but in *Niles's Register* of May 24, 1823, it is stated that 3002 piratical assaults had been committed upon merchant ships in the West Indies since the War of 1812. The "Naval Affairs" volumes of the American State Papers contain many accounts of such assaults, and it appears from these that the pirates not infrequently tortured captured sailors. In March, 1823, the captain and two men of the brig *Alert*, of Portsmouth, New Hampshire, were killed in the mouth of Havana harbor. The captain of the brig *Bellisaurius*, captured near Cape San Antonio, had his arms cut off, after which he was placed on a bed of oakum and burned to death.

The markets of Cuba were frequently flooded with merchandise taken by the pirates, and a number of schooners plied between Cape San Antonio and Regla to carry supplies to the pirate flotilla at work there and bring back captured goods.

The efforts of the Washington authorities to deal with the situation created by the American-owned pirate ships were, as noted, hampered at first by public sympathy for the Spanish-American insurgents. Even after the Spaniards began making reprisals, nothing effective was done until May 15, 1820, when Congress provided for the building of five swift war schooners, a force that was by no means sufficient to cope with the evil. Other ships of the navy were ordered to the region, and these were still further reënforced with a flotilla of small schooners bought in Chesapeake Bay. A number of huge rowboats were built to destroy the pirates operating in small boats near Havana, but the depredations continued; the aid of the Cuban authorities was sufficient to keep the pirates at work. It was not until the independence of the Spanish-American republics was acknowledged, and the Spanish-American privateers thereby lost their commissions, that piracy came to an end in the West Indies.

The last American vessel to suffer at their hands was the *Mexico*, Captain John G. Butman, of Salem. She sailed from home with $20,000 in coin, for Rio Janeiro, on August 29, 1832. On September 20 she was captured by the schooner *Panda*, Captain Pedro Gibert, of Havana. After taking out the coin, Gibert fastened the crew in the forecastle and set the *Mexico* on fire; but the crew released themselves in time to put out the fire. The *Panda* was captured later on the coast of Africa, a number of the pirates were sent to Salem for trial, and Pedro Gibert and four others were hanged. It is an interesting fact that two members of the *Mexico's* crew lived until 1905 and one until 1908. Life at sea agreed well with the New Englanders.

As the facts thus far given show plainly, the slave-trade had intimate relations with the pirates who operated under the Spanish-American flags, and later with those fitted out from Cuba; for the *Panda* cleared out from Havana for a cargo of slaves. But she carried no trade goods; her clearance for the African coast was merely a cover for the real purpose in view. Still, she might have brought a cargo of slaves to Cuba but for the interference of a British war-ship. But the American slave-trade lasted for thirty years after the captain of the *Panda* was hanged, and such acts of piracy as his had long been out of fashion in American waters.

By the act of Congress dated March 2, 1807 (it passed the House by a vote of sixty-three to forty-nine), the importations of slaves into the United States after January 1, 1808, was forbidden. The penalties provided included forfeiture of the vessel, and fines, together with imprisonment, for those involved.

As this legislation had been provided for in the Constitution of the nation, the trade in slaves was naturally brisk in the years immediately preceding prohibition. Thus, from January 1, 1804, to December 31, 1807, 202 ships imported 39,075 slaves into the port of Charleston, South Carolina. Of these ships, 61 were registered at Charleston (though generally owned elsewhere), 59 were owned in Rhode Island, from 1 to 4 in each of several other American ports, and 70 in England. While the prospect of prohibition increased the importations at this time beyond the normal, it is evident that a strong demand for slaves existed among slave-owners. The demand was particularly strong in the Mississippi Valley, where the profits on cotton were enormous. This demand naturally raised the price as soon as lawful importations came to an end. At the same time the existence of the American prohibitory law (England prohibited the trade at about the same time, too) depressed the price on the coast of Africa. Thus a premium was placed on smuggling, and 202 ships were afloat that had been engaged in the trade to one port alone.

All this is to say that while the law drove many ships out of the trade, it added much to the profits of those that remained in it.

Because the trade was continued, an effort was made to strengthen the law in 1818 by increasing the emoluments of informers. Then, by the Act of March 3, 1819, Congress authorized the President to use the naval ships to intercept slavers, and finally by the Act of May 15, 1820, all Americans engaging in the trade were declared pirates, who should be hanged on conviction.

One would be glad to believe that these laws were enacted because the American people had become sufficiently enlightened to appreciate the effects of the trade upon the human race, and especially upon the white people connected with it, but it is impossible to do so. The laws were enacted because of a passing wave of sentiment that had its origin in the work of the pirates herein described. In a dim way people saw that a connection existed between some of the pirates and the slave-trade. The slave-trade was held responsible (properly, too) for some of the horrors of the piracies, and while Congress was legislating against the pirates, it was easy to get acts against the trade passed. Moreover, the desire of the slave-owners to rid their States of free negroes was just then giving strength to the movement for sending those negroes to Africa—Liberia. In short, the prohibitory laws were the result of a sort of hysteria rather than of any real enlightenment of the American people. In truth, we are not so enlightened even now as to appreciate our whole duty toward the inferior race—properly a race of children—we brought from Africa.

As said, prohibiting the trade did but increase the profits of those who disregarded the law, but a more memorable result of prohibition was the effect upon the unfortunate victims of the trade—the increase in the horrors of the middle passage. A brief description of the ships used in the trade will help one to understand how the slaves were affected.

The American slave-ships were usually small vessels, say 100 feet or so long, and 10 or 12 deep. On the way to the coast what was called the slave-deck was laid. By means of beams, stanchions, and rough planks a temporary deck was built 3 feet below the regular deck. The naked slaves were placed upon this deck. In the days of the lawful trade they were compelled to lie down on their backs, shoulder to shoulder, with heads outboard in a row all around the slave-deck. Then other rows of the kind were made on the deck inside of the first row until the deck was entirely covered. When the law prohibited the trade, the slavers increased the number carried to the utmost capacity of their vessels, in order to increase the profits and cover the risks. To do this they compelled the negroes to lie down on their sides breast to back,—"spoon fashion,"—or else they were made to sit in rows, breast to back, from the wall of the ship to the centre. When sitting thus, the only air-space between the two decks was that over the rows of shoulders and between the rows of heads. When lying down, the air-space was greater, but whenever the vessel heeled to the wind, those on the lee side had to lie with their feet higher than their heads, and when the vessel rolled to the waves all of them sawed to and fro over the cracks between the unplaned deck boards. Moreover, the slaves were kept fastened to the deck—they were not allowed to leave their cramped berths for any purpose save only at fixed hours, when they were fed and, in small gangs, were taken to the upper deck for a short airing. In storms the washing of the waves across the deck compelled the crew to put on the hatches and keep them on sometimes for days at a stretch.

Meantime the allowance of water was a pint a day. In short, the slave-ship was a horrible floating cesspool. How the inhuman drivers added to the sufferings of the wretched slaves by the use of the whip, and other means of torture, may be suggested by one story.

When the slaver *Brillante*, Captain Homans, with 600 slaves in her hold, was overhauled by British cruisers during a calm, and Homans saw that the boats of the cruisers would soon come to the vessel, he got the anchor in position as if for anchoring the vessel. Then the iron cable was stretched along the rail outside of all and held in place by slender cords. To this chain all the slaves were carefully secured by means of ropes and chains. Then, just before the cruisers' boats came into view (it was at night), the anchor was cast loose and the 600 slaves were dragged down to the bottom of the sea.

To save a vessel worth at most $5000 from confiscation, Homans murdered 600 negroes. The story is told in detail in the *African Repository*, Vol. XXIII, p. 371.

The profits in the trade are shown by the fact that slaves costing from $12 to $20 on the coast of Africa sold for $350, when delivered alive and able to walk, in Cuba. When smuggled into the United States, they sold all the way from $750 to $1000.

Old ships of known speed were in demand. Speed was necessary because the British government maintained cruisers on the coast that captured and confiscated vessels found with slaves actually on board. Our navy department sold the schooner *Enterprise* (the second of the name) to men in the slave-trade at a small fraction of her value. The swift privateers of the War of 1812 were also bought for the purpose. In later years it was the custom to build swift vessels especially for the trade. Baltimore and New York builders were patronized more than others, New York having the lead in later years. The builders always knew what trade the vessels were to enter, and charged accordingly. No builder ever lost standing in society because he turned out ships for this purpose. In fact, the slave-traders were well known, and they lived among the wealthiest society people of New York—at the Astor House, for instance, where they were in the habit of meeting to arrange the details of their voyages. Public documents show that the most respected merchants of the city were ready to go on the bonds of these slavers, when bonds were required. A New Bedford whale-ship owner who was convicted of fitting out one of his vessels for the trade was afterward elected mayor of his city. Even after the Civil War was begun, a United States district attorney—a man appointed by Lincoln—was seen dining at the leading New York restaurant with a slaver whom he should have been prosecuting at that moment; for while the two ate together, the slaver talked about a slave voyage that he intended to make.

Though American packets had for years controlled the trade between the United States and Europe, and the American clippers were making records that stirred the whole nautical world, the flag from those proud ships was used to cover the reeking slime in the slaver's hold, and it was the only flag that could protect the slaver from inspection on the African coast. These facts were well known, but they roused not a tremor of indignation among the American people, not one, save only in the breasts of a few "fanatics," and the arguments of the fanatics were answered by asking, "How would you like to have your sister marry a nigger?"

The story might well be forgotten—it would have been omitted here but for the fact that the humiliation of it may serve in righting wrongs as yet unheeded, or but partly heeded, which, if less brutal, are born of the same greed and the same disregard for human rights that made the slave-trade possible in the United States until after the middle of the nineteenth century.

CHAPTER XI
THE HARVEST OF THE SEA BEFORE THE CIVIL WAR

IN the year 1772 the people of Marblehead, Massachusetts, boasted that "the number of polls was 1203," and that the vessels of all kinds owned in the port measured more than 12,000 tons. In 1780 the number of polls was 544, the tonnage but 1509. Within the borders of the town were 458 widows with 966 fatherless children.

Marblehead was a type of the New England fishing villages of the day. The nation had won freedom, but the fishing industry from which the American merchant marine had originated was ruined. Moreover, there was no immediate return of prosperity after peace was declared. The gross income of the New England cod-fishing vessels for the year 1787 averaged but $483 each; for 1788 it was $456 each, and for 1789 only $273. The average annual expense during this period was $416 each, and the vessels lost on the average $143 each during the year 1789. In that year the fleet measured 19,185 tons. In the next year the tonnage increased to 28,348, for the fishermen hoped for good times following the adoption of the Constitution, and in 1793, when the fleet received a national subsidy of $72,965.32, the tonnage reached 50,163. But in 1794, although the subsidy amounted to $93,768.91, the tonnage was only 28,671. In short, the statistics show that while the tonnage fluctuated from year to year, there was little prosperity for any of our fishermen in the period between the two wars for freedom.

A similar condition prevailed at Nantucket and other whaling ports. So discouraged were the Nantucket men that many of them migrated to England and France. For the British and French governments, to secure them, offered free transportation, free entry for ships and goods, and sums of money with which to begin life anew. Records show that no less than 149 Nantucket men commanded English whalers before the War of 1812.

The foreign aggressions of various kinds account for a large part of the depression of the fisheries during that unhappy period. The losses sustained by our freight carriers at that time were more than made up by the high freight rates received. But when the fish markets of the West Indies and of Europe were closed by adverse legislation, or by wars, there was no way to repair the loss except by national subsidies, and these, when granted, proved inadequate.

There was one other loss to which too little attention has been paid—the loss of men. The Marblehead men who were killed during the War of the

Revolution were among the most enterprising of the coast—they were killed because of their courage and dash. Lost ships could be replaced in the course of one winter; the lost men were not replaced until their sons became men. Then, too, the prosperity of the carrier fleet drained away the best men among the fishermen; for the owners of the carriers knew where to get able seamen.

After the War of 1812 the cod fleet averaged somewhat larger than it was before the war, but the increase was not at all commensurate with the growth of the nation. The exports of dried fish declined instead of increasing, and in spite of a protective tariff foreigners began (1812) to sell pickled fish in the United States. These imports increased steadily until 1848, when more than 100,000 barrels were brought in, and the imports thereafter remained above that figure. In describing the situation of these fishermen in 1848, Sabine says:—

"Many crews of fishing vessels owned in Newburyport, on settling with their owners for six and seven months' hard toil at sea, received only about ten dollars per month; and on this miserable pittance they were to eke out the year. They had obtained good fares of fish, but were sufferers from the depressed state of the market. With facts like these before us, can we wonder that the more ambitious young men abandon the employment at every opportunity?"

The vessels in the mackerel and other fisheries were, of course, no more prosperous, on the average, than those fishing for cod. From first to last the fisheries of New England are of interest in the story of the American merchant marine chiefly because they afforded an excellent training school for the sailor *of the sail*. It was because of the school afforded that these vessels were subsidized between 1792 and 1866. The annual bounty ranged from $1.60 to $4 per ton, according to the size of the vessel. Pay from the national treasury at the rate of $2 per month has also been given to the crews of fishermen in order to create a sort of sea militia. During the Civil War many recruits for the navy were obtained from the fishermen. Impressed by the precedent thus afforded, and failing to distinguish between the requirements of the old-time and the modern man-o'-war, the Merchant Marine Commission of 1904 proposed to pay bounties to the crews now employed in the fisheries. Of course bounties paid to the crews of tugs and other harbor steamers would be far more effective for the end in view. The tenacity with which our people cling to the idea that a modern sailor needs training on a ship of the sail is one of the discouraging features of the outlook for a revival of our merchant marine. No one would suppose that a training on a Dakota wheat farm was essential to the making of a finished hot-house florist.

During the period before the Civil War the whaling fleet was enjoying what has been called the Golden Era of its prosperity. This fact is all the more interesting because the prosperity was due to the character of the whalemen as developed by their environment. Because Nantucket as farm land could afford no more than a bare living to a small number of people, the more ambitious residents were obliged to look elsewhere for a career; and when they looked they saw right whales just beyond—sometimes in—the surf. A storm—a seeming disaster—was the means of leading the right whalers to go in search of sperm whales, and that cultivated enterprise, because it took them ever farther and farther from home.

The spirit of enterprise was also cultivated by the "lay" system of paying the crew. Every man received a share of the oil instead of set wages. The system sharpened the eyes of the lookout, gave strength to the arm of the man at the oars, and cooled the nerves of the man who thrust the lance under the shoulder-blade of the whale.

When Captain James Shields reached the Brazil grounds too late in the season, the system of "no oil, no pay" drove him around Cape Horn in search of a new ground. When, in 1818, Captain George W. Gardener found the grounds on the west coast of South America barren, he boldly headed across the unexplored Pacific in search of others—with success. In 1819 a merchantman from China stopped at the Sandwich Islands and told a number of whalemen there that he had seen great schools of whales on the coast of Japan. Thereupon the whalemen raced away for the new grounds. In 1843 two New Bedford captains found fortune on the coast of Kamchatka and another in the Okhotsk sea. Two years later still, Captain Royce, of the Sag Harbor bark *Superior*, entered the Arctic by way of Bering's Strait.

The countries of Europe sent naval squadrons at great expense to explore the Seven Seas; the whalemen of America explored the waters of the whole world more thoroughly, if less scientifically, at their own expense, and made money in the quest. One volume of the American State Papers contains a list of more than 400 islands that were discovered by them in the Pacific alone.

Of less importance in its influence, perhaps, but not to be overlooked, was the ease with which the ambitious whalemen obtained promotion. The larger whalers carried three and sometimes four mates, together with a petty officer called a boat steerer for each of the boats. Because the boat steerer hurled the harpoon, his office was important, and many a daring youth who went afloat as a green hand came home wearing the boat steerer's badge. Last of all, but most important in its formation of character, was the danger of the pursuit. The whalers braved the jaws of the vicious sperm bull; they drove their boats under the uplifted flukes, and with a stroke of a boat spade disabled the monster. They pulled to the tune of "A dead whale or a stove boat," and so "made good" in the world's work naturally and easily.

The Golden Era began with the success of the whalers that sailed for the Pacific in 1815, and returned well loaded in 1817. In 1829 the whaling fleet numbered 203 vessels; in 1840, 552; in 1846 there were 680 ships and barks, 34 brigs, and 22 schooners, a total of 736 vessels, hunting the whale under the American flag. New London owned the largest ship of the fleet, the *Atlantic*, measuring 699 tons, and the smallest, the schooner *Garland*, of 49 tons, that was at work on the coasts of Desolation Island.

In 1835 the value of the annual product of the whalers exceeded for the first time $6,000,000. In 1845 the sperm-whale fishery reached its highest point in the amount of product—4,967,550 gallons. The price was then 88 cents a gallon. In 1855 the price was $1.772 per gallon, but the amount saved was only 2,228,443 gallons. Right whale-oil reached record figures in 1840, when the amount saved was 11,593,483 gallons. The price was then 33 cents. The highest income received by the whalers in any one year was in 1854, when the take sold for $10,802,594.20. The years 1854 to 1857, inclusive, paid the whalers $51,063,659.59. The average catch was worth about half the estimated value of the fleet, or say near the actual value. It is certain that a well-handled whaler was a most profitable ship until after the petroleum industry was developed.

A picturesque offshoot of the whaling fleet was the fleet of seal-hunters that came into existence at the end of the eighteenth century. When Captains Gamaliel Collins and David Smith, of Cape Cod, went to the Falklands (1774) in search of whales, they found there thousands of seals, both hair and fur, and sea-lions without end. The oil of these animals being of good quality, the whalers carried some of it home, together with the skins, which were found to serve well for covering trunks. The fur-seals as well as the hair sealskins were used for this purpose. Soon after the War of the Revolution a Mrs. Haley, of Boston, sent a large ship to the Falklands especially for seals. The number taken was 13,000, and the skins sold for fifty cents each in New York. This voyage, like that of the *Columbia* to the Northwest coast, shows well the extraordinary enterprise of the ship-owners of the day.

In 1790 Elijah Austin, of New Haven, sent two vessels to the Falklands for seals, and when they were filled, Captain Daniel Greene, who commanded one of them, took his cargo direct to Canton for sale, because the skins Mrs. Haley's ship had taken had been exported from New York to Canton with profit.

The work of the brig *Betsey*, of Stonington, Connecticut, is perhaps the most memorable of any of the ships that entered the early trade. Though of but 100 tons' measurement, she made two voyages to the southern seal islands, beginning in 1790, both of which were remarkably profitable—the better voyage paid $52,300 net. The outfit, vessel included, probably cost little more than a tenth of this sum.

The *Betsey's* success naturally increased the number of vessels in the hunt very rapidly. Mas-a-Fuera, Juan Fernandez, the South Shetlands, the Prince Edward and Crozet islands, Desolation and Heard's islands, all soon became as well known to the sealers as Long Island Sound was to the coasters. Captain Henry Fanning, of the ship *Catharine*, obtained a manuscript copy of the notes made by the original discoverer of Crozet's Island, and with that as a guide went to the islands and obtained a full cargo.

The most famous of the American seal-hunters was Captain N. B. Palmer, born in Stonington, Connecticut. In 1799 he began his career afloat as the cabin-boy of a coaster at the age of fourteen. At nineteen he was made second mate of the brig *Hersilia*, Captain J. P. Sheffield, bound from Stonington to the Falklands in search of seals. On reaching the Falklands, Palmer and a number of sailors were landed to search the group for seals, while Captain Sheffield went south to search for another group. According to a story told by "gaming" parties on the whalers of the day, a whale-ship that, in spite of a heavy fog, was cruising through the waters to the south of the Falklands, had sailed out of the fog unexpectedly, and found herself almost on top of a mountainous group of islands, the outlying rocks and the beaches of which were alive with seals. The crew of the ship, animated by the danger of their position, hastily tacked and sailed away. Then the fog enclosed them again, and when the captain thought to chart the strange group he had to guess at the position. Sheffield was in search of this group.

A few days after he was left at the Falklands, Palmer saw the brig *Espirito Santo* (owned by Englishmen at Buenos Ayres) come to the anchorage in search of water; and when she was anchored, Palmer noted that she carried a sealing outfit. Thereupon he made friends with the mate, and although sealers had the habit of keeping their destination secret, he learned that the brig was bound for the uncharted islands; also the course she was to steer from the Falklands. Accordingly, when the *Hersilia* returned unsuccessful, Palmer was able to follow the *Espirito Santo* to the new group. These islands are now known as the South Shetlands.

In the following year (1820) thirty sealers gathered at the South Shetlands, including five belonging to the Stonington South Sea Company. One of the five was the *Hero* ("but little rising forty tons," according to one old account), of which young Palmer was captain.

While working the group, Captain Isaac Pendleton, commodore of the five vessels mentioned, on climbing a mountain, saw what he thought was the loom of land far away to the south, and in the hope of finding other rookeries, sent Palmer in the *Hero* exploring.

Land was found, and Palmer soon discovered that it was of continental dimensions. As no seals were found, he finally headed back for the Shetlands, but before he had crossed the intervening water a heavy fog shut him in and he hove to. During the night a ship's bell was heard striking the hour off the port bow, and the stroke was followed by another off to starboard. To the crew these sounds seemed supernatural, for they could not think that real ships were there; but when morning came, they found the *Hero* lying between two war-ships. The story, as told by Captain E. Fanning, of Stonington, to Secretary of the Navy J. N. Reynolds, in a letter written in 1828, is as follows:—

"The two discovery ships sent out by the late Emperor Alexander, of Russia, being between the South Shetlands and Palmer Land, were becalmed in a thick fog; when the fog cleared away they were surprised to find one of the Stonington South Sea Company's barques, a little vessel of about fifty tons, between the two discovery ships, which immediately run up the United States flag, when the frigate and sloop of war set theirs, and the Russian Commodore despatched a boat and officer, with an invitation to Capt. Palmer, of the American vessel, to come on board, which he readily accepted.

"When he arrived on the commodore's deck he was asked what islands those were in sight, and if he had any knowledge of them. 'Yes, sir,' replied Capt. Palmer, 'those are the Shetland Islands. I am well acquainted with them, and a pilot here. I belong, sir, to a fleet of five sail out of Stonington, under the command of Capt. B. Pendleton, whose ship is now at anchor in a good harbor in that island; and if you wish for water and refreshments, I will pilot you in, and my commodore will be much pleased to render you any assistance.' 'I kindly thank you,' said the Russian, 'but previous to being enveloped in the fog we had sight of those islands, and concluded we had made a new discovery; and behold when the fog lifts, to our utter surprise, a beautiful little American vessel, to all appearance in as fine order as if she had but yesterday left her port in the United States, is discovered alongside of my ships, the master of which readily offers to pilot my vessels into port, where *his commodore* will tender me every aid for refreshment! We must surrender the palm of enterprise to you Americans,' said the Russian commodore. 'Sir, you flatter me,' replied the American captain; 'but there is an immense extent of land to the south, and when the fog is entirely cleared away, you will have from your masthead a fine sight of its mountains.' 'Indeed,' observed the commodore, 'you Americans are a people that will be before us; and here is, now, in your information, and in what is now before my eyes, an example and pattern of the oldest nation in Europe. Where I expected to make new discoveries I find the American flag, a fleet and a pilot!'"

The commodore then arose from his seat, and placing his hand upon Palmer's shoulder, continued:—

"I name the land, which you have discovered, Palmer Land, in your honor. But what will my august master say, and what will he think of my two years' cruising in search of land that has been discovered by a boy in a sloop but little larger than the launch of my frigate?"

The land thus named was a part of the Antarctic Continent.

Among the interesting stories of the sealers found in Goode's *Fishery Industries of the United States* is one of the ship *Neptune*, Captain Daniel Greene, of New Haven, which shows very well something of the peculiarities of this branch of the American merchant marine. The voyage lasted from November 29, 1796, to July 11, 1799.

The *Neptune* was a ship of 353 tons, and she carried a crew of 36 all told. Going to the Cape de Verde Islands, Captain Greene bought enough salt to preserve all the skins the ship could carry, and then went to the Falklands, where he arrived February 22, 1797. The first work done there was the building of a shallop for working shoal waters. Then seal-hunting was begun in connection with the crew of a ship from Hudson, New York, which, by the way, had brought a Hudson River sloop as a tender.

The seals were found either on beaches which the hunters reached easily, or on outlying rocks upon which the seas broke with tremendous fury even in the most pleasant weather. Ordinary whale-boats were commonly used in hunting the seals, though dories were preferred for the least accessible rocks. When the weather was at its best, the crews worked the easily reached beaches; incredible as it must seem, it was during the worst storms that the almost inaccessible rocks were visited. The most picturesque and daring work known to the sea was that of taking seals on these rocks. Rowing well out to windward, the officer in command of the boat noted carefully the position of the sunken reefs with which all these rocks were surrounded, selected a safe opening, and waited until the high waves that always come in threes appeared. Upon the crest of the last of a set of these the boat was driven in, and as it was swept along beside the rock the hunters, with clubs in hand, leaped forth to land as best they might.

At other times the boat was rowed up from the lee side to meet the crest of a roller at the side of the rock. The method chosen depended upon the situation of the rock.

Taking the men from the rocks after the killing was often more dangerous, if less picturesque, than landing them. For it was impossible to hold the boat beside the rock, and in leaping out the men often fell into the sea. A favorite way of getting men and dead seals was by throwing a line from the boat to the rock and then, while the boat was held in the lee of the rock, the men and carcasses were dragged through the water by the line.

The crews were continually drenched; the cold winds pierced them to the bone; they fell upon the rocks and were cut and bruised; now and then one fell, helpless, into the sea and was drowned. But the crews of those days were composed of youths who were looking ahead,—the most ambitious and courageous of all who lived around the home port,—and without flinching they took the chances until the ship was loaded.

These were the American fur-hunters of the sea. Rarely if at all elsewhere in the history of the nation can a more instructive contrast be found than that afforded when these men, leaping from the crest of the storm-waves to the seal rocks, are compared with those who traded pot-metal muskets and adulterated rum to the Indians in exchange for beaver skins upon the Western frontier.

Another glimpse of life at sea in those days is found in an adventure of the *Neptune's* men upon the coast of Patagonia. Captain Greene and some of his men went over there looking for seals, and found some Spaniards engaged in seal-hunting not far from Port Desire. The Spaniards said the *commandante* of the fort at the harbor would be pleased to give Greene permission to hunt seals in the region, and Greene, being a law-abiding man, went to the fort to see about the matter.

The *commandante*, however, pretended to believe that Greene was an Englishman; and as England and Spain were at war, the Americans were all held as prisoners, while soldiers were placed in charge of the shallop in which the Americans had come to the coast. As it appeared later, it was to get possession of the shallop that the *commandante* had decided that Americans were Englishmen.

Greene, however, was equal to the emergency. When the priest at the fort gathered the garrison into the chapel at 8 o'clock for the evening services, Greene overpowered the sentinels, ran out of the gate with his men, launched his whale-boat, rowed off to the shallop, set the soldiers ashore, and sailed away.

The *Neptune*, like all American vessels of the period, carried cannon. After seeing that his guns were in service condition, Greene returned to Port Desire and anchored in the harbor just out of range of the fort, and began to take seals from the rocks. The *commandante* came down the beach, and with much gesticulation (and nothing more effective) ordered him away. Greene might have defied him, but instead of doing so sent the purser to offer him the shallop (which was no longer needed) for permission in writing to go on with the hunt. The offer was gladly accepted, and Greene cleaned the coast of seals.

Greene's way of dealing with the official is especially interesting because it was characteristic of the American sea captains of the day in their intercourse with bumptious officials everywhere.

Then the *Neptune* went to Juan Fernandez and Mas-a-Fuera, where the cargo was completed.

"During the latter part of the time ... we frequently stove our boats in the surf," says a letter written by Purser Eben Townsend, and that is the extent of his comment on the dangers of landing on outlying rocks in the midst of a gale.

On June 9, 1798, the *Neptune* sailed for Canton, where she sold her skins for $2 each, and used the proceeds in buying China goods. This cargo, on reaching New York, paid customs duties amounting to $55,438.71, and sold for $260,000. The foremast hands received a "lay" of $1200 each. A paragraph in one of Purser Townsend's letters regarding these foremast hands is worth quoting:—

"Many of our crew were very smart, ambitious young men.... In our voyage across the Pacific they exerted themselves to be qualified for commanding ships, and the captain gave them as much indulgence as he could for that object, allowing them time and giving them instruction. It was quite a regular good school on board, and the progress was even greater than in some literary institutions on shore. Some men that could not do a sum in addition when we left America could now work lunar observations."

By 1825 the seals were so nearly exterminated that the hunt for skins gave no profit, but the amount of sea-lion oil that could be secured was sufficient to keep a fleet cruising in southern seas until 1870, when three vessels fitted once more for a skin hunt and secured 8000. The next year eight vessels obtained 15,000 good fur seals, and in 1876 Captain Athearn, in the schooner *Florence*, took a cargo that sold for $100,000. Between 1871 and 1880 the number of skins taken was 92,756. After that date the hunt again became unprofitable, but the sea-lion oil kept a few vessels busy for some years. The year 1880 may be called the last of the employment of the American seal-hunting fleet.

CHAPTER XII
THE PACKET LINES AND THE CLIPPERS

TWO results of the War of 1812 are of especial interest here. Through good fighting the American ship was at last free to sail upon the high seas unmolested by any power upon earth, and the seafaring people had become aggressive to a degree that was little short of bumptious. In the weary years that had passed since the *Trial* sailed from Boston, our sailors had been engaged in a struggle for mere existence; now they were to enter with eager zest into a contest for the supremacy of the seas.

The first work done to this end was the establishment of a packet line (1816) from New York to Liverpool, by Jeremiah Thompson, Isaac Wright, Benjamin Marshal, and other capitalists of New York under the name of the Black Ball Line. It may interest students of psychology to know that the Quaker religious element prevailed among the stockholders.

The word "packet" had been used theretofore at sea only in connection with certain small but swift vessels (usually brigs) that the British government employed to carry the mail to foreign countries. These vessels sailed from the home port at regular intervals, and the weather was bad indeed when one of them failed to get away at the advertised hour.

In connection with the Liverpool packet service it is important to recall the difference between loading a ship "on owners' account," and carrying freight for any shipper at a rate per ton. The earliest American ships usually carried cargo that belonged to the owners and crews. The ships of Derby's time carried goods partly for the owners and partly for "adventurers," who paid the owners a freight rate. With the further growth of commerce the amount of freight offered for transportation by merchants who owned no ships had increased rapidly, and before, as well as after, the War of 1812 there were ship-owners who made increasing profits by catering to these merchants. The owners of these vessels, it appears, had observed that the regularity of the Hudson River packets had increased the freight and passenger traffic there in a far greater ratio than any one would have anticipated from the growth of population; and this fact led to the conclusion that if a regular day of despatch, with the utmost speed, were provided for the New York-Liverpool trade (the trade in which the freighting traffic was largest), the ships would be able to command the best part of the commerce. The event justified the venture; the Black Ball Line was profitable from first departure. The ships were even able to command higher rates than the ordinary vessels.

The ships employed were among the largest and swiftest of the period (400 to 500 tons each), and the captains were under orders to drive them to the limit. The passages from Sandy Hook to Liverpool during the first 9 years were made on the average in 23 days, the shortest time being 15 days and 18 hours—made by the *New York* in 1822. The westward passage during that time was made in 40 days on the average.

In 1821 the Red Star Line (Byrnes, Grimble, & Co.) entered the Liverpool service with a ship every month on the 24th—a week ahead of the Black Ball Line. To meet this competition the Black Ball began sending ships away on the 16th as well as the first, and then the Swallow Tail Line (Thaddeus Phelps & Co., and Fish, Grinnell, & Co.) made the service weekly.

In 1821 Thomas Cope & Son began a monthly service from Philadelphia to Liverpool, and in 1823 the Swallow Tail Line began sending ships monthly to London. This last service soon had opposition in a line established by John Griswold. Then between 1822 and 1832 three lines were successfully established between New York and Havre.

The success of the transatlantic lines led to the formation of coastwise lines. A number of 180-ton sloops made regular passages from New York to Boston, beginning in 1818. In 1825 packets began running from New York to Charleston; the New Orleans line was opened in 1832, and at the same time another line began running to Vera Cruz, Mexico. These lines added much to the offerings of freight and passengers to the transatlantic lines, and helped the growth of New York immensely.

The New Orleans and the Vera Cruz lines were owned by E. K. Collins, a man of much importance in the history of the American merchant marine, as shall appear. His success in these two lines led him to sail into the Liverpool trade with what was known as the Dramatic Line. The New York *Daily Advertiser*, in announcing this line (September, 1836), said:—

"We notice this new enterprise with pleasure, as it will add another list of fine ships to the sixteen now built. The ships are all to be 800 tons and upward, New York built. The Liverpool lines are composed of 20 ships or about 14,000 tons.... Nor will the establishment of another line injure in the slightest degree the other lines—the more facilities there are afforded the more goods and passengers will be transported."

The number of ships in the packet fleets, as here noted, is worth consideration, for if the ships of the lines to London and to Havre and that from Philadelphia be added, the whole number was no more than 50, the tonnage of which was less than 35,000. In that year the American tonnage in the foreign traffic was 753,094. The packet fleets contained but a small fraction of the American tonnage, but their influence upon the contest for supremacy of the seas was wonderful.

The files of the newspapers of the day give many glimpses of the packet ships as the reporters saw them. Thus the Liverpool Courier, of March 24, 1824, in describing the 500-ton *Pacific*, Captain S. Maxwell, said:—

"This fine vessel has, during the week, been crowded with visitors who have viewed with feelings of admiration the splendid style in which her cabins are fitted up. Her dining room is 40 feet by 14. A mahogany table runs down the centre, with seats on each side formed of the same wood and covered with black hair cloth. The end of the dining room aft is spanned by an elliptical arch, supported by handsome pillars of Egyptian porphyry. The sides of the cabin are formed of mahogany and satin wood, tastefully disposed in pannels and most superbly polished. The doors of the staterooms are very neat, the compartments in each being inlaid with a square of plate glass. An arch extends over the entrance to each room, supported by delicate pillars of beautiful white Italian marble, exquisitely polished. The staterooms are seven on each side; they are fitted up with much taste, and with a studious regard of the comfort and convenience of the passengers. The sideboard is placed in a recess in the end of the cabin. An arch is thrown over it by two pillars of American marble from the state of Vermont.... The *Pacific* is built of live oak, copper fastened, and is now coppering in No. 2 Graving-Dock. Nothing can exceed the politeness of Captain Maxwell in showing her to the public."

In 1838 the New York *Express*, in describing "the last new packet," said:—

"We recollect that thirty years ago, when the *Manhattan* was launched—she was about 600 tons burden—all New York crowded down to see her. She was the wonder of the day; and it was then believed that she was the *ne plus ultra* in ship building; that she was not only the largest and finest ever built, but that ever could be built. From that day to this they have gone on improving and building until they have now got to a point of perfection that one would hardly suppose could be excelled. Our ships, and particularly our packets, are admired by all nations wherever they go; and although we do not admit that we cannot, by our skill, ingenuity and capital, go on improving, the world admits that America is without a rival in the noble art of building this description of vessel.

"We have, from time to time, given descriptions of the various ships that have been put afloat.... We have now another to add—the ship *Roscius*, built by E. K. Collins, belonging to the Dramatic Line, and to be commanded by Captain John Collins. She is the largest that has yet been built, and for strength and beauty is a noble specimen of American ship building. The following are her dimensions:—

"Burden, 1100 tons; length of main deck, 170 feet; length of spar deck, 180 feet; breadth of beam, 36½ feet; depth of hold, 22 feet; height of cabin, 6½ feet; height from keelson to main truck, 187 feet; length of main yard, 75 feet."

Of the velvet used upon the sofas, and the Wilton carpets, the "scarlet marino" drapery, "with white curtains," nothing more need be said, but the facts that she cost $100,000 ($90 per ton) and would "stow about 3200 bales of cotton" are, perhaps, memorable.

With a little imagination a picture that warms the blood is found in the following brief paragraph from a Liverpool paper published in July, 1836:—

"*Ship Race.*—Twelve ships sailed from New York for Liverpool on the 8th instant. Among them were the packet ships Sheffield, Allen; the Columbus, Palmer; and the George Washington, H. Holdredge, and several first-rate vessels, the Star, the Congress, the Josephine, &c. Heavy bets were laid on the respective ships at the time of sailing. The three packet ships having parted company, fell in with each other on the Banks of Newfoundland. Here they parted. The George Washington passed Holyhead on Saturday forenoon; two or three hours afterwards the Sheffield passed the same place. Both ships entered the Mersey in the course of the afternoon, after a run of seventeen days from port to port. The Columbus arrived yesterday morning. None of the other ships have yet appeared."

Fancy a newspaper giving no more space than that to such a magnificent race! Still, races of the kind were common in those days, and the sailor can imagine how the ships were handled. The Palmer who commanded the Columbus, by the way, was Nathaniel Brown Palmer, who discovered the Antarctic Continent while in command of the *Hero*—"a little rising forty tons."

CLIPPER SHIP *SYREN*

In 1837 the papers announced that the *Sheffield*, Captain Allen, that came in second in the race had, within the past 12 months, made the eastward passage five times in succession in an aggregate of 91 days, "being an average of about 18 days each from port to port." In her next passage out she crossed in 16 days, thus creating a record of six passages in 103 days, "being a little over 17 days each."

On April 24, 1836, the Liverpool *Albion*, under the heading "Unprecedented Quick Passage," told how the *Independence*, Captain E. Nye, had "sailed from New York on the evening of the 8th instant, and the interval between her leaving and taking the Liverpool pilot was only *fourteen days* and five hours."

"The passage from port to port has frequently been made in sixteen days; in the year 1822 the packet ship *New York* made it in fifteen days and three-quarters; but the *Independence* is the only ship that ever accomplished it within the fifteen days."

The passengers on the *Independence*, "being desirous of commemorating the unparalleled short passage," appointed a committee to "procure and convey" to Captain Nye "a Piece of Plate with a suitable inscription."

The *Independence* measured only 734 tons. She was built in New York in 1834.

In the course of the packet period five other liners made passages to Liverpool in fourteen days or less—the *Montezuma*, the *Patrick Henry*, the *Southampton*, the *St. Andrew*, and the *Dreadnought*. Under Captain Samuel Samuels the *Dreadnought* was the most famous of them all. She ran in the St. George's line—A. Taylor & Co. Samuels was born in Philadelphia, on March 14, 1823. He ran away to sea when eleven years old, and at twenty-one, after a venturesome career, was placed in command of a ship called the *Angelique*. In 1853 the *Dreadnought* (1413 tons) was built especially for him, and as he told the writer she was a ship of "medium full lines." And yet in her first voyage to Liverpool and back[7] she reached Sandy Hook just as the Cunard steamer *Canada*, which had left Liverpool one day ahead of her, was arriving at Boston.

On Saturday, February 9, 1856, the Liverpool *Chronicle*, under the head lines "Important from America. Five days later—Arrival of the *Dreadnought*," said:—

"The clipper *Dreadnought*, Captain Samuels, ... arrived here this forenoon from New York after a rapid passage of fourteen days and eight hours."

CAPTAIN SAMUEL SAMUELS

By courtesy of *Harper's Magazine*

It took three years to beat that passage, but in 1859 Samuels drove her from Sandy Hook to Rock Light, Liverpool, 3000 miles, in 13 days and 8 hours. And in 1860 he ran from Sandy Hook to Queenstown, a distance of 2760 miles, in 9 days and 17 hours, a record never equalled either before or since.

"She was on the rim of a cyclone, most of the time," said the captain in describing the passage to the writer. The sailors of the day called her the "Wild Boat of the Atlantic," and some unremembered forecastle bard wrote a song of nine stanzas about her, of which the first was:—

"It is of a flash packet,

A packet of fame.

She is bound to New York

And the *Dreadnought's* her name.

She is bound to the west'ard

Where the stormy winds blow.

Bound away in the *Dreadnought*,

To the west'ard we'll go."

Seafaring people are yet alive who well remember the boisterous vigor with which the old-time sailors used to roar out "Bound away in the *Dreadnought*, To the west'ard we'll go," wherein all the crew joined the chanty man.

The counting-house view of the packets must not be overlooked. The earliest ships cost about $40,000, or say $80 a ton measurement. The later ones cost nearer $90 a ton, the *Roscius*, of 1100 tons, as noted above, costing $100,000. The captain usually owned an eighth of his ship, and many a man of good reputation who lacked the money to buy such a share was allowed to buy in with a note that was paid off with his share of the earnings. The captain, who was part owner, naturally handled the ship with greater economy on that account. The salary of the captain was usually $360 a year, but in addition he had 5 per cent of the freight money, a fourth of the cabin passage money, all the money paid for carrying mails (twopence a letter from the British government, and two cents from the American), and the privilege of carrying his wife board free. On the whole, these captains made not far from $5000 a year.

The number of cabin passengers varied from 30 in the earlier days up to 80 in the later, though there were many passages, of course, when the cabin was nearly empty. The price of passage was $140 during most of the time, but competition cut it to $100, now and then. The owners, however, calculated on an income of from $2000 to $5000 per passage from the cabin. The income from freights ran from $5000 to $10,000 per passage. Each ship made six passages a year. Much larger sums were earned in a single passage at times. The *Orient*, Captain George S. Hill, once made a gross income of $50,000 for a round voyage, while the *Webster*, Captain Joseph J. Law, made $60,000.

The proudest seafaring man in the world at that period was the master of a Liverpool packet. When the wind served at the hour of sailing, he set all plain sail on his vessel as she lay at her pier, laid all flat aback, drove her stern first into the stream, turned her around, and then, while the spectators cheered themselves hoarse, he sent her rippling down to the sea. And when he returned he sometimes arrived in the river with royals set and sailed her into her berth with less fuss and jar than the ferryboat in the near-by slip was making. Indeed, tugs were used before 1835 only when the wind was foul or wholly lacking, and for years after that it was a matter of pride as well as profit to save the tug bill ($140) whenever possible.

Most of the newspapers that have been quoted in this chapter were printed in England. It is a significant fact that the English papers, which represented the attitude of the English merchants of the day, gave the American packets unstinted praise. The acrid jealousy that English merchants had shown during all the long years before the War of 1812 was silenced. How did it happen that these "Yankee" seamen were treated so well?

The British House of Commons having appointed a committee in 1835 "to inquire into the cause of shipwrecks in the British merchant service," the London *Courier*, on August 18 and 20, 1836, printed a number of extracts from the committee's report. One of the paragraphs in that report is of special interest:—

"45. *American Shipping.*—That the committee cannot conclude its labor without calling attention to the fact, that the ships of the United States of America, frequenting the ports of England, are stated by several witnesses to be superior to those of a similar class amongst the ships of Great Britain, *the commanders and officers being generally considered to be more competent* as seamen and navigators, and more uniformly persons of education, than the commanders and officers of British ships of a similar size and class, trading from England to America; while the *seamen* of the United States are considered to be more carefully selected and *more efficient*; that American ships sailing from Liverpool to New York, have preference over English vessels sailing to the same port, *both as to freight and to rate of insurance*; and *higher wages being given*, their whole equipment is maintained in a higher state of perfection, so that fewer losses occur; and as the American shipping have increased of late years in the proportion of 12¾ per cent per annum while the British shipping have increased within the same period 1½ per cent per annum," the superior growth of the American merchant marine, as well as the higher wages paid, was taking the best of the British sailors into the service of the American ships.

All of this is to say that while only twenty-one years had elapsed since the American sailor had won, by good fighting, the right to cross the seas unmolested by foreign war-ships, his chief competitors openly acknowledged that in the trade between New York and Liverpool (the most important trade route in the world) he had won unquestioned and even uncontested supremacy. The American packets received cordial praise in Liverpool because no British ship-owner so much as thought about entering into competition with them, and this, too, at a time when the British tonnage, in the aggregate, was far greater than that of the United States.

In the meantime the American whalemen had won supremacy, as already noted, in the work of gathering the harvest of the deep seas, and the most splendid conquest of all, the supremacy of the sea in the trade of the Far East, was at hand.

The most interesting feature of this contest was the evolution of a class of ships called clippers. Curiously enough, it appears that one aggressive naval architect, John W. Griffiths, of New York, was responsible for the introduction of this remarkable type of ships. Griffiths was of the opinion that a ship having "hollow" or concave water-lines, especially at the bow,— "hollow entrance lines,"—would sail more swiftly than one with ordinary convex lines, no matter how fine the convex lines might be. In 1841 Griffiths exhibited a model of a ship shaped according to his ideas, at the American Institute, and he also delivered a number of lectures on the subject. The nautical world became greatly interested, and in 1843 William H. Aspinwall ordered a ship of 750 tons built to designs by Griffiths. She was named the *Rainbow*, and when sent, under Captain John Land, to Canton on her maiden voyage, she arrived back at the end of 6 months and 14 days. In another voyage she sailed to Canton in 92 days and made the passage home in 88, breaking the record each way.

The *Howqua*, the *Samuel Russell*, and the *Sea Witch* were also built to the new designs,—the clipper model, as it soon came to be called,—and all made swift passages. The *Russell* is of special interest because she was commanded by Captain N. B. Palmer, who now left the packet service to engage in that of the Far East. His first run was made to Hongkong in 114 days, which was slow time for a racer, but in the course of the voyage he covered 318 miles in a day; and in 30 consecutive days he sailed 6722 miles.

To complete Palmer's record it may be said here that in his last ship, the *Orient*, he covered 328 sea miles in a day, and made the run home from Canton in 81 days.

The *Howqua's* best work was the run from Shanghai to New York in 88 days. The *Water Witch*, called "the swiftest ship of her day," was commanded by Captain Robert H. Waterman ("Captain Bob"). She set the pace when she sailed from New York on December 23, 1846. In 25 days she hove to off Rio Janeiro long enough to send mail ashore on an inbound ship, and in 104 days she reached Hongkong. Her return run from Canton was made in 81 days. In the next voyage she returned from Canton in 77 days, her best day's run being 358 sea miles, something then unheard of.

There were a number of other celebrated clippers in the China trade, but none of them was swifter than the *Shooting Star*, with a passage record of 88 days from Canton, and the *Atlanta* with a record of 84; none equalled Waterman's passage of 77 days.

When the captains of these clippers, dressed in "lustrous, straw-colored, raw-silk suits," paraded the water front of New York, they were more admired and envied by the loungers than any prince or potentate on earth. They were the kings of the sea by right of conquest. Imagine what Captain Waterman would have done if told that he reigned by grace of "a system of national protection deliberately initiated in 1789!"

In 1849 the British government, in a desperate determination to place British shipping ahead of American in quality as well as quantity, repealed the old navigation laws. British merchants were not only permitted to buy American ships, but American ships were permitted to enter all trades to the United Kingdom. The British ship-builders declared their business would be ruined; and the building of the old-style wooden ships was ruined. The ship-owners, too, saw disaster staring them in the face, and, for a time, there was reason for their fears. For where the British ships in the tea trade received from £3 to £4 per ton (50 cubic feet) from Canton to London, the American clippers received six and even more.

The little Baltimore clipper *Architect*, having made a run from Canton to London in 107 days, beating the fleet by about a week, she was paid £8 a ton when next she applied for a cargo of new-crop teas. The ordinary ships were glad to get the common £4.

In the meantime the California territory was acquired from Mexico by the treaty proclaimed July 4, 1848. Placer gold had already been discovered in El Dorado county (January 24), and when official reports confirmed the wide-spread rumors of the "find," a migration of gold-seekers such as the world had never seen was begun.

The growth of population in the territory was phenomenal, and the growth at once created an insistent demand for many products of civilization, especially for such things as were needed by miners and town-builders; for the whole region was a wilderness. This demand was backed by gold washed from the placers, and the prices seem now almost beyond belief.

"On the 1st of July, 1849, lumber was selling at San Francisco for $500 per 1000 feet. A better quality of lumber could be purchased in New York for $12—in Maine for $10." (Ex. Doc. 2, 32 Cong. 1 sess. p. 306.) At the same time, (Phil. Quar. Reg., Dec. 1849), eggs were selling as high as $2 a dozen, hens for $4 each, butter at $1.50 a pound, and potatoes, by the pound, 6 to 8 cents; turnips and cabbages still higher.

The merchants made haste to forward the needed supplies; thousands of eager gold-hunters sought passage on the outbound ships, and the one demand of the merchant and the passenger was for speed.

The number of ships obtainable being inadequate, the merchants went to the shipyards, and it was then that the most famous of all the American clippers were built.

The records of some of the old ships that were at once put into the California trade were not bad. The *Colonel Fremont* reached San Francisco after a passage of 127 days, and the *Grey Eagle* in 117. But the *Flying Cloud*, built by Donald McKay of Boston, and sailed by Captain Josiah P. Creesy, of Marblehead, in 1851, made the passage in 89 days, and in one day covered 374 sea miles. The length of this passage is given as 84 days in some accounts, but *A Description of the New Clipper Great Republic*, a pamphlet printed at Eastburn's Press, Boston, in 1853, for Donald McKay, says the time was 89 days. This pamphlet also says that the outlook for profits led McKay to build the *Sovereign of the Seas*, a ship of 2400 tons, and then the largest, longest, and sharpest merchant ship in the world. "Contrary to the advice of his best friends, he built her on his own account; he embarked all he was worth in her, for no merchant in this vicinity would risk capital in such a vessel, as she was considered too large and costly for any trade.... To the surprise of even those who knew him best, he played the merchant and loaded her himself. And well he was rewarded. He not only sold her on his own terms, but her performances exceeded his expectations."

Captain Lachlan McKay, brother of Donald, commanded this famous clipper. In August, 1851, she left New York for San Francisco, and until well beyond the Horn made record speed; but off Valparaiso, while the captain was driving her through a gale by night, an extra heavy squall carried away her fore and main topmasts. Captain McKay was sitting in an arm-chair on the quarter-deck at the time, and that chair was his only bed for the next two weeks. During that time new masts were made and got on end, the yards were crossed and sail was made. She reached San Francisco in 102 days from New York in spite of the disaster.

Going to Honolulu, the *Sovereign of the Seas* loaded whale-oil for New York. In the course of the passage she sailed 3144 sea miles in 10 consecutive days, and arrived in New York in 82 days. There she loaded for Liverpool, sailed on June 18, 1852, and anchored in the Mersey 13 days and 19 hours later. During this passage she covered 340 sea miles in a day. Her next voyage was to San Francisco, and during the return passage, "in 24 consecutive hours she ran 430 geographical miles." (Eastburn pamphlet.)

The *Antelope* and the *Surprise* are credited with making passages from San Francisco to New York in 97 days; the *John Gilpin* and the *Sweepstakes* in 94; the *Flying Fish* and the *Great Republic* in 92, and the *Sword Fish* in 91. Professor J. Russell Smith's *Ocean Carrier* says the *Comet* made the passage in 76 days. Her record is disputed (see *Shipping Illustrated*, New York, April 3, 1909), but the *Nautical Magazine*, April, 1856, confirms it. It is not disputed that the *Northern Light* ran from San Francisco to Boston in 76 days, and Captain A. H. Clark, in *Harper's Magazine*, June, 1908, says the *Trade Wind* made the San Francisco-New York passage in the same number of days.

CLIPPER SHIP *WITCH OF THE WAVE*

The *Great Republic*, built by Donald McKay, was the largest American clipper ship. She was "325 feet long, 53 feet wide and her whole depth is 39 feet." She was "of 4000 tons register and full 6000 tons stowage capacity." She had four masts, the after, or spanker, mast carrying fore and aft sails only. Her main-yard was 120 feet long. After she was loaded at New York for her maiden voyage she was accidentally burned, the total loss, as insured, amounting to $400,000. The sunken hull was raised, rebuilt at a cost of $27,000 and she was then rigged as before. In rebuilding her, a less depth of hull was given, but she was still able to carry 4000 tons dead weight. With 3000 tons in her hold she ran from New York to the coast of England in 12 days. In the Guano trade from the west coast of South America she was credited with making 412 miles in one day. (Admiral Preble in *U. S. Serv. Mag.*, July, 1889.) The *Red Jacket* once covered 413 sea miles in a day, and the *Flying Scud* claimed a day's run of 449, but this was disputed. (See *Nautical Magazine*, June, 1855.) The undisputed record day's run was made by the *Lightning*, built by Donald McKay, for English capitalists. A letter from McKay which appeared in the *Scientific American* on November 26, 1859, says:—

"Although I designed and built the clipper ship *Lightning*, and therefore ought to be the last to praise her, yet such has been her performance *since Englishmen learned to sail her*, that I must confess I feel proud of her. You are aware that she was so sharp and concave forward that one of her stupid captains, who did not comprehend the principle upon which she was built, persuaded the owners to fill in the hollows of her bows. They did so, and according to their Bullish bluff notions, she was not only better for the addition, but would sail faster, and wrote me to that effect. Well, the next passage to Melbourne, Australia, she washed the encumbrance away on one side, and when she returned to Liverpool, the other side was also cleared away. Since then she has been running as I modelled her. As a specimen of her speed I may say that I saw recorded in her log (of 24 hours) 436 nautical miles, a trifle over 18 knots an hour."

A few records will give an idea of the profits of the best of the clippers. The *Sovereign of the Seas* received $84,000 freight money for the passage when she was dismasted, and her owner says she earned $200,000 in the first eleven months. The *Surprise*, Captain Dumaresque, in a voyage from New York to San Francisco and then by way of China home, made a net profit of $50,000 above her cost and all expenses. The *Great Republic*, according to Preble, received $160,000 freight in a passage from New York to San Francisco. It seems worth noting here that the insurance rates on these hard-driven clippers were far lower than can now be obtained by the best of modern sailing ships.

The most interesting period in the history of the American merchant marine is the clipper ship era. The story has been told over and again, but the interest never flags. And yet while those ships were sweeping the seas and lying in port where their captains walked the piers in suits of lustrous China silks; and while the newspapers of Europe as well as America were printing in leaded lines the details of their wonderful passages, *the seafaring people of the United States were living in a fool's paradise*. The work that was to drive the American flag from the principal trade routes of the seas had been begun before the keel of the clipper *Rainbow* was stretched. Our seafaring people saw it, too, and even helped it on, but with but one notable exception, so far as the record shows, they utterly failed to comprehend its significance.

The character and effect of that work shall be described in another chapter. It remains to consider here one other interesting fact about the clippers. It is demonstrable that the shapes of the much-lauded clipper hulls had only a trifling, if any, influence upon the speed attained. Indeed the lines upon which the builders of the most famous of them all relied for speed were inferior, as modern designers know, to those of some ordinary ships wholly unknown to the record.

As a first bit of evidence in proof of this assertion here is the story of the *Natchez* in which Captain "Bob" Waterman first won fame. In 1843 Waterman sailed her around the world and made the passage from Canton to New York in 94 days. The whole voyage required only 9 months and 26 days. In 1844 he drove her from New York to Valparaiso in 71 days, thence to Callao in 8, and thence to Hongkong in 54. She then loaded teas at Canton and he drove her from that port to New York, 13,955 miles, in 78 days. This last passage was but one day longer than Waterman's record passage of 77 days made in the *Sea Witch*, "the swiftest clipper of her day." But the *Natchez* was not a clipper, although she has been described as one. She was built with full lines and a flat bottom in order that she might carry huge loads of cotton from New Orleans, across the shoals at the mouths of the Mississippi, and around to New York; and while engaged in that trade, she had earned the reputation of being one of the slowest ships on the American coast!

As to the lines of the clippers note that while Donald McKay supposed that the *Lightning* made her great speed because she was "hollow" at the bow, the modern yacht designers, who have tried out the hollow lines for years, have entirely abandoned them. The famous *America* had hollow lines; no modern yacht has anything of the kind.

The *Dreadnought*, with her unequalled North Atlantic record, was called a "semi-clipper," in her day. Her lines, as printed in Griffiths's *Nautical Magazine*, show that she was as full as many ships that were never classed as anything but plain cargo carriers. In connection with this fact recall the records of a ship or two built long before the clipper era—Derby's *Mount Vernon*, for instance, with her passage of 17 days from Salem to Gibraltar. The *Silas Richards*, formerly a packet between New York and Liverpool, left New York in June, 1836, for Canton, and she was back in New York at the end of March, 1837. Her run home was made in 91 days. Even the old *Desire* (high in poop and low in spars, when compared with the clippers) made the passage, away back in 1640, from Boston to Gravesend in 23 days.

Out of 157 vessels that arrived at San Francisco in 1852, no less than seventy had been designed as clippers, of which, however, only three or four made notable passages.

No complete list of the ships built with clipper lines was ever made, nor can one be made now; but out of the 2656 ships and barks launched between 1843 and 1855, which was the clipper era, it is certain that at least 10 per cent—256—were of the clipper model. But only a few more than a score ever made better records than the previously built packets had made. Indeed, many of the leanest and sharpest of the clipper hulls, together with (curiously enough) others that were built from the drawings of some of the successful clippers, were absolute failures, so far as speed was concerned.

This is not to deny that the clippers were in some respects grand ships. They were superior in the strength of hull, *in the breadth of beam*, and, consequently, *in the spread of canvas under which they could stand*. In the *general proportions* of their hulls many of them were right—as was the old frigate *Constitution*, which had a bow as round as an apple and yet had a record of better than 12 knots an hour. But even when all of that is said, the fact remains that the full-lined *Natchez* was but a day behind the record from Canton.

If it was not to the model of the ships, to what, then, were the splendid records due? The answer is of the utmost importance in any study of the American merchant marine. The records were due to the fact that our seamen were the most ambitious and the most efficient sailors *of the sail* that the world has ever seen. While the gale permitted the ship to hold her course, the captain paced the deck the whole night long and caught his sleep by day in short naps under the weather rail in order that he might see that she was kept going. The sheets and halyards of the important sails on those record ships were made of chains, and they were locked fast in place—held by padlocks, so that frightened sailors, unseen by the master, could not let them fly when the ship, rolling to the blast at night, dragged her lee rail through the solid water. When the captain gave an order, the crew ran with all their might to do the work—or they were knocked across the deck with a pump-brake in the hands of the nerve-racked mate. Captain Waterman even shot men off the yards because they seemed to be handling the sails slowly. Studding sails were spread to the zephyrs when the ship crossed the equator, and they were yet seen in place while she sailed with trade-winds so strong that ships from Europe close-hauled were reefed down to the cap. Indeed, all sail was often carried when ordinary ships were seen reefed down on the same course. As Clark Russell notes in one of his novels, the skipper of the ship from Europe, as he paced the deck with anxious eyes upon his shortened canvas, fearing that it would be blown from the bolt ropes, very often saw a tiny white speck upon the horizon, watched it grow into a splendid ship with "every rag set," saw her fling the Stars and Stripes to the gale, as she went roaring by, and then with feelings that cannot be described, gazed after her until she disappeared in the mists far down the lee.

If the two crews thus meeting in mid-ocean could have changed ships, the bluff-bowed hulk from Europe would soon have gone smoking away while the clipper would have rolled her spars over the lee rail before her new crew could have learned the lead of a single sheet or halyard.

It was the man on the quarter-deck—he who had handled ships among the rocks of the South Shetlands, or had lanced whales in the North Pacific, or had skimmed the sands of Cape Hatteras, in order to learn the arts of the sea as handed down from the beginning—it was the master mariner evolved by two hundred years of battle—with the sea and its people—who made the American flag supreme upon all the seas of the whole world.

CHAPTER XIII
DEEP-WATER STEAMSHIPS—PART I

IN order to comprehend the story of the efforts to establish lines of steam packets under the American flag between the United States and various ports in Europe, it is necessary at this point to review briefly our foreign relations in the period between the War of 1812 and the Civil War, and then to consider what was done by the British in the early development of steam navigation.

In the year 1818, in the course of what is known as the Seminole War, General Jackson, at the head of a strong body of troops, invaded the Spanish territory of Florida, captured a number of fortified places, and ruthlessly hanged one British subject named Arbuthnot and shot another named Ambrister on the unproved charge that the two had been "stirring up the Indians to war with the United States." No war followed this outrage, but the ill feeling which had animated the British after the War of 1812 was greatly intensified.

Trouble over the northeast boundary of the United States followed, and when the king of the Netherlands was asked to arbitrate the matter, he laid down a line which was not satisfactory to the English. At the same time it was exasperating to the Americans, especially to the people of Maine. In fact, open hostilities in a small way occurred near the boundary.

In 1837 the British manner of ruling the Canadian region created so much opposition among the settlers there that a small insurrection broke out. It was suppressed, but only to break out again, and at this time a number of American sympathizers joined the insurgents. A band of the insurgents having taken possession of Navy Island, in the Niagara River, the American sympathizers went in the American steamer *Caroline* to join them, and carried arms and supplies. The steamer then returned to American waters, but the British loyalists crossed over the line, captured the steamer, set her on fire, and sent her over Niagara Falls. One American was killed in the attack. Later a Canadian deputy sheriff boasted that he had killed the man whose life was taken, and then, in 1840, incautiously came across to Lockport, New York, where he was arrested for the murder. His name was Alexander McLeod. Thereupon the British government, with the aggressive Palmerston in the lead, avowed that the *Caroline* was seized on the authority of the nation, and peremptorily demanded McLeod's release. The Washington authorities were disposed to yield, but Governor Seward, of New York, declared that McLeod should stand trial; and he did. But having proved an alibi, he was acquitted, and on October 12, 1841, he was returned to Canada. In the meantime an American had been seized as a hostage to abide McLeod's fate. He was of course released at last.

In the course of the year 1841 an American coaster named the *Creole*, while carrying a cargo of slaves from the breeding grounds in Virginia to the ever eager market in the Southwest, was taken from her officers and crew by the slaves, who then ran the vessels to the Bahamas, where the slaves, 125 in number, were protected. The slave owners of the United States had been restive because of frequent reports that British cruisers, engaged in suppressing the slave trade upon the coast of Africa, had "exercised the right of search" by boarding ships under the American flag, and when the story of the protection of the *Creole's* cargo reached the country, the excitement rose toward the war heat.

In the meantime, the United States had annexed Florida. Then the Texans set up an independent government, and it was recognized as an independent nation, but with its people openly anxious for annexation to the United States. The statesmen of England saw that annexation was inevitable and that a war with Mexico would follow, with the result that the territory of the United States would be enlarged in the Southwest and along the Spanish Main, where British subjects were looking for a further extension of territory and influence. For at about this time the ancient settlement of logwood cutters at Belize was developed into the colony of British Honduras (1845). Although England had subscribed to and helped to enforce the Monroe Doctrine, her statesmen were looking to an extension of British Honduras as far south as the mouth of the Rio San Juan, in Nicaragua. To secure this extension a protectorate over the Mosquito Coast Indians was declared, and the coast was assumed to be territory entirely independent of Nicaragua. On August 19, 1841, British war-ships captured San Juan del Norte, at the mouth of the San Juan, drove away the Nicaragua officials, and installed Mosquito Indians. The Nicaraguans soon drove away the Mosquito forces, but the interest in the place having been intensified by projects for building an interoceanic canal across the country, the British returned, late in 1847, and on January 10, 1848, placed the Mosquito chiefs once more in possession.

With the rush of emigrants to California, the United States became interested in this aggression. It would never do to allow the British to control such a highway as was then in contemplation. The British naturally held on to what they had secured at the mouth of the San Juan, however, and then, with a view of obtaining control of the other end of the canal route (the Gulf of Fonseca), they began to press Honduras for the payment of certain claims of British subjects, the nature of which is of no importance because the claims were merely a pretext for an aggression that would have been made had no claims been in existence. To back these claims a British warship appeared, but when the Honduranians were in straits, the American envoy to Nicaragua heard of their trouble, hastened to meet them, and then negotiated a treaty (September 28, 1849) by which a part of Tigre Island and a part of the coast of the Gulf of Fonseca were granted to the United States for a naval station. When the British envoy learned how he had been outwitted, he ordered some of the naval force at his command to seize Tigre Island in contempt of the acquired rights of the United States. (See Keasbey's *Nicaragua Canal* and Pims *Panama*.) That the British fully expected a war with the United States, is beyond dispute. In fact, they had been prepared for war ever since 1840, but the Nicaragua matter it was supposed would surely bring on the long-looked-for contest.

To add to the dangers of the situation, a dispute had arisen, meantime, over the northwestern boundary of the United States, a controversy commonly referred to in history as the Oregon Question. The United States claimed the territory as far north as the south line of Alaska, then belonging to Russia, in latitude 54° 40'. The British claimed as far south as the Columbia River. The claims created great excitement in this country in 1845, and the cry of "Fifty-four forty, or fight" was heard throughout the nation.

To show the state of feeling in England at that time, here is a quotation from a letter written by Louis McLean, American Minister to London, to the Secretary of State, January 3, 1846.

"I sought an interview with Lord Aberdeen, in order that, in conformity with your instructions, I might bring to his notice the warlike preparations making by Great Britain, and, if possible, ascertain their real character and object.... In introducing the subject I adverted at the same time to the information the President had received from various sources, of the extensive preparations making by Great Britain, and the natural inference upon his part that, in the present pacific state of the relations of Great Britain with all the powers of Europe, they could only look to a rupture with the United States.... Lord Aberdeen said very promptly and frankly that it would be improper to disguise that, with the sincerest wish to avoid it, they were obliged to look to the possibility of a rupture with the United States, and that in such a crisis the warlike preparations now making would be useful and important.... He stated that the most extensive and formidable parts of their preparations were the fortifications of the principal and exposed stations ... and to *the increase of the number of steam vessels in lieu of the old craft.*" (See Cong. *Globe*, February 6, 1847.)

In short, during the whole period under consideration, the Americans and the British were constantly animated by intense antipathy and even animosity, each toward the other.

While turning, now, to the story of the evolution of British steamships, it will be worth while to recall first what has already been said about the environment that developed the character of the American sailor. From the day when the men of Massachusetts Bay built ships and launched forth in them to catch fish and trade with foreign countries, until such men as Palmer, Samuels, and Waterman made marvellous speed with whatever form of ship they happened to command, the whole environment of the American seafaring population had served to develop excellence in handling ships of the sail.

With this fact in mind, note that steamers made an extraordinary change in the conditions of transportation by ships. These conditions were so far removed from the old that a portrait-painter who had never learned any of the arts of the sea designed the first commercially successful steamer in the United States. The keeper of a bathhouse performed a similar service for the British public. When steam navigation had become an assured success, the splendid skill of the sailor *of the sail* was no longer needed. The man at the throttle usurped the place of the man on the weather yard-arm, and this is true in spite of the curious and absurd fact that even now the captains of steamships do not reach the bridge by way of the stokehole.

Then recall the fact that while the United States had produced excellent sailors of the sail, there was such a dearth of mechanics in Fulton's day that he was obliged to import the *Clermont's* engine from England; and Stevens, though he built his own engines, was obliged to train men to work in iron before he could do so. The British had been building efficient engines for twenty years before Fulton bought his. In every application of steam power, the British were that much in advance of the Americans.

As Day points out in his *History of Commerce*, inventors living in the United States, as well as in other countries, went to England to perfect their inventions, because of the superior facilities afforded in British machine shops; and this was done as late as 1836—even later. Some of the best machinery invented in the United States, in the period under consideration, was first put in use in Great Britain.

The fact that abundant supplies of coal were to be had at low price in Great Britain is not to be overlooked in connection with this argument. With the consequent great progress in factory industries, the time was close at hand when all England was to become "a free port" for all the world, as well as a place for working up the raw materials of all other countries.

Still another important fact is this, that the American capitalists who began to invest in steamships at an early day, found immense stretches of inland waters upon which to develop the carrying trade, while the inland waters of Great Britain were of insignificant extent, and the capitalists there were soon engaged in the coasting trade where the waters were by no means pacific. In 1818 the *Rob Roy* was put on the route between Glasgow and Belfast, and a little later she was sent to ply between Dover and Calais. In 1822 a line was established between Liverpool and Glasgow, and this was followed in 1826 by a line plying between Edinburgh and London. These last ships were 160 feet long and were provided with engines of 200 horse-power; they were regarded as such marvellous ships that people came from all parts of the kingdom to look at them. And it is to be noted that all the coasters so far mentioned were provided with a form of engine (the side lever) which was efficient for deep-water service.

Following the success of the Glasgow line, other lines were established to various ports of Europe, including one to Bordeaux, the ships of which had to cross the stormy Bay of Biscay and traverse a route 1600 miles long. All of this is to emphasize the fact that while the steamship men of the United States were making records upon the Hudson and other *inland* waters, those of Great Britain were engaged almost exclusively upon waters with a rending power little, if any, less than that of the Atlantic. The environments of the men engaged in steamboat traffic in the two countries were so different that widely different classes of ships, engines, *and engineers* were developed. The British had been navigating the Bay of Biscay with success for several years before the Americans put the *Home* upon the route around Cape Hatteras.

And yet it was an American that first stirred up the British to embark in the transatlantic steamer trade—Dr. Junius Smith, who graduated from Yale in 1802, and then went to London as representative of some American merchants. The success of the British coasters led Smith to believe that transatlantic steamers would prove successful, and in 1832 he came to the United States to look into the matter more fully.

"My friends in New York make no doubt of the practicability nor of the success of such an undertaking," he wrote to a director of the London and Edinburgh Steam Packet Company, "and have assured me that they will build two steam vessels suited to the object in view," provided English capitalists would build two more for use in the same line. Mr. Smith's letter was written to invite the directors of the company to join in the enterprise, and to charter to him one of their steamers for a demonstration trip, to New York. The directors replied with a cold refusal. Smith, however, tried elsewhere, and when his plans were presented in the newspapers, the professional humorists gave much attention to the "Yankee" innovator. In 1836 a noted scientist of the period, Dr. Lardner, in a lecture at Liverpool, declared that any effort to make direct passages from New York to Liverpool would prove "perfectly chimerical, and they might as well talk of making the direct voyage from New York or Liverpool to the moon."

When this lecture was reported in the papers, a number of steamship men showed by arguments drawn from the experience of the coasters that Lardner was wrong, but even with their assistance Smith made two vain efforts to organize a company. But in July, 1836, when the books were again opened, enough shares were taken to enable the company to build a good ship which in time proved successful. But because there were long delays in getting this vessel afloat, Smith's company chartered the steamer *Sirius*, a packet plying between London and Cork, for a voyage to New York.

The *Sirius* was of about the size of a large sailing packet of the day. She measured 700 tons and had engines of 320 horse-power. On April 4, 1838, she left Cork for New York.

In the meantime, I. K. Brunel, who was then chief engineer of the Great Western Railroad, had become convinced of the feasibility of transatlantic steam navigation, and with a few associates he had built at Bristol a ship named the *Great Western*, especially for traffic between Bristol (the end of the Great Western Railroad) and New York. This ship was 212 feet long by 35 wide and 23 deep. She registered at 1340 tons. She was provided with side-lever engines of 440 horse-power, the cylinders being 73½ inches in diameter by 7 feet stroke.

As it happened, the *Great Western* left Bristol for New York on April 7, and transatlantic steam navigation was thereby begun with a race. The *Sirius* arrived first, anchoring off the Battery, New York, early in the morning on April 23. The excitement in the city was extraordinary, and the water about the ship was soon covered with small boats carrying people for a look at her. And then at about 11 o'clock, when the throngs around the *Sirius* were densest, a lookout announced another steamship in sight down below, when the crowd began to shout:—

"The *Great Western*! The *Great Western*!"

It was she, and in the middle of the afternoon she anchored off Pike Street.

The British consul, in a letter congratulating Lieutenant R. Roberts, R. N., commanding the *Sirius*, on arriving first, said:—

"I have a further cause of rejoicing, that the honor of accomplishing the enterprise has been achieved by a son of the British navy, and that it was completed on St. George's Day."

It was five years after this arrival that the keel of the first American clipper was laid, but *with the termination of the passages of these two ships* the dawn of the day of British supremacy upon the high seas appeared.

Special attention seems due to the *Great Western*, because she was the first ship built for the traffic. She had steamed 3125 sea miles, making an average of 208 miles per day, or 8.2 knots an hour. The total consumption of fuel was 655 tons, less than a day's consumption in some modern ships. She returned home with a consumption of only 392 tons, prevailing winds and a large spread of canvas helping her to save coal. The cost of this ship was £50,000, of which £13,500 was paid for the engines. She continued to ply regularly on the route, and on September 25, 1838, the New York *American* had this to say:—

"The arrival of the steam packet *Great Western* puts us in possession of intelligence to the 8th.... The great success of this enterprise has confirmed the timid and almost crazed the sanguine. She brings *one hundred and forty passengers*. All her berths were engaged before she arrived at Bristol." Then an article from the London *Times* is quoted as follows:—

"Upon the eighty-seven passengers home, and the 130 out, at 40 guineas passage money per head in the saloon, and 35 guineas in the cabin, each way, the directors of the Great Western will have received upwards of £8000, exclusive of the benefit derived from the conveyance of goods, of which the *Great Western* brought from New York to the extent of about 200 tons' measurement."

The Liverpool *Albion* is then quoted as saying that "the last trip of the *Great Western* netted £6000."

The *Great Western* continued in the New York and Bristol and the New York and Liverpool trades until she had made seventy-four passages, and she was then sold for use between England and the West Indies. These facts are of importance to the history of the American merchant marine, because our writers who have favored paying subsidies to American steam lines have asserted that in those days it was not possible to run steamship lines between the United States and England without a subsidy. The *Great Western* made money without a subsidy. So did many other steamers that followed, as shall appear.

We now come, however, to the story of the first lines of subsidized transatlantic steamships. One Samuel Cunard, a wealthy merchant of Nova Scotia, had been dreaming about steam navigation since 1830, and when the Great Western Company had shown the way, he went to England in order to arrange for a line from Liverpool to Halifax, and thence to Boston. After consultation with eminent men of experience in steam navigation, he gave an order to Robert Napier, the foremost designer and builder of steamships in the kingdom, for four steamships of about 900 tons each. But before the work was begun, Napier convinced him that larger ships would prove more profitable, and as the larger ships would cost more than

Cunard had to invest, George Burns, of Glasgow, and David McIver, of Liverpool (both of whom were men of experience), were united with him in forming what is now known as the Cunard Company. The *Britannia*, the first ship built for this company, was a wooden vessel 207 feet long by 34 wide and 22 deep, registering 1156 tons. She had engines of 423 horsepower. The other three ships built at that time were slightly smaller.

It is to be noted that this company was formed to run ships in opposition to the *Great Western* and to Smith's lines. They were to depend upon what traffic they could get for success and upon nothing else. But in the meantime the British government had been considering the advisability of employing steamships to carry the royal mail across the Atlantic. Theretofore certain brigs had been employed by the Admiralty for this purpose, and beginning in 1821, government-owned brigs were employed exclusively. This proving expensive, the plan of hiring privately owned brigs was resumed in 1833, and these brigs were in use at that time. The success of the *Great Western* having proven the efficiency of steamships in the transatlantic trade, the postal authorities, in connection with the Admiralty, decided to use steam, and when Cunard came into the field, bids were invited for a mail service under certain burdensome conditions among which were these: The ships were to be fit for war use, carrying heavy guns, a naval officer was to be carried to care for the mail, and the ships were to be sold to the Admiralty on demand at a valuation. The Great Western, as well as the Cunard people, put in bids. The Great Western did not know that they would have opposition, and bid accordingly, with the result that Cunard made the better offer and got the contract. The full story is told in Lindsay's *History of Merchant Shipping*. Cunard was to receive at first £3295 per voyage, but, the plans having been modified, the subsidy was raised to £81,000 a year. For this he was to maintain a fortnightly service from Liverpool by way of Halifax to Boston, and with a line of smaller steamers from Halifax to Quebec. The *Britannia* left Liverpool upon her first voyage on July 4, 1840. No American writer has as yet pointed out that this was "a beautiful coincidence of nominal dates."

SAILING OF *BRITANNIA*, FEBRUARY 3, 1844

From a contemporary engraving

A few months later the Royal Mail Steam Packet Company was organized especially to carry the mail to the West Indies, including St. Thomas, Haiti, and Cuba, and to Chagres, to Mexico, and to the south part of the United States, as well. A branch line was to be maintained from the West Indies to Brazil. The contract (made in March, 1841) called for fourteen steamships built so as to carry "guns of the largest caliber" then in use in the navy; and the frames and planking were of a thickness to resist shot as well as a frigate—as, indeed, were those of the Cunard line. The commanders of the ships were to be naval officers. The subsidy paid was £240,000 a year.

It is important to note that this line was to run regularly to Chagres, where there was not enough traffic to pay the expense of the ship while lowering a boat to carry the mail ashore, and, further, that there was not enough traffic anywhere on the route to pay any considerable part of the expense of the line. Indeed, the traffic and subsidy together proved insufficient to pay expenses. Further than that, the time allowed in all the ports was limited— to six hours at the important island of Barbados, for instance, and to twenty-four at Port Royal, Jamaica, where there was an important naval station. It was impossible to handle any valuable quantity of West India cargo in such short periods. It is therefore certain that frequent and swift voyages were wanted in the establishing of this line, rather than the carrying of cargo. And this is to say that it was established for the same reasons that brigs had been used in carrying the royal mail theretofore. It was a political and military service that the ships were to perform.

Consider all these facts in connection with the political complications with the United States that have been mentioned. It was in 1840 that the British government demanded the release of McLeod on pain of war. It was at that time that the people of Maine and New Brunswick took up arms in connection with the boundary dispute. At the same time the British government was looking ahead to an increase of territory along the Spanish Main, including a canal across Nicaragua in contempt of the Monroe Doctrine.

Then recall the fact that the use of steam for driving war-ships was yet in the experimental stage. Many able naval men believed that sails were yet to be preferred, but the English were especially anxious to learn all about the new power in order to keep abreast with the progress of the age—to preserve their *naval* superiority. It is of significance that young naval officers were detailed to command all of the West India ships and to accompany those of the Cunard line. Further than that, it is to be noted that the Admiralty insisted that the subsidized ships be built of wood not only then, but for years after iron had proved cheaper and more efficient for merchant ships, and this was done because it was fully believed that a wooden ship was best for naval uses.

In short, the subsidizing of ships was begun chiefly as a military and diplomatic measure. Any candid review of the facts shows it. It was done, too, with a full knowledge that paying a subsidy was against the interests of the other owners of steamships that were already plying between Liverpool and New York. In fact, the Cunard line had hardly learned the way to Boston when the Great Western line made such loud complaints about the destruction of private enterprise through the subsidizing of the Cunard that a committee of Parliament took up the whole matter and concluded that the other steamers would not be put out of the trade.

There were men on both sides of the Atlantic who saw at that time that steam would eventually drive sails from the packet routes. E. K. Collins was one of these men. But no one supposed at that time that subsidizing a single mail line from Liverpool to Boston would do it. And even the optimistic Cunard directors made no effort to interfere with the traffic of the New York and Liverpool sailing packets until it was seen that American capitalists were about to put on a line of steamers between New York and Liverpool.

With these facts in mind, we may now comprehend the full story of the first American steam-packet lines that ran across the Atlantic Ocean.

CHAPTER XIV
DEEP-WATER STEAMSHIPS—PART II

THE success of the British steamers that crossed the Atlantic in 1838 led a number of New York capitalists to form what they called the American Atlantic Steam Navigation Company, of which James de Peyster Ogden was chairman, and on March 22, 1839, calls for subscriptions to the capital stock were published in the New York papers. The answers to the calls were few, and the enterprise was abandoned.

Out of several reasons for this failure, consider these: The American people had but little capital, and there were calls in many directions for every dollar obtainable. The calls from the railroads were particularly insistent, for while the first railroad to use steam (the Albany and Schenectady) was completed in 1833, the steam mileage in 1840 was 2380. The inland water traffic was most attractive. In 1839 the enrolled steamers measured 489,879 tons, and they were worn out so rapidly that every vessel had to be replaced (on the average) within four years. Then the deep-water sailing ships absorbed much capital, the tonnage in 1839 being 829,096, while the coasting tonnage measured 1,032,023 tons, and all these vessels were, on the average, highly profitable.

Of the other attractive calls for capital, nothing need be said, but a brief reference to an attempt to form a company to run transatlantic steamships from Philadelphia may be quoted from *Niles's Register* of August 25, 1838:—

"At a meeting of the citizens held in the Merchants' Exchange, Philadelphia, to take such measures to forward the plan for a communication by steam between that city and Europe ... the following resolutions were unanimously adopted: ... Resolved that we have learned with lively satisfaction the willingness of our brethren of Great Britain to coöperate with us in this great enterprise" by making a liberal subscription for the construction of "such steamships as might be needed."

The "brethren" were not quite as willing to "coöperate" as was supposed, but the "great enterprise" was taken in hand a few years later by a man named William Inman, with notable results.

In considering their failures to organize transatlantic steamship companies, these business men did not fail to refer to the fact that the British government was paying subsidies to the Cunard and the Royal Mail steamship companies. The fact that the Cunard subsidy was a hardship for the owners of the unsubsidized steamers in the American trade was not dwelt upon. The people were told that subsidies were given in order to build up a steam merchant marine. Then Congress was invited to consider the fact that in subsidizing two lines of steamships Great Britain had secured eighteen fine ships fit to add to her growing steam naval fleet. Naval officers were carried on all those ships, and they were not only learning how to handle steam, but they *were learning to navigate American waters*—and all this at a period when England and the United States were on the verge of war.

Thereupon Thomas Butler King, chairman of the House Naval Committee, brought forward a plan for a subsidized mail line under the American flag. (Ho. Reps. 681 and 685, 28 Cong. 1 sess.) His arguments in favor of a subsidy were: That a reduction might be made in the rate of postage, and yet the income from the mails would soon pay all the subsidy that would be required. That our naval officers would learn how to handle steam. That we should learn how to build efficient steamships for deep water. That a line to the north of Europe would promote emigration and trade. In connection with this last argument it was stated that the British post-office authorities were in the habit of holding up all mails bound across England to the continent until the British merchants had had time to read and act upon their advices from America, and the newspapers had had time to print all the American news. After considering the matter for four years, Congress acted, on March 3, 1845, in a bill providing—

"That the Postmaster-general ... is hereby authorized ... to contract for the transportation of the United States mail between any of the ports of the United States, and a port or ports of any foreign Power, whenever, in his opinion, the public interest will thereby be promoted ... for any greater period than four years and not exceeding ten years. All such contracts shall be made with citizens of the United States, and the mail to be transported in American vessels by American citizens."

Thereupon the Postmaster-general contracted with Edward Mills of New York, who agreed to build ships to plans approved by the Secretary of the Navy, and run a steam-packet line from New York to Southampton and Bremen, twenty voyages a year, for a subsidy of $400,000. If alternate voyages were made to Havre instead of Bremen, the subsidy was to be $350,000.

Mills and his associates were incorporated (May 8, 1846), as the Ocean Steam Navigation Company. Contracts were let for the building of two steamships, and then the troubles of the company began. On learning that an American company was to enter the transatlantic trade, the Cunard Company began running packets regularly to New York. The opposition of this established line increased the timidity of capitalists so much that in spite of the guaranteed income of at least $350,000 a year, it was impossible to obtain the needed money in the United States, and "money was furnished for the undertaking by the little government of Bremen, and by individuals connected with the enterprise on the other side of the Atlantic, and pretty largely furnished, too." (App. Cong. *Globe*, September 4, 1850.)

The one deadly misfortune of the company, however, was found in the fact that the Americans had not yet learned how to build ocean-going steamships. Said the *Merchants' Magazine*, May, 1849, regarding the first ships of the line:—

"The models of the *Washington* and *Hermann* were quite defective, particularly so in having a very narrow bottom, which made them load deep and be tender or even crank at all times.... *Their engines also were not quite strong or stiff enough.*"

The boilers were not large enough to furnish an adequate supply of steam and the paddle-wheels were too large for the engines. The *Scientific American*, October 7, 1848, said:—

"The great cause of our unsuccess in our Atlantic steamers is owing to our short acquaintance with the building of marine ships. There is science and genius among our nautical engineers, but *they want experience.*"

When our first American mail steamer sailed for Europe no practical marine engineers could be found to work her engines. She took a first-class engineer and corps of assistants from one of the New York river packets; but as soon as the ship got to sea, and heavy breakers came on, all the engineers and firemen were taken deadly seasick; and for three days it was constantly expected that the ship would be lost. (Rainey's *Ocean Steam Navigation*.)

It is to be noted here that John L. Stevens, the ablest American marine engineer of his day, was one of the directors of this company.

The *Washington* sailed for Southampton and Bremen on June 1, 1847. Her passengers and crew looked forward to a cheering reception on the other side; for when the *Sirius* and the *Great Western* arrived in New York the people of the city turned out to honor them, and the city authorities and such bodies as the Chamber of Commerce gave public receptions in honor of the event. Then when the Cunard's first liner the *Britannia* was frozen in at Boston the merchants of the city contributed $10,000, for which a contractor agreed to saw a channel for her to clear water. The contractor spent $20,000 in doing the work. He spent $10,000 out of his own pocket without a murmur, and the Cunard Company without a murmur let him do it. But the only official action taken on the arrival of the *Washington* at Southampton was in the sending of a notice to the American mail agent that he would have to pay full sea postage on all mail landed, as well as the usual inland rates. And the only word of welcome spoken in the port was uttered by the officials of the dock company with whom the ship was berthed.

Because of their financial difficulties the company organized a separate corporation to build and run ships to Havre. The *Humbolt* and the *Franklin* were put on this route in 1849. The *Humbolt* was wrecked at Halifax, December 5, 1853, and the *Franklin* stranded on Montauk Point, July 17, 1854. The *Arago* and *Fulton*, built to replace these two, were somewhat better than any ocean-going steamships theretofore built in the United States, and they were able to continue the service until the government chartered them for use in the Civil War (1861). The two Bremen ships were laid up after their subsidy ceased—1859. All six of these ships used by this corporation were slow as well as expensive to operate. The time used in the Bremen passage was about fourteen days; that to Havre, twelve.

The Collins Line (New York and Liverpool U. S. Mail Steamship Company), was the most famous of the subsidized lines. E. K. Collins was a Truro, Cape Cod, boy, who, at the age of fifteen (1817), became a clerk to a New York merchant. Five years later he was sent to sea as a supercargo, and a little later he became a partner in the business. His first memorable stroke of business was made in 1825, when cotton took a sudden rise in the Liverpool market. The news of the rise reached New York on the day that the regular Charleston, South Carolina, packet was to sail, and a number of New York merchants took passage on the ship, intending to buy all the cotton in Charleston before the news of the rise could be learned there. As the packet passed the bar at Sandy Hook, bound out, the merchants on her deck saw a pilot-boat, with young Collins on her deck, head away down the coast; and with one accord they made jeering remarks at the idea of a little schooner trying to beat the regular packet in such a race. But when they reached the Charleston bar they met the boat with Collins on board coming out. He had bought all the cotton.

With money made in that deal and with some obtained by marrying a rich wife, Collins started the New Orleans packet line, and another line thence to Tampico. These having proved successful, he then established the famous Dramatic Line to Liverpool. In 1840, Collins said:—

"There is no longer chance for enterprise with sails. It is steam that must win the day. I will build steamers that shall make the passage from New York to Europe in ten days and less."

In the winter of 1846-1847 Collins and others persuaded Congress to pass the act dated March 3, 1847. It provided for the construction of four naval steamers in place of ten that the naval committee had asked for; for a contract between the Secretary of the Navy and Collins & Co., for transporting the mail between New York and Liverpool; for a contract between the Secretary of the Navy and A. G. Sloo for transporting the mail between New York and New Orleans with a stop at Havana, and from Havana to Chagres, on the Isthmus of Panama—known as the Law Line, from George Law, the leading capitalist; for a contract with unnamed capitalists (C. H. Aspinwall was the leader), for a mail service between Panama and the ports of San Francisco and Astoria.

Collins's company had a paid-in capital of $1,200,000. By his contract, signed in November, 1847, he was to receive $19,250 per voyage for making two voyages per month for eight months of the year and one a month during four winter months. For this service Collins was to build four steamships measuring "not less than 2000 tons each," and complete them ready for sea within eighteen months; also a fifth ship "as early as may be practicable thereafter." Each ship was to carry a naval officer, as mail agent, and four passed midshipmen to serve as deck officers.

Contracts were made for the four ships, and many different statements have been made regarding their size and cost. Chief Engineer Isherwood, of the navy, put the size of the *Atlantic* and the *Pacific* at 2686 tons each; the *Arctic* and *Baltic* at 2772. Senator Rusk, of Texas, who vigorously supported the line in all its appeals to Congress, said the four measured 11,131 tons in the aggregate. The *Merchant's Magazine* (Vol. 22, p. 682) rated them at 3500 tons each and said they cost $650,000 each. G. S. Houston, in a speech in Congress on July 7, 1852, quoted the company to prove that the average cost of the ships was $736,035.67 each.

With a paid-up capital of $1,200,000, four ships were built that cost at least twice as much as the money in hand would pay for, and they were each at least 700 tons larger than the contract called for. The builders gave Collins credit, and thereby secured the work on their own terms. And yet while thus paying the highest prices for his ships, and with an ever growing debt staring him in the face, Collins was recklessly extravagant in furnishing his cabins, and in every department of the company's management.

As a result, within six months after the contract was signed with the Secretary of the Navy, Collins was back in the lobby at Washington, "begging and boring" for further help. By the act of August 3, 1848, the Secretary of the Navy was authorized to advance $25,000 a month on each of the four ships until they should be put into commission, and the time for completing them was extended to June 1, 1850. Under a subsequent agreement this advance was paid back in small instalments.

And during all this time Collins walked the streets, telling all who would listen that he was going to run the *Scotch-built, Scotch-managed* Cunarders off the sea!

When done, the ships were found to have fine models—they rode the waves in a way that excited the admiration of all sailors. But the keelsons under the engines were only forty inches deep, while the keels were 277 feet long, and there was "give" enough to rack the engines to pieces—a fact showing conclusively the ignorance of the designer so far as ocean steamships were concerned. And yet George Steers, the famous designer of the yacht *America*, was the responsible man! As the *Scientific American* had said of our engineers, he "wanted experience."

The *Atlantic* began the service on April 27, 1850. It was in this year that the average American sailing ship was making three voyages where foreign ships made but two. For thirty years our sailing packets had carried the broom on the North Atlantic. The captains of the Canton tea clippers, dressed in raw silk, were strutting about the water front, boasting of passages that were the wonder of the world. And here was a new line of steamers with a managing owner who had won fame as the owner of swift ships, and who had been assuring the whole world that he was going to beat all creation with steam!

In the mind of the captain of the *Atlantic* the honor of the Stars and Stripes was in his custody, and he could keep it safe only by driving the ship to the utmost limit of speed. And each of the other ships was also driven to the last gasp. In May, 1851, the *Pacific* ran from New York to Liverpool in 9 days, 20 hours, and 16 minutes. In August, 1852, the *Baltic* crossed from Liverpool to New York in 9 days and 13 hours. Collins had kept his promise to drive a ship across the Atlantic in less than ten days.

In the meantime, the Cunard Company, to meet the determined opposition, built new ships, and the British government raised the subsidy to $16,500 per voyage. Orders were issued in England to drive the new Cunarders, too, but it was impossible for them to equal the rampant Collins liners at that time.

For a time it seemed to the American people that the supremacy upon the seas was to be maintained with steam, and not a few Englishmen, including the editor of the *London Times*, took a pessimistic view of the situation. A little later, however, the situation was seen in its true light. On February 15, 1851, when the *Atlantic* had been in commission but ten months, the *Scientific American* said editorially that "it is very foolish to push through a steamship on a long passage by dint of coal." The *New York Herald*, a nautical specialist, was complaining, meantime, that the American firemen were wretchedly inefficient. It was admitted by the company, later still, that for the first twenty-eight voyages of the line the average cost of coal was $8612.28, the amount consumed being well up toward 2000 tons.

And yet the big coal bill was one of the least of the evils of the situation. By driving the engines to the limit on every mile of the route the weak timbers under the engines were needlessly strained, with the result that the engines were racked out of line and torn to pieces. No sooner did a ship get rid of its passengers at the pier than an army of machinists came on board to make repairs; and they were employed in relays, day and night, until the passengers came to the pier for the next passage.

"Either the scale upon which it was planned was not required, and could not be sustained by the country, or it has been most shamefully mismanaged," said Congressman Borland, in a speech in the House, on May 17, 1852, in reference to the Collins Line. Collins had come to Congress for an increase in the subsidy, and a statement of the company's affairs which he submitted shows that Borland was right in both ends of his statement. (See App. *Cong. Globe*, 32 Cong. 1 sess.) The statement is dated December 15, 1851. It showed that the expenses for the first twenty-eight voyages had averaged $65,215.59. The income was—for passengers, $21,292.65; freights, $7,744.20, subsidy, $19,250,—a total of $48,286.85, leaving a net loss of $16,928.74 per voyage.

Because Collins had broken some records, and because it was believed that his ships would serve in case of war, and because he had reduced the cost of carrying package freight, and because Congress heartily hated everything British, the subsidy was increased to $33,000 per voyage for twenty-six voyages a year. (Act of March 3, 1854.)

For a time thereafter Collins was free to continue his extravagant career. Having luxurious furnishings, he gained in the cabin passenger trade. He also gained somewhat in the package freight business. The advent of the Crimean War (March 27, 1854, to March 31, 1856), helped him because the British government took and used several of the Cunard steamers as transports (as *war-ships*, even the Cunarders were a sham). The Cunard service was thereby reduced and he thus had opportunity to sail in alternate weeks with the remaining Cunarders. But even then no profits were made. The line never paid a dividend.

In the meantime, the Scotchmen were learning to race their ships, and in 1855 they built the *Persia*, an iron ship of 3300 tons, and 3600 actual horse-power; and with her, in September, 1856, they crossed in 9 days, 2 hours, and 40 minutes, thus making a new record.

Collins built the *Adriatic*, the fifth ship under the contract, and the records agree that she was a very swift ship, but by no means a profitable one. Moreover she appeared too late; for by the act of August 18, 1856, Congress gave notice to Collins that the subsidy would be reduced, a year later, to the original sum of $19,250 per voyage. At the same time it became certain that no subsidy would be paid after the end of the original term of the contract—ten years.

In the meantime the line lost the *Arctic*. While running at a speed of thirteen knots an hour through a heavy fog, forty miles off Cape Race, and making no sort of signal to notify other vessels of her presence in those waters, she was rammed by the French steamer *Vesta*, and sunk with a loss of 307 lives. It has been asserted that she went down because the modern system of bulkheads had not been invented. As a matter of fact, the Norwich liner *Atlantic*, a ship built in 1846, had a collision bulkhead, and other ships had been divided by several bulkheads before the time of the *Arctic*, but experience shows that no system of bulkheads as yet installed has been able to save a ship when rammed in the engine-room. Then on September 23, 1856, a little more than a month after Congress decided to reduce the subsidy, the *Pacific* sailed from Liverpool, and was never heard from afterward. The two ships thus lost were together insured for $1,250,000, chiefly in England, and the money was paid to the company.

The line continued its service after the subsidy was cut (June 30, 1857), but a financial panic swept over the commercial world in the fall of that year, and with the consequent loss of business the line failed. The last voyage was made in January, 1858. In April, following, the sheriff sold the ships (subject to claims of $657,000) for $50,000. Collins died at his home in Madison Avenue, New York City, in June, 1878, and was buried in Woodlawn Cemetery.

"I knew the Collins line very well.... They burned an immense quantity of coal; they were fitted out and fitted up in the most sumptuous manner; they had large crews, a large number of officers and a large number of engineers, for they had most powerful engines. They were run at full speed, and the company had not enough ships on the line to enable them to have proper relays so that they began to deteriorate very rapidly, and they ran them out in a very short time. They had very large buildings in New York, a great many officers and a great many people connected with them. All these had to be paid. Then there were a great many deadheads, so that I used to be astonished how they kept running at all." (Admiral Porter, H. R. Rep. 28, 41st Cong. 2 sess. p. 192.)

Two other lines, subsidized under the act of March 3, 1847, need a brief consideration. One was the Sloo Line, which, as noted, ran steamships from New York by the way of Havana, to New Orleans, with a branch line to Chagres, on the Isthmus of Panama. The subsidy paid was $290,000 a year. The first ship (the *Falcon*), left New York in September, 1848. The Pacific coast contract went to the Pacific Mail Steamship Company at

$308,000 per year. The first ship on this line left New York on October 6, 1848.

In providing for these lines Congress had been influenced chiefly by a desire to meet the British diplomacy in establishing the Royal Mail Line to the West Indies, the Isthmus, and Mexico. But the desire to provide ships fit for war was also in mind, and some enthusiasts supposed that the line would in some way increase American commerce with the countries of the Pacific coast, especially those at the south of the Isthmus, where an American named William Wheelwright had established a coast line with British capital. It is seen now, that neither of these lines could have made money under the contracts, and that none of the hopes of Congress would have been satisfied but for the discovery of gold in California and the consequent rush of emigrants to the gold-fields. Because of the traffic thus supplied both lines were immensely profitable. The Pacific Mail made money in spite of the fact that coal cost $30 a ton (one lot $50), and there were no shops anywhere on the coast for the repair of ships until the company established works of the kind. In fact, the enormous profits brought unsubsidized steamers into competition with both the lines. Commodore C. Vanderbilt, who had earned fame as a steamship man on the Hudson River and Long Island Sound, was one of the "interlopers," and he was paid, at one time, $56,000 a month to keep his ships out of the traffic (*Cong. Globe*, June, 1858). The Panama railroad, which was completed at midnight, January 27, 1855, was built as a connecting link between these two lines; and one gets an idea of the extent of the traffic thereafter from the fact that in the first seven years it was operated (including the traffic on the uncompleted line beginning in 1852) the earnings amounted to $5,971,728.66 (Otis, *Isthmus of Panama*).

Brief space will suffice for the stories of the unsubsidized transatlantic steamships of the period. In 1848 the owners of the Black Ball Line of sailing packets attempted to substitute steam for sail by building the steamer *United States*, a ship of 1904 tons, which they despatched to Liverpool. But because of the competition of the subsidized ships it was not possible to make her pay. The subsidized ships were able to cut rates on all kinds of traffic, of course, and this was naturally done when the new ship was seeking cargo.

This fact seems to be of much importance. It is a fact beyond dispute that subsidies to a few favored lines greatly injured all other shipping trading to the same ports—it injured British as well as American shipping. In fact, the British ship-owners, as already noted, were injured so much that they made emphatic protests to their government, but they were, in the long run, able to survive the effects of the unfair practice. In the United States the paying of subsidies to the few lines simply killed private enterprise on the North Atlantic.

In the meantime, Captain R. B. Forbes, of Boston, built the auxiliary screw steamer *Massachusetts* (1845), a ship with full sail-power and a screw that could be lifted out of water when the wind served. She made two voyages between New York and Liverpool, after which she was sold to the government for use in the war with Mexico. A number of ships have been built on this principle since then, and there are several in the lumber trade on the Pacific coast at this time (1910), but for some unexplained reason auxiliaries have never become fashionable.

In 1850 William Inman, of England, established the line for which the Philadelphia merchants had hoped in 1837, and two American steamships, the *Pioneer* and the *City of Pittsburg*, made a voyage or two each in the service, but they were then withdrawn and used in more profitable traffic on the Pacific coast.

In 1855 Commodore Vanderbilt offered to establish a Liverpool line, to run in alternate weeks with the Collins Line, if a subsidy of $15,000 a voyage were paid him and he were allowed to make no shorter passages than the Cunard Line; if Collins Line speed were demanded, he wanted $19,250 a voyage. This was when Collins was receiving $33,000. The only result of the offer was to help turn public sentiment against Collins. Vanderbilt had already constructed two large steamers (the *North Star*, called his yacht, and the *Ariel*) for use in his Isthmian competition, and when he failed to get a subsidy contract, he made a few voyages in the Bremen route and to Havre, omitting, however, all voyages in the winter months. With a view of increasing his service he built a still larger ship, called the *Vanderbilt*, and he was able to arrange with the Post-office Department for the sea and inland postage on all mail carried. During the four years (1858-1861) during which this arrangement lasted, his mail receipts amounted to $360,730.48, according to Morrison. He made some money, and it is likely that the service would have developed into a permanent line but for the Civil War.

CHAPTER XV
THE CRITICAL PERIOD

IF ships under the American flag are ever again to obtain any share of the deep-water carrying-trade of the world, it is of the utmost importance that the American people should learn first of all why American ships lost the trade they once enjoyed.

To enable us to comprehend the reasons for the decadence of our merchant marine it is necessary to have well in mind the fact that we obtained our supremacy by actual merit. It was an economic development, not the result of any kind of political or other stimulation. We did not gain or hold supremacy because we could build ships cheaper than they could be built elsewhere. Cheaper ships could be had in the north of Europe and in Canada. Moreover our most profitable ships were those that cost the most per ton. The American ships were supreme, too, rather because the wages paid were higher then in spite of that seeming handicap. In short, the whole environment of the American seafaring population had evolved a ship and crew which, taken together as a unit, were able to give more ton-miles for a dollar than any other similar unit in the world.

At first the advent of steamships changed these conditions in but one respect; it gave greater regularity of passage. The swiftest sailing ships could cross the Atlantic, now and then, in as short a time as the steamer, and they carried more cargo at the same time. But the steamer instantly commanded the cream of the traffic, and received higher rates for it, because the merchant could calculate, within a day, the time required for the passage. The time of even the swiftest of sailing ships was sometimes extended by adverse winds to fifty or sixty days.

This is to say that even the first crude steamships took the best of the trade because they were more efficient.

With the inevitable improvements in steamships came an encroachment upon the cheaper traffic that had been carried on sailing ships, and the most important of these improvements was made when the screw propeller was adopted.

Stevens had driven a small boat with screws before Fulton built the *Clermont*, but John Ericsson, a Swede, was the first to develop screw propulsion in a practical manner. His first work was done in England, where he built a screw steamer 45 feet long with which he made a speed (April, 1837) of ten miles an hour on the Thames. Then he towed the American packet ship *Toronto* at a speed of four and a half miles an hour.

On July 7, 1838, an iron vessel 70 feet long by 10 wide, and having a draft of 6 feet 9 inches, named the *Robert F. Stockton*, was launched at Laird & Co.'s yard, Birkenhead, England, for Captain Robert F. Stockton, U. S. N. It was fitted with an engine and an Ericsson screw. It was then brought to America under sail, and set to work under steam as a tug on the Delaware River, where it earned much money for many years.

In 1839 Ericsson came to the United States and built the screw steamship *Princeton* for our navy, the first warship of the kind in commission.

In the meantime Francis P. Smith, an English farmer, was developing screw propulsion, and succeeded in convincing the Admiralty that the screw was a practical device, with the result that many experiments were tried and the screw was much improved.

In introducing the screw, two difficulties were encountered. The engines of the day gave only about twenty-five revolutions to the minute, and it was therefore necessary to introduce some sort of multiple gearing between the engine-shaft and the screw shaft; for a screw should turn at seventy-five times a minute, or more. The other defect of screw propulsion was found in the strain of the shaft upon the stern of the ship. No combination of timbers in a wooden ship could resist that strain for any great length of time. To the English, however, this was a matter of no moment, for iron had already been used for building hulls. The first of these iron ships was the *Aaron Manby*, launched in London, in 1820, but the iron ship that first really influenced the British merchant marine was the *Great Britain*, built for the Great Western Steamship Company at Bristol, in 1843. She was a big ship for her day (322 feet long), and she was not only a profitable cargo carrier, but, having been stranded on the coast of Ireland, she endured the poundings of the storms of an entire winter, and was then hauled off, repaired at small expense (considering the storms she had endured), and when put at work again was found to be as serviceable as ever.

As the *Great Britain* was driven by a screw the use of iron screw ships soon became fashionable in the British merchant marine, and the more rapidly because they were much more economical in the use of coal.

Lindsay (*History of Merchant Shipping*) says that the repeal of the ancient British navigation laws helped to turn British merchants to the screw steamer. They were unable to compete with the Americans in the use of sails, and had to take up the new ship or abandon the sea. The Cunard Company would have adopted iron ships promptly but for the contract with the Admiralty. The naval officers supposed that wooden walls were better for keeping out shot than iron, and it was not until 1855, as noted, that this company was allowed to use the best material. The fact that a subsidy thus restrained enterprise seems important here.

For a number of years the iron screw steamer had small effect upon the transatlantic trade. The owners of the sailing packets were making as much money as ever—perhaps more than ever, for they were building larger ships. In 1850, however, William Inman, an Englishman who had been interested in sailing ships, put on a line of iron screw packets between Liverpool and Philadelphia, as noted, and that line sealed the doom of the sailing packet. For the Collins, the Bremen, and the Cunard lines had taken, or were to take, only the cabin passengers and the express freight from the sailing packets, while Inman was after the steerage passengers and the coarser freight. The emigrants were all travelling from Europe to America. The greater part, in bulk, of the freight carried across the Atlantic travelled from America to Europe. Inman filled his ships with emigrants bound west, and with coarse freight bound east. Having a cargo both ways is a most important feature of successful navigation. Inman made money from the first voyage, and he did so *without a penny of subsidy*. The *City of Manchester*, of his line, made a net profit of 40 per cent the first year.

For the sake of emphasis let it be said that our transatlantic sailing packets lost their trade, not because the Cunard Company received a subsidy, and not because Collins lost the subsidy he had been receiving, but because of the evolution of a cargo carrier that was far more efficient than the American ship of the sail at its best. And the Collins and Bremen lines were beaten because they, too, were much less efficient than their competitors.

The reader may now ask why the American ship-owner did not adopt the iron screw steamer. A brief review of the conditions will answer the question. He could secure all the capital he needed for the well-tried sailing ship, but no one would advance money for what seemed to be, then, an experiment with a curious device not yet well tried out. Almost incredible as the statement may seem now, the most influential American ship-owners, during the years before the Civil War, refused to have anything to do with the screw propeller. In an essay on "Screw Propulsion in the United States," read before the American Society of Naval Architects and Marine Engineers, at a meeting held in New York in November, 1909, Mr. Charles H. Cramp, vice-president of the Society, said (see *Shipping Illustrated*, November 20, 1909):—

"The supremacy of British propulsion practically began with the advent of the fine screw steamship *Great Britain* in 1844, but New York interests would not consider any other than the paddle-wheel, with its walking-beam engine; and as they knew nothing of any other type, they loudly and persistently proclaimed its superiority over all other types, and carried with them the ship-owners, shipbuilders, shipping men, mariners, and all others in general, and the screw propeller was sneered at by them."

Mr. Cramp, having been a shipbuilder in Philadelphia during the period considered, spoke from personal knowledge.

Of equal interest is the state of the iron trade in America at that time. The clippers that were the pride of the nation were bolted together with British iron. All the large castings used in the Collins steamers were imported from England. In his essay quoted above, Mr. Cramp had this to say on iron ship-building:—

"A short time after iron construction was introduced abroad, certain engine builders here commenced iron construction. The first one in America was built in Kensington at the boiler works of Jesse Starr, several squares from the water, and was hauled down there by a large number of horses and then launched.... The first iron steamers here were fearful specimens of naval architecture; the workmen were the boiler-makers of the works, and the vessels were looked on by these engine-builders as merely exaggerated boilers. At first they employed commonplace shipwrights to do certain woodwork that the vessel needed. The British soon began to build the entire ship complete by first-class ship-builders, and the finest specimens of war-ships and merchant ships were turned out by them. In this country iron ships were built with their engines by the boiler-makers and machinists with the most indifferent results."

Said John Roach, a most noted ship-builder, in testifying before the committee of Congress that investigated the state of American shipping in 1869 (H. R. Rep. 28, 41 Cong. 2 sess.):—

"The high cost of iron, produced by the tariff upon it, was one of the principal difficulties that our commerce had to contend with.... If Congress will take off all the duties from American iron, reducing it to the price of foreign iron, then we are prepared to compete with foreign ship-builders. The labor question is misstated. We are prepared to meet that difficulty, and to ask no further legislation upon the subject."

The tariff was not as high before the war as it was after, but the inability of the American ship-builder to obtain iron at home for any purpose at a living price had great influence in preventing the adoption of iron screw steamers.

Of the influence of lack of experience in building sea-going steamships, something more must be said here, and leading authorities of the period shall tell the facts:—

"Hitherto our steamboats have been built for short and comparatively unstormy voyages. The navigation of the Atlantic is quite a different affair from that of the Hudson or the Erie. Now in England they have had the practical experience of thirty-six years in building *sea-going* steamers." (*Scientific American*, October 7, 1848.)

Charles H. Cramp, another noted ship-builder, when testifying before the committee of Congress mentioned above said:—

"Great Britain now had the advantage of this country in the carrying trade of the world, not because the vessels constructed were superior to ours *in model*, but *because of the great superiority of their marine engines*. The English have built the finest and best marine engines in the world. *We have always been inferior to her in that respect.*"

Senator Rusk, of Texas, who was chairman of the Senate "Committee on the Post Office and the Post Roads," in the course of a report made to the Senate under date of June 15, 1852, described at some length the difficulties under which the Collins Line was then laboring in spite of the subsidy it was receiving. In laying special stress upon the expense of running these ships he said that it was in part due to "the well-known fact that, at the period when they were commenced, there were no machine shops in this country in which castings of the size required could be made, *nor were there on this side of the Atlantic, experienced practical engineers competent to take charge of marine engines of such immense size....* It is not to be supposed that engines of such vast dimensions could have been constructed in a country *where there were, as yet, no workshops adapted to the purpose* and where labor is very high, as cheaply as in a country where every appliance of the kind already existed and where the prices of labor are proverbially low. *Nor can it be reasonably imagined that vessels of this description could have been navigated upon as good terms by men taken from this country.*" (Sen. Rep. Com. 267, 32 Cong. 1 sess. pp. 3-4).

That the iron screw steamer was steadily driving all American ships from the sea, was plainly seen several years before the war, and sufficient warnings were printed in the periodicals of the day. Said the *Scientific American* on May 16, 1857:—

"There are no less than thirty steamships now running between New York and different ports in Europe. These are regular steamers carrying passengers and merchandise, beside which *there are a number of transient ones that carry cargo only*. But ten of them are American vessels, while the Boston, Portland, and Philadelphia lines are entirely European. *The Atlantic trade is departing from us*, and unless our shipping merchants exhibit more practical wisdom and enterprise *they will ultimately be vanished in this contest*. The whole number of steamships engaged upon the routes between Philadelphia, New York, Boston, Portland, Halifax, and Quebec, on this side of the Atlantic and the ports of Havre, Bremen, Hamburg, Southampton, London, Liverpool, and Glasgow, on the other side, is fifty-one. Of these only seventeen have paddle-wheels: all the others—thirty-four—are *screw propellers with iron hulls.* They are the most economical of steamships; their steam power is but small in proportion to their tonnage; they make very regular and quick passages, carry large cargoes, charge but little more freight than sailing vessels, and *merchants prefer them for carrying goods. These* are the steamers that are fast 'routing out' our sailing craft in the Atlantic trade."

Of the foreign ships mentioned above, only the *Cunard* received a subsidy.

That was in 1857. On March 31, 1860, the *Scientific American* again referred to the subject:—

"Three years ago we directed attention to the great increase of foreign screw steamers, and showed clearly how they were rapidly taking away the trade that had been formerly carried by American ships.... Our merchants did not heed this injunction, and, as a consequence, their rivals have grown stronger, while they have become weaker. To-day nearly all the mail and passenger, besides a great deal of the goods, traffic, is carried by foreign ships, *the great majority of which are iron screw steamers.* These facts are indisputable; how can we account for them but upon the theory that iron screw steamers are the cheapest and best for the traffic?... We exhort our shipping merchants to examine the question candidly for themselves, ... for we assure them that 'the Philistines are upon them!' We have not a single new Atlantic steamship on the stocks, from one end of the country to the other, while in Great Britain there are 16,000 tons of new iron screw steamers building for the American trade."

It was in those days that the "New York interests," as Mr. Cramp says, "carried with them the ship-owners, ship-builders, shipping men, mariners, and all others in general," while they sneered at the screw propeller.

Other quotations to show how and why the British secured supremacy are worth making. Said the *Nautical Magazine* (New York) for February, 1856, regarding two steamers that had been compared in all particulars:—

"The extraordinary fact which presses itself upon our notice from the foregoing details by trials consists in the difference in power required in the two vessels to produce nearly identical speed ... 2050 H. P., economized by the screw, propelled the *Himalaya* at about the same speed as 3016 H. P., transmitted by paddles, propelled the *Atrato.*"

The *New York Journal of Commerce* published the following warning in 1857:—

"While we are learning [to build steamships] England is using her advantages. Their merchants, captains, engineers, and sailors are carrying on our trade, and taking the bread from our mouths."

Congressman Nelson Dingley, Jr., of Maine, a prominent advocate of the subsidy system, in an article in the *North American Review*, dated April, 1884, said:—

"At the time Great Britain accepted our invitation to participate, on equal terms in the business of" transportation (it was in 1849), "experiments in iron ship building and steam propulsion were going on in that country, which, *as early as 1855, began to work a revolution in marine architecture.... This revolution* from wood to iron and sails to steam *at once* began to deprive the American merchant marine of" the advantages it had enjoyed.

The total number of British steamers receiving mail pay, or subsidy, in 1857, was 121, including the vessels plying to Ireland, the Isle of Man, the Orkneys, and other near-by points; among which was one line sending two steamers a day over its route. (See *Nautical Magazine*, September, 1857.) The total number of steamers under the British flag, in 1857, was 2132 (Rep. Com. of Nav. for 1901, p. 472). It is manifest that the mail pay aided the 121 steamers thus favored; it is equally manifest that the 2011 unsubsidized steamers were not only obliged to depend on their intrinsic merit for profit, but they were obliged to compete on unfair terms in all the trades (like that from Liverpool to New York) where the subsidized steamers were employed.

The progress made by the British iron screw steamer thereafter was pointed out by John Roach, in the course of his testimony, quoted above, when he said (p. 177) he "had found out by personal examination that there were 119 iron steamships plying between the ports of America and Great Britain. Of that number 110 were running to the port of New York."

A brief space must be given to a commonly accepted statement to the effect that the members of Congress from the South, in the decade before the Civil War, were opposed to the payment of subsidies to American steamers because of prejudice against the North. Marvin, in the *American Merchant Marine*, names Jefferson Davis and three of the men who were afterwards associated with him in his cabinet as president of the Confederacy, as leaders in this assault upon a Northern industry. The reader who is interested in making a candid study of the facts can find many speeches made by Congressmen from all parts of the country, in the *Globe* for the period in question. Part III, for 1857-1858, will be found most interesting in connection with this charge against Mr. Davis. On page 2832, third column, are the following words uttered by him (he was then a senator), on the method of paying subsidies:—

"Having established the mail line the question is, how shall the compensation be stated. In one of these amendments it seems it is to be the postal receipts. I think that altogether an objectionable method, and I shall vote against that amendment for the reason that this is to be a fluctuating amount.... The company cannot bear the fluctuation. The depression of commerce, the existence of war, or some other cause, may limit the correspondence, and cut off passenger and light freight, and then a line relying on postage receipts might not be able to run; whilst if the government allowed from year to year a fixed sum ... it might keep up the line."

Later Mr. Davis voted as he had talked. It is but fair to say that he, together with other senators and members of Congress, believed that the payment of subsidies, as a national policy, was objectionable, but so, too, did Ben Wade of Ohio, and other pronounced opponents of the "slave oligarchy." Senator Rusk, of Texas, was as firm in his support of the utterly reckless Collins Line as was Seward of New York.

The assertion, so often made at the North, that Congressmen from the Southern States, during the years immediately preceding the Civil War, were united in a conspiracy to injure Northern industries in order thereby to weaken the North and make the work of secession easier, is absolutely without foundation in fact. It is as absurd as the similar statement to the effect that the Secretary of the Navy (Toucey, a Connecticut man) had scattered the ships of the navy all over the world to weaken the fighting power of the general government. The truth is the ships were not as badly scattered in 1860 as they had been in several of the preceding years. Thus there were twelve ships upon the home station in 1860, but only five in 1851. Further than that, Toucey had for two years urged upon Congress the building of seven sloops of war of a draught of only fourteen feet, and Congress, on February 21, 1861, appropriated the money for that purpose. These shoal-draught vessels were admirably adapted for use in the waters along the Southern States, and that fact was pointed out during the discussion in the House. *Nevertheless several members from the Southern States voted for the bill.*

The subsidy policy was never treated as a sectional issue in Congress. Hamlin, of Maine, Vice-president under Lincoln, voted with the opponents of the subsidy men. (*Globe*, June 9, 1858, p. 2837.)

Hamlin's opposition is especially significant because he represented the great mass of unsubsidized ship-owners whose business was injured by the subsidized ships, and who were hot in their opposition to Collins.

Then it is to be noted that a chief argument urged by these Southern men against the payment of subsidies to the lines then in question was based on the belief that the ships were not fit for war-ships—were, in that respect, the shams they are now known to have been. In short, any candid reading of the speeches shows that in this question they were inspired by a desire to do what was best for the whole nation.

That one kind of sectional jealousy hurt the Collins line has been pointed out by Smith, in *The Ocean Carrier*—the well-founded jealousy of the ship-owners of Boston, Philadelphia, and Baltimore. The clipper ship-owners of New York also bitterly opposed the Collins Line. In fact, these unsubsidized ship-owners combined to fight the Collins lobby at Washington, and it was their influence that struck the "terrible blow" which Marvin says was inflicted by the Southern members of Congress.

The influence of the Civil War upon the merchant marine must now have consideration. First of all, the appearance of Confederate privateers upon the ocean at once doubled the rate of insurance on all American merchantmen. Then, when Commander J. D. Bullock, of the Confederate navy, was sent to England to buy iron-clad war-ships with which to raise the blockade of Confederate ports, and was induced to build swift cruisers with which to raid the North's merchant marine, a still heavier blow was struck. In all, the Confederates had 19 cruisers at sea, and they captured 257 merchantmen. The loss of these ships, however, was the smallest part of the injury suffered. The possibility of capture deprived American ships of the opportunity to obtain cargoes, and led to a cessation of building in American shipyards. It led many owners to transfer their vessels to foreign flags. It changed the currents of commerce. Naturally the British merchants took every advantage of their opportunity, as the Americans had done in the troubled days of the war with Napoleon.

One might suppose that the demand for naval ships would have given prosperity to the shipyards and engine works, but John Roach testified before the committee mentioned that "out of ten marine engine shops that were in existence in New York at the commencement of the war, his was the only one remaining in existence."

Though iron was largely used in the government ships, Nathaniel McKay, the ship-builder, told this committee that "*we have got to have some experience in building iron ships*. We have built but few iron ships, and most of them were failures."

Mere mention only of the transfer of American capital from the sea to the shore need be made here. With the depreciated currency there was plenty of opportunity for "wildcat" speculations; for government contracts, and for other kinds of investments more to the taste of honest capitalists.

The whole seafaring population spent the war period in acquiring new habits, while the British ship-builders were busy perfecting their arts, and the British merchants were establishing themselves firmly in the trades from which the war drove the Americans.

As a final reason for the decadence of the American merchant marine, note that the conditions of life in the American forecastle had greatly changed, and that this change began when the American ships were winning their laurels. With the advent of the packet system the "private venture" method of adding to a sailor's income disappeared, and with it one strong inducement to the young men who thought of going to sea. Then the old custom of making the forecastle a schoolroom, with the ship's officers serving as instructors in navigation, died out. The very prosperity of the American merchant marine served to deteriorate the quality of American seamen, for the number of ships increased much more rapidly than the seafaring population. Foreign sailors were employed for lack of enough Americans. In time even the number of experienced foreigners was insufficient. Captain J. S. Clark testified before the committee of Congress mentioned above that he had taken a ship to sea with "but two men out of a crew of sixty who could steer."

With the employment of foreigners the pleasant relations that had existed between the forecastle and cabin came to an end. The officers who had been shipmates with crews of ambitious young Americans found the foreign sailors, with their lack of ambition—with a certain slowness of movement, in fact—exasperating, especially when topsails were to be reefed after "carrying on" somewhat too long! This exasperation, with race or national prejudices to increase it, was what led to the use of the belaying pin and the pump-brake for the "encouragement" of sailors who failed to "show willing." Naturally, as time passed, the treatment of sailors grew worse, and an American statute which required the sailor to prove malice or revenge on the part of an assailing officer, when he had the officer arrested for ill treatment, did but add to the horrors of a passage on a driven ship. Dana, in his *Two Years Before the Mast*, describes mildly the treatment which common sailors received in American ships in his day. Jewell's *Among Our Sailors* describes the cruelty more in detail. It was a common thing for captains to torture men, and men were sometimes killed by the brutality which they could not escape. And while the conditions in the American forecastle were growing worse, those in the British were growing better. In 1869 Captain Cyrus F. Sargeant, the well-known ship-owner, testified that "the wages of sailors are lower in an American ship than in an English ship." It is well known that the port makes the wages for the forecastle, but it was true, then, that seamen on British liners, at least, saved more money in a year than the men on American ships.

The testimony taken before the Merchant Marine Commission, in 1904 (p. 1263), contains the following paragraph, the truthfulness of which was not disputed:—

"The condition of sea life under the American flag repels the American, boy and man. These conditions are mainly—we might say solely—due to the state of the navigation laws of the country. These laws are antiquated and disgraceful, compared to American standards: they were designed to govern slaves, and are maintained for the purpose of making slaves. No American boy with any spunk in him will submit himself to the conditions created by the maritime law, except (as frequently happens) as the alternative of a term in prison. Take any trade that now attracts the American boy and now holds the American adult, apply to those who follow it a special code of laws obnoxious to all conceptions of Americanism, repugnant to the dictates of humanity and condemned by the instincts of decency, and it may be regarded as certain that that trade would speedily be shunned by American labor. And if consulted about it the American people would be very likely to declare that if such laws are really necessary to the continuance of the trade in question, it would be a mercy to let the trade die in order to be rid of the laws.... To create a healthy popular interest in the whole subject of American shipping it is necessary to alter the laws affecting American seamen, thus, by inducing Americans to accept service at sea, creating an interest in the vital element of the subject, and also by reflex action, in the physical considerations involved."

This matter is of much importance here because, while life at sea was becoming absolutely unendurable, by a self-respecting American youth,—in an American ship, that is,—the opportunities for a career on shore were becoming more alluring. The young men who might have become leaders in our seafaring population—who might, perhaps, have found a way to maintain our supremacy at sea—were forced to suppress a natural liking for salt water; so they took the farms which the government gave away too freely; or they raised cattle on the unfenced plains; or they located mines; or they became managers and owners of factories where "protected" goods were made; or they obtained power and fortune from the railroads. While the British were strengthening their hold upon the sea, the Americans were steadily losing the sea habit.

It is manifest from any candid review of the facts that the decadence of the American merchant marine was wholly due to natural causes—to conditions of national development (the Civil War was a feature of our national development) that were unavoidable. It is unpleasant, but absolutely necessary, to face the facts. When the American merchant marine lost the command of the sea and the British gained it, the result was due to the working of the immutable law of the survival of the fittest.

CHAPTER XVI
DURING A HALF CENTURY OF DEPRESSION

IN 1866, just after the end of the Civil War, the American steam fleet registered for foreign trade, measured 198,289 tons. The steam vessels enrolled for coasting traffic measured 885,223 tons. In 1879 the steam tonnage in the foreign trade had fallen to 156,323, while the coasting tonnage had passed the million mark. In 1896 the coasting fleets measured more than 2,000,000 tons, while the foreign trade ships measured 264,289 tons. In 1908 the coasting steamers reached a tonnage of 4,055,295,—double the figures of 1896, and the registered tonnage was 598,737,—more than double that of 1896, but so far below that of the coasting tonnage as to warrant a serious inquiry into the causes which had created the contrast.

Four-master *DIRIGO*

First steel ship built in the United States

Before entering into this inquiry, however, it will be of interest to consider several features of the growth of the coasting traffic. First note that the cheap rates of transportation afforded by the ships running from such Southern ports as Savannah, Charleston, and Norfolk to Boston and New York have had a most remarkable influence upon the agriculture of the Southern coast States. Where once cotton only was raised, or cotton and tobacco, the land-owners are producing cargoes of vegetables at a season when such truck can be produced at the North only by the use of hothouses. The health of millions of people at the North, and the prosperity of other millions at the South, have been greatly promoted by the coasting steamers. At the same time the coast lines of railroads, to secure a share of the traffic which was originated by steamers, have improved their service so far that strawberries and string beans have right of way over passengers.

A natural evolution of traffic alongshore has been seen in the extension, so to speak, of the railroads across both salt and fresh water. Soon after the Boston and Providence Railroad was opened (June 15, 1835), its directors made an agreement with a line of steamers to New York under which the vessels of rival lines were excluded from the terminal facilities of the railroad, and the passengers from the rival lines had to wait hours for a train on which to continue their journey. In 1845 Daniel Drew, a director of the Providence and Stonington Railroad, became the president of the line of steamers running from Stonington to New York, and the two companies, for the purposes of traffic, were operated as one.

The railroads that terminated on the shores of Lake Erie engaged in the Lake traffic at an early date by establishing ship lines that gathered freight at all Lake ports of importance for transportation to the East, and, of course, carried the traffic from the East to the farthest points on the Lakes. These steamers had a marked influence on the development of the West. Of such lines as that which runs from Galveston and New Orleans to New York in connection with the Southern Pacific Railroad, only mention need be made, but the fact that the extension of railroads in this way across wide stretches of the waters of the country, has had a marked influence upon the prosperity of the country as well as upon that of the railroads, is memorable.

Another notable feature of the coasting trade is a revival of the old system, practised by such merchants as Derby, of Salem, when they built ships especially to carry their own goods to market. Thus, when petroleum was found in Texas, the Standard Oil Company built many vessels to carry the crude oil from the wells to the refineries at New York. The oil was taken through pipes from the wells to the ship, and it was pumped from the ship into tanks at the refineries. With the aid of such port facilities the cost of transportation was reduced to the lowest figure.

The United States Steel Corporation, owning ore beds near Lake Superior and mills near Pittsburg, built a fleet of ships to carry the ore to points on Lake Erie whence it could be shipped on a private railroad to the mills. The ore in the beds was scooped up with steam shovels and dumped into cars, by which it was transported to high trestles on the edge of the harbor. On the trestles it was dumped into pockets, from which it fell through chutes into the vessel, the hatches of which were spaced to correspond with the spaces of the chutes. A cargo of more than 10,000 tons has been loaded in two hours. At the port of discharge other scoops (a sort of dredge), made to operate through the hatches, lift the cargo out of the ship at a rate of more than a thousand tons an hour.

The great coal companies of the East deliver their coal in similar pockets on the coast, but they transport a large portion of it thence to the consumer by means of tugs and barges. In proportion to the coal carried, the tug-and-barge system costs less than cargo-carrying steamers. The tugs, with their high-priced crews, are kept moving; they tow the barges in "strings" to their destinations, dropping one here and another there, until the last is at the pier. Then they return, picking up the barges that have been unloaded, and take them to the pockets for more coal. The barges have small crews of low-priced men. The expense of waiting for the discharge of the coal is therefore less than if a steamer had carried the coal; it is even less than the expense of a schooner lying thus. The systems of handling cargoes in coarse freight trades of the American coast are, perhaps, the most perfect in the world.

Naturally, extensions of the railroad lines have been made across deep water. The Pennsylvania Railroad established the American line from Philadelphia to Liverpool in 1871. The Baltimore and Ohio established the Atlantic Transport line to Europe. The Louisville and Nashville created lines from Pensacola to several countries, including Japan and China. The Illinois Central has lines from New Orleans. The Occidental and Oriental Steamship Company was organized to carry the freight of the Pacific railroads from San Francisco to the Far East. Near the end of the nineteenth century the Southern Pacific Railroad bought an interest in the Pacific Mail. The Northern Pacific was served for years by the Boston Steamship Company, and the Great Northern Railroad built two of the largest cargo carriers in the world for an extension of service across the Pacific. Most of the ships in these extensions of railroads have been of American build.

In oversea traffic the through bills of lading and special terminal facilities gave the ships owned by railroads special advantages in the world's traffic. A great corporation is able to purchase supplies at the lowest prices. Further than that, it is not infrequently advisable to carry freight on ships at an actual loss in order to provide freight for the cars in which it can be carried with profit.

Another American adventure at sea that is of interest here was the evolution of the United Fruit Company. Individual dealers in perishable products of the tropics found it profitable to unite in gathering bananas and other fruits, and in chartering ships to bring them to the United States. As the business continued to increase, the need of swift ships, and for fittings to preserve the fruit in the best condition, led to the building of special kinds of ships (chiefly under foreign flags) and of machinery for loading and unloading the cargoes at the terminals. In the meantime, the speedy ships employed had proved attractive to passengers, and because passengers could be carried without decreasing the efficiency of the ships as fruit carriers, efforts were made to increase this branch of the traffic. In time the company built hotels for the comfort of the passengers at points in the tropics where a comfortable hotel was a surprise to the experienced traveller. Then because the well-contented fruit farmers of the tropics were unwilling to keep up with the demands of the trade in either the quantity or the quality of the fruit, the company bought land and produced the cargoes needed by their ships.

The Standard Oil Company employs nearly a hundred ships (chiefly under foreign flags), which it has built for the purpose, to transport its products to foreign countries. And there are other corporations that own ships as parts of their business equipment.

These American enterprises are of the utmost importance to the story of the American merchant marine, because they are the most modern features of our water-borne traffic. The great corporation is doing an *ever growing* share of the world's work, and the growth is an economic evolution that must be forwarded as well as controlled. In spite of the prevailing fear of great aggregations of wealth, it is worth while to inquire whether a further combination of corporate interests might not help on a revival of the American merchant marine. Suppose that a ship-building "trust" were united with the steel-making "trust" and the aggregation were to make a traffic agreement with a combination of railroads extending from the Atlantic to the Pacific, under which special low freight rates were obtainable; is it not conceivable that this powerful corporation might solve the problem of ships able to compete on deep water? Although the law now prohibits such combinations as this, may we not hope that the American people will yet learn how to preserve themselves from oppression, and the fear of it, without hampering the men who are able and eager to do the world's work on the world's terms?

In any consideration of a revival of the American merchant marine, it is necessary to view candidly the conditions which our ships must face. Emphasis is laid upon the need of candor, because in such discussions of the matter as have been had in periodicals, and before committees of Congress, the plainest facts of history have been frequently misstated, and, at times, deliberately misrepresented. If one-half the ingenuity and energy that have been used in arguing for the subsidy policy had been expended in evolving a revolution-making type of ship, we should have had, long since, a merchant marine worthy of the flag. Further than that, while an appeal to sentiment is justified, the matter ought to be viewed first as a cold matter of business.

Is the deep-water carrying trade worth the attention of American capitalists? It is a curious fact that in the hearings before the committees of Congress that have investigated the state of our shipping since the Civil War, not one word has been said about the dividends paid by the ocean carriers of the world. The reports of the committees assume that there is great profit in such shipping. One adroit advocate of the subsidy system says "the European steamship combinations ... now derive an income of about $200,000,000 a year from their control of our carrying trade" (*Atlantic Monthly*, October, 1909), leaving the reader to suppose that that great sum is divided as net profits.

As a matter of fact, the International Mercantile Marine Company, one of the larger corporations thus engaged (it is largely in the hands of American capitalists, too), has paid no dividends as yet (1909), and even its bonds sell below par. When the Cunard Company wished to build two ships to excel the swiftest of the German liners, it was unable to do so until the British government loaned it the necessary capital under conditions that amounted to a gift of the total cost of the ships. According to the *Financial Times* (London), dated Wednesday, April 14, 1909, the highest dividend paid by this most highly favored of all the British subsidized lines during the last fourteen years (1895-1908) was 8 per cent, which was distributed in 1900. The average distribution for the fourteen years has been 3.17 per cent a year. In 1895, instead of making a profit, the company lost £40,000. In 1904 there was a loss of £66,700. In 1908, while operating the two splendid and thoroughly well-advertised record breakers which it had received as a free gift from the British government (the *Mauretania* and *Lusitania*), it made the enormous loss of £249,800. A letter from the company to the writer admits that these figures are correct.

Said James A. Patton, then one of the foremost grain exporters of the United States, in a hearing before the Merchant Marine Commission of Congress in 1904 (Sen. Rep. 2755, 58 Cong. 3 sess. p. 714):—

"The ocean freight market has been so low during the past two years that at times the ship agents have offered to transport grain to Liverpool and London for nothing, to take it as ballast. Recently we have shipped corn from Boston to London at a price less than that ... less than nothing, owing to duties the port dues in London, which absorbed more than the freight rate received."

The conditions described by Mr. Patton are out of the ordinary, of course, but conditions which have kept the dividends of the well-subsidized

Cunard Company under 3 per cent have prevailed for thirteen years. The company was able to earn the 8 per cent dividend in 1900 only because the war with the Boers created an extraordinary demand for ships to be used as transports, and these having been taken from the general carrying-trade freight rates rose to an abnormal point. Leaving out the abnormal dividend of 1900, the average distribution has been but 2.8 per cent.

The ocean carrying-trade is performed by two distinct classes of services; the line traffic, like that of the Cunard Company, and the independent cargo carrier or tramp service. The tramp will go anywhere and at any time for a charter price. The income received by the tramps is as uncertain as that of a prospector in the mining region. In spite of the ease with which the demand for tonnage is telegraphed around the world the tramps accumulate on this or that coast in numbers far beyond all needs of the trade, and rates drop to a point where many of them are glad to get away in ballast. At such a time, however, a lucky (perhaps a far-seeing) owner has a ship at a port barren of tonnage, and receives for a cargo that must go quickly a price that pays half the cost of the ship. It is the lucky stroke that keeps the seafaring people hoping against hope, just as the prospector remembers how Creede, of Colorado, made a million out of the Amethyst.

Then consider the effect of the tides in the business world upon the carrying-trade. After the war with the Boers the freight rates went to pieces. Owners ceased building new tonnage. The ship-builders, to keep their forces together, offered to construct the best of modern vessels at cost of construction. Thereupon new capital came into the trade, and some men of experience also placed orders. In this way an excess of tonnage was kept afloat. Meantime much old tonnage in the progressive countries like England and Germany was placed on the market at forced sale, and these ships were bought by continental owners who patched them up ("cheap repairs for the cheap ones"), and sent them, with cheap crews, looking for cargoes. It must be kept in mind that Chinese owners, who can hire stokers at $6 a month, are competing in the world's traffic, as well as owners who have to pay $40 a month for the same kind of work. Where the Chinese owner can make money, and the owner of the best of modern freighters can live, and even make a lucky stroke, now and then, the owner of the average tramp keeps her running because the losses while she is in commission are less than when she is laid up in ordinary. The tramp traffic is precisely like mining in that the luck of the few keeps the many trying. Moreover the trend of business has been, for some time, away from tramps and into regular line ships, and that is a fact worth serious consideration.

The average profit of the lines of steamers is well set forth in the statement of the Cunard Company, unless, indeed, that statement is more favorable than the average facts warrant. The Hamburg-American Line dividends during the past fourteen years have averaged 5¾ per cent per annum, and it is likely that but one other ship-owning corporation has done as well on deep water. It is a world's traffic even for a line that plies between New York and Liverpool only. The price that a Swedish tramp will accept for wheat in the River Plate, and the rate which the Japanese will accept on the coast of China, both affect the North German Lloyd at Bremen. A few lines, especially those having special trades, make good dividends. The United Fruit Company's ships are among the exceptions because of the peculiarities of the business. But every ship-owner knows that on the average there is no great part of the world's work that pays smaller dividends than carrying cargoes across deep water.

The people of the United States, before taxing themselves to add to the congestion upon the high seas, should ask themselves whether success, when attained, will be worth the cost. Would a sensible American farmer, able to earn $3 a day grafting orchards, work overtime in order to compete with a foreign ditch digger receiving $1.50?

If we decide to make the fight for a share of the business of the sea it will then be of the utmost importance to consider the strength of the opposition to be overcome. In this inquiry no account will be taken of ships of the sail. For while schooners fit to carry from 3000 up to perhaps 10,000 tons' dead weight came into use in the coast coal trade at the end of the nineteenth century, and proved profitable, it is absurd to think of any kind of sailing ship in connection with future traffic on deep water.

According to the last Report of the Commissioner of Navigation (1908), the United Kingdom had, in 1907, 4105 steamships, measuring 9,156,356 tons, with crews aggregating 185,867 men (this "includes masters as well as Asiatics and Lascars"), in the foreign trade, besides 239 ships of 240,983 tons, manned by 5362 men, engaged partly in the home, and partly in the foreign, trade. The tonnage of 1907 was about four times as great as it was in 1880.

The German Empire had, in 1908, 2521 steamships, of 4,070,242 tons, manned by 65,568 men. This tonnage was twice as large as the tonnage of 1900.

In 1908 the Japanese had 626 steamships of 1,076,070 tons, which was twice the tonnage registered in 1900. The number of men in the fleet is not given, but it was at least 16,000.

The steamships of the world, exclusive of those of the United States, measured, in 1906, more than 30,000,000 tons. Perhaps 800,000 men were employed on these ships, and there was an experienced force of owners and managers on shore to look after the interests of the fleet.

The quality of this vast sea power must now be considered. In this point of view it is a most discouraging fact that about all important improvements of recent years in the steam engine have been made by Europeans. Between 1855 and 1865 steam pressures in boilers ranged from 20 to 35 pounds per square inch, and the consumption of fuel was about 3 pounds per horsepower-hour. Compound engines came into general use between 1865 and 1875, when boiler pressures rose to 125 pounds, and the consumption of fuel decreased to 2.2 pounds and even less. Between 1885 and 1895 twin screws and quadruple expansion engines were adopted for the swiftest ships, and the improved engines were used on many cargo carriers. Boiler pressures reached 225 pounds and upward, and the coal consumption dropped as low as 1.4 pounds. Then came the far-reaching change to the steam turbine, on ships of 14 knots and upward. For slower ships the turbine in combination with reciprocating engines has been found more efficient than the old-style engines, while a combination of the turbine with the dynamo for still slower ships is now in hand and sure to make headway. In all these matters Europe has taken the lead.

In the turbine, with its combinations, it is believed that the steam-engine reaches its highest possible efficiency, just as sails reached their highest efficiency as used on the American clipper. But a new machine, still more economical, has been invented—the gas motor. Coal is used for the generation of gas, which drives internal-combustion motors, much like those seen on automobiles. The consumption of fuel is thereby reduced far below that of steam engines.

While the marine steam-engine has been perfected in Europe, it is worth noting by the way that the producer-gas engine, though yet in the experimental stage for ship use, has been brought to a higher state of perfection for land use in America than in Europe. Magazine articles by marine engineers have been published, urging American ship-owners to adopt this new method of propulsion, because it is to make a revolution almost as far-reaching as the iron screw steamer made in 1855. But the American ship-owner refuses to see his opportunity. Having certain profits with old-style engines in the coasting trade, he is willing to let foreigners do the experimenting.

All of this is to say that the ship-owners of foreign countries are at least as far-sighted and enterprising as those of the United States.

Some of the facts in the story of our coasting steamer trade are of interest in this point of view. The most interesting division of this fleet is found upon the Great Lakes. The screw propeller and the compound engine were successfully introduced on the Great Lakes before 1850—several years before the iron screw steamer of the British began its deadly inroads upon our salt-water trade—but the Atlantic coast remained indifferent.

After the Civil War tugs came into use for towing the sailing vessels through the Detroit and Huron rivers, and from these the use of barges in "strings" behind steamers that carried cargoes as well as served as tugs, was developed. This system ruled upon the lakes until the evolution of the iron ore trade led to the building of ships so large that they were unable to handle barges. In 1902 the ship able to carry 10,000 tons arrived.

Still larger ships have been built since 1902. A ship that can carry 12,000 tons' dead weight needs but thirty-five men, all told. The average cost of carrying freight on the best ships of the lakes is less than .8 of a mill per ton-mile. Through natural development this splendid efficiency has been attained, and the fleet in 1908 numbered 1942 ships measuring 2,341,686 tons.

SEVEN-MASTED SCHOONER *THOMAS LAWSON*

A feature of these ships to be considered is that they are all built for passing through certain shoal channels, the Welland Canal, and the canal at the rapids at the outlet of Lake Superior, for example. These channels have compelled the designers to adopt one cross-section of hull for all ships (at least below the water-line), and that cross-section is the largest that will pass through the channels. Because of this similarity of models the lake builders have been able to carry specialization in the work of construction as far as any builders in the world, and much further than it is carried in the Atlantic coast yards, where builders may have a battleship, a harbor tug, and a side-wheel passenger boat on adjoining ways. The lake ships can be built for the lowest price of any in the United States.

Contemplation of these facts, and upon the further fact that lake engineers seemed to be about the best the world had ever seen, led the lake capitalists to organize the American Navigation Company, which built two large cargo carriers, sent them down to salt water, and entered the general cargo trade. Those vessels were among the most economical ever built in the United States, all things considered, *but they were unable to compete with the European ship.*

A story told by A. B. Wolvin to the Merchant Marine Commission is significant here. A company of which he was president operated a line of steamers from Duluth and Chicago to Montreal and Quebec. The steamers numbered ten of the maximum size for passage through the Welland Canal—250 by 42 feet large, with a draft of fourteen feet, and a carrying capacity of 2200 tons. The cost of these ships, built under the best American conditions of specialization, was $140,000 each, and the operating expense was $135 a day each. While the company was engaged in its work, a steamship man from Sweden came and offered to put on twelve ships of the same size, each at a charter price of $2900 per month. His ships cost but $90,000 each, and the wages of crew and other operating expenses were so much lower than the American standard that he could make money at a charter price of $1000 a month less than the cost of operating the American ships. Having used these Swedish ships long enough to know them (for it was necessary to accept the offer to keep the Swede from starting in opposition), Captain Wolvin testified:—

"They are better from the standpoint of construction.... The vessels carry well; they run well. We have no trouble with the crews."

The crew of the Swedish ship numbered seventeen; that of the American, twenty-two. And the Swedish wage was far less.

The bearing of these facts in any consideration of the power of the ship-owners who are now in control of the deep water traffic of the world is obvious.

Other views of the world's carrying trade are of interest here. The Hamburg-American Company runs steamships in sixty-eight different lines. There is a line of its ships from Europe to each port of importance from Montreal to Newport News. It maintains other lines to the important ports of the West Indies, to Ports Limon and Colon on the narrow mainland, and to every important port on the north, the east, and the west coasts of South America. It reaches nearly every port of importance on the coasts of Europe, and down the west coast of Africa. Indeed, on the west coast of Africa the natives see two German steamers to one under the British flag. It sends other ships through the Suez Canal to skirt the coast of Asia as far as Vladivostok; it maintains cargo gatherers among the islands along shore, and then, from Japan, it reaches across to Portland, Oregon, where it connects with our Northern Pacific Railroad. It runs every kind of ship from the 23-knot passenger packet to the economical cargo carrier that uses perhaps little more than ten tons of coal a day. The traffic of the world is, in a way, within the touch of this one corporation. The worldwide tides of commerce are felt and noted daily in the home office, and while losses are suffered, here and there, through depressions in business, *or through competition*, the profit made by the vast fleet as a whole is sufficient to yield regularly the modest dividends that satisfy the owners.

The fact that the powerful North German Lloyd is allied with the Hamburg-American in all matters that affect German commerce and trade is also a matter of interest in this place.

To show now how an effort to force a new company into an established trade affects freight rates, it is necessary only to refer to such an instance as the "war" that prevailed in the trade from New York to South Africa in 1902. As Smith notes in *The Ocean Carrier*, the rival steamships lost from $10,000 to $15,000 on every trip. Moreover, the low rates were of no advantage to commerce, for commerce demands stability first of all. It is worth noting, too, by the way, that in the course of this war, goods were carried by English steamers from New York to Africa for less than was charged by the same companies on ships from London to the same destination.

When American capitalists tried to establish a line of ships from New York to Brazil some years ago, the venture failed. One reason for this was the higher cost of American ships and crews. Another was extravagance, especially in providing terminal facilities at Rio de Janeiro. Old merchants in Brazil still smile when they talk of what the American line did in that way. But the most important reason for failure was the advantage enjoyed by British rivals in the triangular line route followed by their steamers. In the currents of commerce on the Atlantic the British manufacturer ships large quantities of goods to South America, the South American producer ships large quantities of coffee to the United States, and the American producer ships large quantities of food-stuffs to Great Britain. The British ships had profitable cargoes from home to Brazil. At Rio de Janeiro and Santos they cut the rates far below cost, and then on arrival in the United States they secured cargoes for home at a profitable rate. The profits on the two trips enabled them to endure the cut on the middle passage. But because American manufacturers had little to ship to Brazil the American ship lost money on both passages.

Every business man understands the advantages of one who is well-established in any trade, over one who is just beginning, but one method by which established lines of ships hold their trade must have mention. The merchant who sends all his goods by the established line receives a rebate of 10 per cent on the amount of his freight bill, the rebate being calculated once in six months, say, and the payment being made six months later. If the merchant ships an ounce of stuff by a rival line he loses all the rebate, and he may be punished in addition, if the rival is a new line. The merchant, having rivals in trade, feels the loss of the rebate seriously; his rivals by loyalty to the established line continue to enjoy the rebate even when rates are cut below those of the new line, and below cost. In such trades as that between New York and Rio de Janeiro, where a number of lines are plying, the established lines unite their entire resources to kill off a new line trying to enter the trade.

When the American people have before them any proposition for the revival of the American merchant marine, they should keep in mind that ships designed for the purpose and at least in sufficient numbers, are afloat in every trade of the world; that the freight rates are maintained at a point where the profits are as low as any afforded by any branch of the world's work; that the men doing the work have been developed with the steam carrying trade, just as the splendid American sailor of the sail was developed by his environment, and they are therefore at once well-informed, alert, enterprising, resourceful, persistent, and merciless. Observe, too, that in the work of the high seas man faces primeval conditions, brute force prevails as nowhere else, and the fittest survives.

Perhaps a definition of terms is needed here. By fitness we mean the ability to do the world's work on the terms which the world offers. We have learned to build bridges and locomotives on those terms, but, in spite of the fact that our ship-builders and ship-owners are fully protected in the "home market," they have not yet learned how to combine the locomotive and the bridge into a ship fit to compete with the unsubsidized ships—the cargo carriers—now in the world's traffic.

In connection with the known degree of efficiency of the world's merchant marine, as now afloat, consider a statement that can be found on page 1248 of the *Report of the Merchant Marine Commission*. It is, perhaps, the most discouraging statement that has been made in connection with our merchant marine.

"The statistics of loss of ships at sea afford matter for reflection.... They show, as the United States Commissioner of Navigation has summarized them, that out of every 100 American seagoing steamships over 100 tons, for the past seven years, on the average 2.24 have been lost each year; that out of every 100 foreign seagoing steamers over 100 tons, for the same period on the average 1.98 have been lost each year." (See also An. Rep. Com. Nav., 1904, p. 19.)

A MODERN CLIPPER SHIP AND A MODERN BRIG

By courtesy of *Munsey's Magazine*

When American ships were supreme they were insured at a less rate than those of any other nation, and the insurance was placed, to a large extent, in England. Because the American sailor of the sail, who had been evolved by 200 years of American environment, was able to handle his ship better than any other, he paid lower premiums to the underwriters. But if this be true (and no one disputes it), it follows that the higher percentage of losses among modern American steamers proves that the American environment, since the steamer era, has produced a steamship sailor who is less efficient in his work than our old-time sailor of the sail was in his, and less efficient, too, than the foreign steamship sailor of the present day. It is an important fact that a man may win laurels upon the weather yard-arm in reefing topsails and yet be of no particular value as an oiler or an assistant engineer in the engine-room. At any rate, any effort to revive the American merchant marine will have to be made in the face of the record of American losses, and the influence of that record upon insurance rates.

Then in spite of the "boundless resources of our country," and "the intelligence of the masses," and a "protective tariff" of twenty-five cents a bushel, the farmers of "the overcrowded nations of Europe" are able to sell potatoes in New York at a profit. And millions of dollars' worth of factory goods made in Europe pay ocean freights, pay the tariff tax, pay the commissions of agents, pay the freight rates on our railroads, pay the margin of our retail merchants, and are then sold at our doors in competition with the products of our workmen.

The fact that the tariff wall fails to keep out foreign goods is a matter for serious attention in every point of view, but it seems especially necessary here to consider the influence of "protection," as it is called, upon those features of American character which we call self-reliance and the spirit of enterprise. Under the prevailing system how is it possible for the American people to develop the aggressive manhood that is needed?

One other feature of the opposition that will be encountered in any effort to create a new American merchant marine is yet to be described—the support which the existing carriers will receive from their governments during the conflict; but before that is considered it may be well to review the means by which it has been proposed to increase our shipping.

Naturally a people accustomed to "protection"—a people who make boast of a system that is at best a confession of a lack of ability to meet open competition—have turned, first of all, to "government aid."

Among the first provisions of Congress for the benefit of American shipping after the adoption of the Constitution was a 10 per cent discriminating duty on all goods imported in foreign ships. It is asserted that this discriminating duty supplied our ships with cargoes from foreign ports to American, and was thus a feasible and satisfactory "protection." A 10 per cent duty amounted then, and it would amount now, to more than the whole freight, upon some goods. It is also asserted that this discrimination was made in order to "protect" our shipping. But in an extended argument, which was made before the Merchant Marine Commission (in the *Report* of which the curious reader can find it), by Hon. E. T. Chamberlain, Commissioner of Navigation, it was proved that "in the minds of those that applied" it (Jefferson, Clay, Gallatin, John Quincy Adams, etc.), the law was provided as a means of retaliation only—for the purpose of preventing discrimination against American shipping. The fact that our government anxiously strove from the first to secure fair reciprocity confirms this view. Further confirmation is found in the fact that our old-time ship-owners were unanimous in their support of the government in its efforts to secure reciprocity.

Those who advocate the policy of discrimination for modern application assert that our shipping reached supremacy at sea while the discriminating policy prevailed as to Great Britain, and that is true, because the British did not accept our offers of reciprocity until 1849. But the assertion that our shipping became supreme *because* of this policy is made only by those who are unable to appreciate in full the facts of the case. For our ships that were engaged in the trades between foreign countries, beyond the reach of any "protection" afforded by "discrimination" or any other artificial stimulation, at one time measured a million tons. Why were those ships favored beyond all others by the merchants who loaded them? Why did merchants of rival nations—why did the British merchants, for instance—charter these "Yankee" ships, if it were not because they were the most efficient in the world?

It is a slander upon the American sailor of the sail to say that he won the long pennant through coddling.

As a system for modern adoption "discrimination" is objectionable for three reasons. One is that it provides at best for keeping our ships in trades between home and foreign ports only; it does not provide for trade between foreign ports. Next it is a system for supporting ships that are confessedly inferior to those already in the trades—it places a premium upon inefficiency. Last of all it is a system that must excite all foreign governments to retaliation; and that those governments will be eager to retaliate, and that they will find ways enough for doing so, is beyond doubt. In connection with this statement it is necessary to keep in mind that we shall soon cease to export wheat in any form, and the growth of population is so great that we shall soon cease to export other, perhaps all other, food products. Before inviting retaliation we must look ahead.

Indirect discrimination has been proposed. Under this the ships of any country were to be permitted to bring in without discrimination goods produced under their flag; but goods brought from any other country were to be subjected to a discriminating tax. Any analysis of our imports, however, shows that if British goods were taxed when brought here in any but British ships, all such goods would be forced into British ships at once, to the great advantage of the British shipping. They could not at present, nor for years to come, be forced into American cargo carriers. As the system would in like manner help German shipping, the policy would but make our task the harder.

Before considering the policy of paying direct subsidies a glance at the oft-repeated assertion that our shipping is "our one unprotected industry" seems necessary. What does "protection" provide for any industry, or what does it pretend to provide? Simply the home market—this and nothing more, at best. This is done by laying a tariff upon imports. But the American shipping is now and always has been protected that far—absolutely protected, in fact, by prohibition. The importation of ships has been forbidden, and the use of foreign ships in the "home market" has been reserved to home-built ships for nearly 100 years. If "protection" could enable any industry to expand from the "home market" to the foreign, then the coasting trade industry should have expanded long since over all the world. Unhappily, however, the profit found in well-protected industries does but tend to make the beneficiaries contented, and willing to let well enough alone.

Ever since the Civil War efforts have been made to induce Congress to modify the navigation laws far enough to enable Americans to buy ships in the cheapest market and sail them under the flag. It is said that this would give our shipyards so much employment in repairing the foreign fleet so to be purchased that our builders would soon learn how to set afloat ships as cheap as any in the world. It is not easy to treat seriously one who supposes that repairing tramps would develop the distinctive type of ship able to produce results in ton-miles, which is imperatively needed; but when it is remembered that free trade in ships quickly drove the British from the sailing ship to the screw steamer, the proposition looks attractive. For free trade—the necessity of swimming unaided in rough water or drowning—might compel the American builder to produce the revolution-making ship for which we are to hope.

We now come to the policy of paying direct bounties as a means of creating a merchant marine; and nowhere are candor and accuracy of statement more important.

Bounties were paid in the colonial days. Virginia gave a subsidy of tobacco to induce her people to build ships, and they built one ship. When the whale fishery was depressed, just after the Revolution, Massachusetts gave a bounty on Massachusetts oil, with the result that the market was flooded, and the fishery was depressed more than ever. In spite of a bounty paid on oil by Rhode Island, her sailors continued to favor the slave-trade. For some reason those who favor subsidies as a means of reviving our shipping never quote these facts.

Of the effect of subsidies upon the Collins Line and of other subsidies, something has already been said. The first grant to the Cunard Company was made for military and diplomatic purposes only, but when subsidized American ships appeared, the Cunard grant was increased to maintain the British flag in the trade. That is a fact beyond dispute.

It is manifest that the subsidy was of benefit to the receiver. It helped the company to build improved ships. It gave the builders some experience. It provided schools for the instruction of seamen in the art of handling steamships. The subsidizing of the Royal Mail, and of the lines to other parts of the world, where private enterprise was unequal to the occasion, created an increase of commerce as well as some addition to the shipping of the country.

With equal candor the evils of the system apparent in those days ought to be told. The subsidized Cunarders not only drove off the American subsidized lines but they drove away the unsubsidized Great Western line. *They depressed all British shipping that entered the trade to New York and Boston.* If they had had a larger subsidy they would have spread to Philadelphia, and thus would have prevented or delayed the establishment of the Inman Line. The British shipping in the trade to the northern ports of America was not increased by the subsidy to the Cunard Company; it was, on the contrary, restricted. Paying a subsidy to establish a line where no steamers had traded before, and none could trade without government aid, was a very different thing from forcing a new line of steamers into trade already supplied with shipping, and even congested. Paying a fair price per pound to a ship for carrying the mail ought not to be confused with paying a subsidy. The first Cunard mail pay was not a subsidy; it was a low price for the work done. Senator Rusk declared, in the document already quoted, that the British Post Office Department "derived a *clear* income of no less than $5,280,800" from the contract in the first six years it was in force. After Collins began running his ships by aid of a subsidy the British subsidized Cunard to enable him to compete.

When the Collins Line reduced freights from £7 10*s* to £4, *commerce* was certainly benefited, but the reduction was ruinous to *shipping*. It was especially injurious to the American packet lines. The advent of the subsidized Collins Line did more to injure the American *shipping* of its day than any other influence except that of the iron screw steamer.

Then the effect of admiralty supervision upon the subsidized ships was an incubus upon progress. Naval men are usually conservative, and conservatism often means stupidity. Thus, after the British *Dreadnought* had demonstrated the efficiency of the turbine engine our American naval engineers provided one battleship with turbines and another of the same model with reciprocating engines in order to learn whether the turbine was worth installing in future ships! The Cunard ships were built of wood, long after iron was known to be a better material, because of naval stupidity. Worse yet, when the requirements of the merchant service became imperative the rules of the admiralty were evaded—ships were reported to be fit for war cruisers when in fact they were useful as transports only.

After the Civil War, Congress provided subsidies by which a line from New York to Rio Janeiro, another from San Francisco to China and Japan, and a third from San Francisco to Hawaii, were established. Under these contracts the policy did not have quite a fair trial. The beneficiaries by activity in politics created so much opposition that the subsidies were withdrawn before the effect was fully apparent.

By the Act of March 3, 1891, a subsidy was again provided under the thin disguise of paying for carrying the mail—a reprehensible plan, because if subsidies are justified, they ought to be paid openly. The fact is that the methods of indirection employed by the advocates of subsidy have done much to discredit their system. Under this act ships of 8000 tons and a speed of 20 knots receive $4 a mile "by the shortest practicable route for each outward voyage." Ships of 5000 tons and a speed of 16 knots receive $2 a mile. Ships of 2500 tons and a speed of 14 knots receive $1 a mile, while those of 1500 tons and a speed of 12 knots receive "two-thirds of a dollar a mile." This act was designed to maintain lines of ships which would be useful as scouts, transports, etc., in time of war.

Before stating the effect of this law upon American shipping, certain facts in connection with the subsidizing of ships by the continental nations of Europe will be useful. It is a curious fact that while the annual reports of our Commissioner of Navigation have for years given much space to the "progress" of the British, the German, and the Japanese shipping, nothing has been said about the "progress" of the shipping of France, of Italy, or Austria. The progress of the shipping of England, Germany, and Japan is stated because government aid is given to shipping in those countries and shipping makes progress; but in the other countries, where still more liberal aid is given to shipping, no progress worth mention is made. The annual report of the Commissioner of Navigation is made a vehicle for the dissemination of arguments in favor of the subsidy policy.

A candid examination of the policy of Germany shows that some aid has been given to lines of ships in the form of liberal pay for carrying mails. The North German Lloyd receives $1,330,420 per annum for its service to China, Japan, Australia, and the German possessions in the Pacific. The Germans thought it better policy to subsidize a line of merchantmen than to maintain a line of transports to its colonies as the United States has been doing in connection with the Philippines. The payment to the North German Lloyd is properly called a subsidy; to give the name of subsidy to all payments made to German steamers for carrying the mail is to misrepresent the facts in a way that injures the cause of the subsidy advocates materially in the eyes of all who know the facts.

The German railroads, which are owned by the government, not only give low rates on goods intended for export, but extremely low rates are provided for all materials used in building ships. The fact that special rates on railroads are used to promote the German merchant marine is worth serious consideration in the United States, even though such rates are here viewed with suspicion. The national laws governing our railroads, as enforced now (1910), are in some respects an incubus upon legitimate and praiseworthy enterprise. Through ignorance and prejudice the efforts of our transportation lines to increase our export trade have been seriously hampered.

Unquestionably subsidies and special rates were provided to extend German influence by means of shipping. The payment of bounties has been one feature of the expansion of German shipping. To assert that the bounty has been the sole, or even the chief, cause of that expansion, however, is to misstate the facts. The experience of France, for instance, shows conclusively that a subsidy in itself is not enough to create a merchant marine. Although the French subsidy is so liberal that French cargo carriers are able to sail half-way around the world in ballast to get a cargo at rates that would be less than cost of maintenance for any other ship, the French merchant marine grows so slowly as to justify the assertion, made by the late Captain John Codman, that the French mariners are working against a fiat of nature. The tonnage of 1881, 914,000, was but 1,952,000 in 1908.

Further than that the German subsidies have been less than those paid by the British (especially those paid to the Cunard Company), and yet German steamers are steadily encroaching upon those of the British. The reason for the progress of German shipping is readily found in the spirit and habits of the people. Consider the work of the patient, spectacled scientist in his laboratory—his methods and his aims; consider the growth of the factory system; consider the effect of the training which all men receive in the army or navy—how the whole people learn to move as one man, and as comrades, for the attainment of a worthy national object; consider how all the people—the men with the hoe as well as the men behind the guns—are stirred by an attack, or a seeming attack, upon the Fatherland.

The effect of government bounties upon German shipping is like that seen when the spectacled German professor of agriculture applies inorganic fertilizers to crops planted in well-cultivated, humus-filled soils. The effect in France, and other nations not well prepared for expansion, is like that when those fertilizers are applied to arid, acid, uncultivated land. In Germany the soil for the production of shipping was in excellent condition before the fertilizer was applied. What is the condition of that soil in the United States?

The American subsidy law has been in operation since 1891. For the service rendered it provides more liberal compensation than that given to any German ship. The American Line (now operated as a part of the fleet of the International Mercantile Marine Company), owns two American ships that were built for the line and two British ships that were placed under the American flag by special act of Congress. The subsidy maintains this line in existence but does not increase it. The Mallory line has been extended somewhat since the subsidy was given to it. Elsewhere ships that were maintained under the subsidy have been driven from their route by foreign competition. The ships run in connection with the Great Northern Railroad, for instance, were unable to compete with the Japanese line between the same ports, partly because the Japanese subsidy was more liberal, and partly because of the greater expense of running American ships. In short, the law of 1891 has failed to provide an American merchant marine.

Further measures for providing subsidies have therefore been proposed. The Merchant Marine Commission, after a lengthened inquiry, offered a bill to Congress which was to provide a line from "a port of the Atlantic coast of the United States to Brazil," with "ships of not less than fourteen knots speed," at a subsidy rate of $150,000 a year, "for a monthly service," or $300,000 for a fortnightly service. A similar line to the River Plate was to receive $187,500 and $350,000 according to the service. The same subsidy was to be paid to a 12-knot line to South Africa. Three lines from Gulf ports to Cuba, Brazil, and Mexico were to be paid sums in proportion to the service rendered, and three lines were to be provided for the Pacific on similar terms.

In addition to providing these lines an attempt was to be made to set afloat cargo carriers by giving an annual bounty of $5 a ton gross measurement to all cargo ships continuously in service. On the whole ten new lines of ships were to be established at an expense of $2,590,000, and it was supposed that $10,000,000 might be the necessary limit of the subsidy for the tramps. In the meantime it was supposed that the existing lines working under the law of 1891 would continue in the service for the compensation provided.

Passing over the claptrap in the bill about the use of these liners as scouts,—fancy a 16-knot merchantman scouting around a squadron of Dreadnoughts!—the bill ought to be considered on its merits because it sets forth the amount of subsidy supposed to be sufficient to create a real revival of our shipping, and thus gives an idea, perhaps, of what sum would be adequate.

Accepting the Commission's statement that the subsidies would prove sufficient to place the more expensive American ships upon an equality with the foreign, and "a little more," as was said, it may be assumed that the new lines would eventually employ sixty or seventy ships. At $5 a ton the $10,000,000 might put afloat from 300 to 400 modern cargo carriers. Thus we should, at best, about double our present registered fleet, which, in 1908, numbered 478 ships. But if we compare that fleet with the German, which now numbers more than 2500 ships, or with the British, which now numbers more than 4000, we shall see that even under the best circumstances we should yet be a far cry from the supremacy of which we made boast in other days. Indeed, the fleet of liners would not number as many ships as the Standard Oil Company now employs to carry abroad its products, while the fleet of cargo carriers could not be compared, with any satisfaction, to the fleet now in use by the allied German companies of which mention has been made.

And the ships thus to be set afloat, as they crossed the seas, would proclaim to the world that they were in the carrying trade, not by right of efficiency, but by grace of a subsidy.

But now we are to consider whether any subsidy heretofore proposed would really be sufficient to sustain either liner or tramp. The effect of such ships upon freight rates, for instance, was stated before the Merchant Marine Commission, by B. N. Baker, formerly president of the Atlantic Transport Company, and an advocate of the subsidy system. He said:—

"If you added any more to the open sea traffic (the foreign traffic) of the United States than 100,000 tons a year you would so demoralize the general carrying business in rates, both as to freight and passengers, it would be so unprofitable that no one could go into it, *unless you would double, and triple that compensation.*"

The effect of that building programme upon the organized mechanics of our shipyards—the strikes for higher wages, and the consequent increase of prices—need only be mentioned.

Then figure up the expense of the war between the lines from New York to South Africa in 1902, wherein ships lost $15,000 in a single voyage. Manifestly the American liners would need all of their subsidy ($15,625, per voyage) to meet the reductions in freight rates which the opposition would make. They would thus be no better off than they would be if they were permitted to enter the trade on even terms with the present lines—without war and without subsidy. The line to Brazil would yet have to face the disadvantages due to the triangular service which British ships maintain, though the decreasing exports of American food products would reduce those disadvantages somewhat.

In short, one may well doubt whether the proposed subsidy would enable our ships to overcome the opposition of the powerful foreign interests that are already in the trade. But if we suppose it to suffice that far, we have yet to inquire what the governments behind those powerful corporations would do. Recall the story of the Cunarders *Mauretania* and *Lusitania*. The British government gave those two ships to the company outright on the understanding that it should operate and maintain them in a condition fit to cross the Atlantic at a speed of 25 knots an hour. This was done at the time that American capitalists acquired control of a number of British lines, under the name of the International Mercantile Marine Company, and formed a working agreement with the two leading German companies. This combination threatened British supremacy on the North Atlantic, or was believed to threaten it, and the whole British nation rose up to defend, figuratively speaking. If that were possible under those circumstances, it is certain that the "subventions" now given to the British lines would be increased the moment any American subsidized ships began to cut into the British carrying trade. Increased subsidies would then be needed by the American ships. If the American people were to enter into a subsidy war it is likely that they could endure the strain longer than any other nation; but is such a war worth while to secure a part in a traffic that pays the well-subsidized Cunard line no higher profit than 2.8 per cent a year?

CUNARD S. S. *LUSITANIA*

By courtesy of the Cunard Steamship Company

One more argument in favor of subsidy is yet to be considered. With the Panama Canal and the Monroe Doctrine to defend, it is necessary to provide sufficient transports and colliers for the exigencies of war. The spectacle of our splendid war fleet steaming around the world with its fuel carried in ships under foreign flags, was humiliating to the nation. Congress should build auxiliaries more rapidly by direct appropriation, or it should give ample subsidies, however great the sums needed, to maintain auxiliary ships in the merchant service. Many Americans would gladly pay their share of the tax for the pleasure of seeing the American flag above a ship's taffrail, now and then on salt water, in spite of the humiliation of the fact that it was the tax and not efficiency that kept the flag in place. A merchant fleet so provided would be a kind of insurance against the exigencies of war, and even against war itself. With a thousand American merchant ships afloat on deep water there would be less danger of an aggressive nation of Europe invading Rio Grande do Sul or menacing the Panama Canal.

Whether to provide the auxiliaries by direct appropriation or by subsidy is, or should be, a question of relative expense and efficiency. Such a question, one would think, might be solved by the rules of arithmetic; at any rate it is not necessary in the discussion to misrepresent the attitude of senators from Southern States, nor to say that the former American supremacy was due to "protection" instead of the ability of the sailor of the sail.

There are excellent and perhaps imperative diplomatic and military reasons for maintaining at least one line of swift steamers from the Pacific coast to the coast of Asia and the Philippine Islands. The ships of this line, if established, should be fitted, as battleships are, for a cruising speed of say sixteen knots, with a reserve of power for an emergency, when they should be able to develop real scout speed—should be able to run away from the modern twenty-one knot battleships. The value of a fleet of ships of this kind, in a military point of view, and especially upon the Pacific, is obvious. A dozen ships of the kind would not be too many. A fleet of smaller ships, fit for use as naval colliers, might well be maintained to gather and distribute cargo along the Asiatic coast and among the islands. We have undertaken the work of developing civilization in the Far East, and we need to do everything possible to prevent an attack upon our position there. After squadrons of war-ships nothing will create a higher respect for our flag among the people of that region than a fleet of superior merchantmen *avowedly maintained for diplomatic and military reasons*. In fact a fleet so maintained would impress other peoples than those of the Far East.

The same argument may be made for the maintenance of swift lines to both coasts of South America, where we have the Monroe Doctrine and the Panama Canal to defend. If we establish these lines, a war of subsidies is to be expected, and the well-established and powerful companies already in the trades will be wholly unscrupulous in their opposition, not because their present profits are high, but because they are low; a division of the traffic will still further reduce the profits which are already too narrow for comfort. We may be sure, too, that extravagance and inefficiency of the Collins kind will be found in the management of some of our companies;

but as a diplomatic and military measure the experiment seems to be worth making. We have a very good precedent in the action of Germany in establishing a line to its Pacific possessions by a subsidy of a million a year, which is given for the precise reasons urged herein. It will cost the United States many times as much as it does Germany, but one who looks at the matter broadly may well suppose that such an increase of expenses, avowedly made as a measure for increased military efficiency, might be worth while, in the end, as a peace measure. For we shall be obliged in any event, to go on increasing our naval budget to keep even with the growth of European navies, until the war burden becomes intolerable in Europe as well as in the United States; and then we shall have measures for preserving peace more rational than those now in vogue. The sooner the burden is made intolerable the better.

But while we can provide an ample fleet of naval auxiliaries by means of subsidies, if we are willing to pay the price, let no one suppose that such a measure will give the country any share of the world's traffic worth consideration, not to more than mention supremacy upon deep water.

One method by which the Merchant Marine Commission thought to increase American sea power is memorable. A heavy tonnage tax was to be laid upon all ships coming from foreign countries to American ports, and the money so raised was to be paid to American ships in the foreign trade in return for carrying a certain proportion of American citizens enrolled as members of a corps of naval volunteers. The measure looked toward an increase in the number of American seamen, but it did not become a law.

The communities that have supported nautical schools (New York and Boston, for example) have had the end in view for which the measure of the commission was designed. Graduates of these schools are among the best officers in our merchant marine, and this, too, in spite of the fact that antiquated ships of the sail formerly served as school rooms, and the boys were taught to handle the obsolete marline-spike instead of the throttle. But, at best, these efforts to turn ambitious young Americans from the opportunities they find on land are inadequate. Congress might have turned the naval academy into a splendid nautical university for the education of all Americans who wish to learn the ways of the sea. We appropriate millions a year for the farmers, not as bounties on their products, but to teach them, *through experiment stations*, how to do their work. No one seems to have thought it worth while, however, to make a national appropriation for the education of merchant seamen.

To confess the truth we have done nothing adequate to the situation since the Civil War, nor has anything adequate been attempted; but the people who have promoted the work of our nautical schools have seen dimly what the whole story of the American merchant marine proclaims. The pretty pinnace *Virginia* thirty feet long, as she crossed and recrossed the Atlantic; the *Trial* in the Azores and the West Indies; the *Mount Vernon* as she dodged pirates, privateers, and war fleets in her seventeen-day passage from Salem to Gibraltar; the *Empress of China* in her venture to the Far East; the sealers among the icy rocks of the Antarctic; the whalers beyond Bering's Straits; the packets of the sail as they crossed from New York to Liverpool; and the clippers that flaunted the Stars and Stripes off the weather beam of every ship they met on the Seven Seas,—in short, the whole story of the American merchant marine has been worth consideration here because it sets forth unmistakably that the superior intrinsic efficiency of the American sailor of the sail, during the contest that culminated with the perfection of the ship of the sail, gave supremacy to the American flag. We can buy ships—whole fleets of them—if we are willing to pay the price, and we can maintain them upon the high seas in like manner; but we shall never again see the Stars and Stripes triumphant upon the high seas until the American environment evolves, once more, by natural process, the nautical unit as efficient for the modern day as was our ship of the sail in the days long past.

Footnotes

[1] This board was created by an Order in Council dated July 4 (nowhere mentioned as "a beautiful coincidence"), 1660, "to receive, hear, examine and deliberate" upon all matters concerning the colonies, and report the facts and their conclusions to the king.

[2] *The Story of New England Whalers* gives a satisfactory history of the American whale fishery.

[3] Many vessels went out without cannon, expecting to capture guns from the enemy.

[4] The following is the inventory of the cargo of the sloop *Charming Sally*, which "cleared out from Dominica to Newfoundland," and was eventually considered as a prize by the Continental Congress: "1300 bushels of salt; 14 hogsheads of molasses; 120 gallons of rum; 65 reams of writing paper; 1 hogshead and 27 demijohns of claret wine; 27 bottles of French cordials; 5 cases of oil of olives and anchovies; 4 ankers of brandy; 150,000 pins; 24 pairs of wool cards; 10 pieces of linen and checks; 500 pounds of shot; 1 cask of powder; 150 pounds of coffee; 4 umbrellas; 100 yards of osnaburghs; 4 beaver hats; 1 Negro man; 1 suit of velvet; 1 suit of black cloth; 1 suit of light-colored cloth; 1 suit of purple cloth; 2½ dozen of shirts; 2 dozen of neck cloths; 3 dozen of handkerchiefs; 4 dozen of silk and thread stockings; 3 dozen of linen waistcoats and breeches; 2 chintz nightgowns; several short coats; great coat and cloak; ½ piece of cambrick; 8 yards of crimson silk; 1 dozen pair of French laced ruffles; bedding; table linen; musket sword; pistols; 2 blunderbusses; quadrant and other instruments; small library of books."

[5] The sea letter given to Captain Green read as follows: "Most serene, most puissant, puissant, high illustrious, noble, honorable, venerable, wise and prudent emperors, kings, republics, princes, dukes, earls, barons, lords, burgomasters, councellors, as also judges, officers, justiciaries, and regents of all the good cities and places, whether ecclesiastical or secular, who shall see these patents or hear them read:

"We the United States in Congress assembled, make known, that John Green, captain of the ship called the Empress of China, is a citizen of the United States of America, and that the ship which he commands belongs to citizens of the said United States, and as we wish to see the said John Green prosper in his lawful affairs, our prayer to all the before mentioned and to each of them separately, where the said John Green shall arrive with his vessel and cargo, that they may please to receive him with goodness, and treat him in a becoming manner, permitting him upon the usual tolls and expenses in passing and repassing, to pass, navigate and frequent the ports, passes and territories, to the end, to transact his business where and in what manner he shall judge proper, whereof we shall be willingly indebted."

This letter was signed by the president and the secretary of Congress.

[6] See *James Rogers and His Descendants*, by James Swift Rogers, Boston, 1902. There is also other evidence that it was Captain Moses Rogers, but the New York papers of the period do not give the first name of the captain in what they say about this first passage. Captain Rogers left the *Clermont* on reaching Albany.

[7] To show what the packets carried, here is the invoice of the *Dreadnought's* first cargo: 3827 barrels of flour, 24,150 bushels of wheat, 12,750 bushels of corn, 304 bales of cotton, 198 barrels of potash, 150 boxes of bacon, 5600 staves, 60 tons of ballast, a total dead weight of 1559.65 tons.

The ship was 200 feet long on deck, 40.25 feet wide, 26 feet deep. With this cargo on board she drew 21½ feet of water aft and 21 forward. Her main yard was 79 feet long.

Milton Keynes UK
Ingram Content Group UK Ltd.
UKHW030906151124
451262UK00006B/978